Byronism, Napoleonis
Nineteenth-Century R

Byronism, Napoleonism, and Nineteenth-Century Realism offers a fresh analysis of the nineteenth-century European novel, exploring the cultural images of Byron and Napoleon as they appear in the construction of 'bourgeois heroism.' Utilising a unique pan-European perspective, this volume draws together concepts of heroism with theoretically informed questions of form, particularly the role of the hero-protagonist and development of literary realism. Observing Byron and Napoleon as parallel entities, whose rise and twin fame cast long shadows in the first decades of the nineteenth century, this text exemplifies the force of personality which made them heroes. Even where they were reviled, their commitment to challenging moribund cultural and social values make them touchstones for all those who attempted to understand the nineteenth century's modernity. Integrating the study of heroism in the nineteenth-century novel with key developments in critical theory, *Byronism, Napoleonism, and Nineteenth-Century Realism* is essential reading for students and scholars of the bourgeois hero, as well as those with a wider interest in nineteenth-century literature.

Tristan Donal Burke studied at the University of Manchester, and his thesis, funded by the Arts and Humanities Research Council and the University of Manchester's President's Doctoral Scholarship, was entitled 'Mutations of Heroism in Nineteenth-Century Modernity.' He is currently Teaching Fellow in Victorian Literature at the University of Leeds. He recently published on Dickens's Bleak House and political violence in *The London Journal*, and his work with the Everyday Analysis Collective is published by Zer0 Books.

Among the Victorians and Modernists
Edited by Dennis Denisoff

This series publishes monographs and essay collections on literature, art, and culture in the context of the diverse aesthetic, political, social, technological, and scientific innovations that arose among the Victorians and Modernists. Viable topics include, but are not limited to, artistic and cultural debates and movements; influential figures and communities; and agitations and developments regarding subjects such as animals, commodification, decadence, degeneracy, democracy, desire, ecology, gender, nationalism, the paranormal, performance, public art, sex, socialism, spiritualities, transnationalism, and the urban. Studies that address continuities between the Victorians and Modernists are welcome. Work on recent responses to the periods such as Neo-Victorian novels, graphic novels, and film will also be considered.

Titles include:

Virginia Woolf's Unwritten Histories
Conversations with the Nineteenth Century
Anne Besnault

Illegitimate Freedom
Informality in Modernist Literature, 1900–1940
Gaurav Majumdar

Byronism, Napoleonism, and Nineteenth-Century Realism
Heroes of Their Own Lives?
Tristan Donal Burke

Strange Gods
Love and Idolatry in the Victorian Novel
Timothy L. Carens

For more information about this series, please visit: https://www.routledge.com/Among-the-Victorians-and-Modernists/book-series/ASHSER4035

Byronism, Napoleonism, and Nineteenth-Century Realism

Heroes of Their Own Lives?

Tristan Donal Burke

Routledge
Taylor & Francis Group

NEW YORK AND LONDON

First published 2022
by Routledge
605 Third Avenue, New York, NY 10158

and by Routledge
2 Park Square, Milton Park, Abingdon, Oxon, OX14 4RN

Routledge is an imprint of the Taylor & Francis Group, an informa business

© 2022 Tristan Donal Burke

Library of Congress Cataloging-in-Publication Data
A catalog record for this title has been requested

ISBN: 978-0-367-74903-3 (hbk)
ISBN: 978-0-367-74905-7 (pbk)
ISBN: 978-1-003-16016-8 (ebk)

DOI: 10.4324/9781003160168

Typeset in Sabon
by SPi Technologies India Pvt Ltd (Straive)

Unhappy the land that is in need of heroes.
—Bertolt Brecht, *The Life of Galileo*

Contents

Figures

Acknowledgements

This book started life as a PhD thesis, written at the University of Manchester, between 2012 and 2017, and I am grateful to so many people I worked with during this time. My supervisor, Alan Rawes, provided acute and perceptive advice and criticism and taught me something of the rigour and precision which characterises his own approach to writing. Jeremy Tambling, who supervised the first 15 months of the thesis, is a great inspiration in both his teaching and writing. And the members of my supervisory panel, Liam Harte, and Rachel Platonov, offered robust, challenging, and always helpful critiques and suggestions. I am also grateful to Mike Sanders and to Simon Bainbridge of Lancaster University, whose scrutiny of my work in the *viva voce* examination was so illuminating.

Thank you to Rachel Platonov and Dan Kennedy who offered me advice on the Russian language. Any errors are, of course, my own.

I am grateful to the members of the Theory Since 2000 reading group at the University of Manchester: Lucy Burns, Edmund Chapman, Anirudha Dhanawade, Zoe Gosling, Luke Healey, Şima İmşir, Joe Morton, Hazel Shaw, William Simms, and Laura Swift. I'm also grateful to other friends in Manchester: Dan Bristow, Mareile Pfannebecker, Jo Rose, James Smith, and, especially, Jack Sullivan.

More recently, thank you to Sam Ridout, Deborah Koh, Hannah Gascoyne. And thank you to the English departments of the University of the West of England and the University of Leeds where I have had wonderful working environments since finishing my PhD.

Thank you, too, to the organisers and attendees of the Gladstone Centre for Victorian Studies Colloquium, where I presented an early version of the chapter on Thackeray.

Finally, thank you to Alan Burke, Eirian Burke, and Jenny Burke.

Introduction

> Napoleon [and] Byron [...] are the representatives of our age. They will show the next generation its secret, and reveal to them how in our time human spirit wanted to triumph over fate, and how it was exhausted by a battle with fate that was beyond its strength.[1]
>
> Alexander Nikitenko

I

This book explores the way writers of the early to mid-nineteenth century conceptualise heroism. In response to a number of canonical texts of nineteenth-century European literature, Alexander Pushkin's *Eugene Onegin* (1825–1832, first complete edition 1833), Mikhail Lermontov's *A Hero of Our Time* (1839–1841), Charles Dickens's *David Copperfield* (1849–1850), Stendhal's *The Red and the Black* (1830) and William Makepeace Thackeray's *Vanity Fair* (1847–1848), I argue that all of these texts exemplify Europe's need to invent new conceptions of heroism under changing economic and social pressures associated with the rise of the bourgeois class, in its various manifestations, across Europe. What unifies these texts is their conceptualisation of new forms of heroism through an engagement with two towering figures of the early nineteenth century, who, in their lifetimes, were figured as heroic and who have become bywords for certain forms of heroism: Lord Byron (1788–1824) and Napoleon Bonaparte (1769–1821). I show how the figures of Byron and Napoleon are adopted by writers later in the nineteenth century in order to produce mutations in heroism: Byron and Napoleon no longer exclusively figure the values that they did during their own lifetimes but are deployed in order to imagine new forms of heroism adapted to the bourgeois or nascent-bourgeois modes of life.

In addressing the literary creation of heroism through a response to the historical figures of Byron and Napoleon, a number of aesthetic and historical issues present themselves. Particularly these concern theoretical questions to do with the novel as a key cultural form through which the bourgeoisie ideologically expresses and consolidates itself, questions such

DOI: 10.4324/9781003160168-1

as 'what is realism?'; 'how does the novel respond to historical events?'; 'can the novel be thought of as a radical or reactionary form?'; 'what is its relationship to revolution?' In answering these, in conversation with the work of Karl Marx, Sigmund Freud, Walter Benjamin, and Jacques Rancière, I put forward a reading of exactly how an emergent bourgeois subjectivity can be imagined, recognised, and theorised.

II

Karl Marx, in his writings on the coup d'état of Napoleon III in 1851 offers a key conceptualisation of heroism in the nineteenth century. Describing Napoleon III in the 1869 preface to 'The Eighteenth Brumaire of Louis Bonaparte,' he writes that 'the *class struggle* in France created circumstances and conditions which allowed a mediocre and grotesque individual to play the hero's role.'[2] Though Marx still sees a place for heroism in the bourgeois world, the figures who play the hero are not suitable for that role. Heroism has become a problematic category. If the class struggle in France made it possible for a mediocrity to play a hero's part, this suggests that the whole notion of heroism is giving way to the movements of broad swathes of people. Hero etymologically derives from the Latin *heroes*, 'man of superhuman strength, courage or ability' (*OED*). This spectacular subjectivity of a lone individual no longer counts for much when it is mediocrities who play these roles. For Marx, of course, the motive force of history belongs to classes rather than heroes. This erosion of heroism in the bourgeois world is repeatedly insisted on by Marx in 'The Eighteenth Brumaire.' Yet, he observes that 'unheroic as bourgeois society is, it still required heroism, self-sacrifice, terror, civil war, and battles in which whole nations were engaged, to bring it into the world' (p. 148). Again, this statement is complex, for similar reasons to the last. On the one hand, Marx is stating, quite clearly, that bourgeois society is unheroic but has emerged from heroism, which, having served its purpose, has now become obsolete. The last flourishing of heroism is that which brings bourgeois society into being, after which it withers and dies. Yet even here, in the growth of bourgeois individualism, heroism is not that of an exceptional individual. Rather, Marx gestures towards the disappearance of the hero as an exceptional individual. The heroism that brings bourgeois society into existence is figured in the collective terms of battles and wars rather than the actions of individuals.

In 'The Eighteenth Brumaire,' Marx returns again and again to the disappearance of heroism. Elsewhere he describes the whole historical scene in mid-nineteenth-century France as being characterised by 'heroes without deeds of heroism, history without events' (p. 170). Heroism has disappeared in favour of a broader sense of the populace. At some points, Marx implies that perhaps classes have become heroic, rather than individuals. At others, Marx casts doubt on whether the category of heroism

obtains at all. In a political pamphlet that insists on the historical importance of the existence of heroism in the revolutions of the past, Marx
remains concerned about how past and contemporary heroism is figured
in the mid-nineteenth century. How is this heroism figured? Heroism,
though it is now unheroic and being supplanted, according to Marx,
establishes itself by the new actors of history 'timidly conjur[ing] up the
spirits of the past to help them; they borrow their names, slogans and
costumes so as to stage the new world-historical scene in this venerable
disguise and borrowed language' (p. 146). Unheroic heroism in bourgeois
society legitimises itself as heroic by depending upon, by dressing itself up
as, the heroism of the past.

   This book takes this problematic as its starting point. It works on
a period that slightly predates Marx's observations, and the novels it
deals with actually reflect the period during which the bourgeoisie are
consolidating their cultural dominance and defining themselves in light
of it. This is a period, according to Marx, in which heroism and the
unheroic coexist in uneasy, shifting mutations. In the context of the
Russian texts discussed, bourgeois society is in its nascent phase and
developing in somewhat different patterns from the rest of Europe; the
French text deals with the historical consolidation of bourgeois hegemony in France after the 1830 revolution; the English texts, whilst
written against the backdrop of the revolutionary events that Marx
describes between 1848 and 1851, project themselves backwards in history and are concerned with the emergence of the nineteenth-century
bourgeoisie at the beginning of that century, using this to comment on
the total hegemony of the British bourgeoisie at the time they are written, when the revolutionary movements which swept Europe fail to fully
emerge in the United Kingdom. In various ways, these texts are both
attempting to lend heroism to the bourgeois characters that they depict
and interrogating the very possibility of that heroism. In terms of these
texts' role in the culture of bourgeois life, they establish new notions
of the bourgeois hero. It is my contention that this does not simply
represent a shift from the individual hero to heroised classes, as Marx
suggests, but that individual heroism takes new forms that withdraw
from an active participation in world-historical events. Certain aspects
of individualised bourgeois life become heroised by these novels but
with no aspirations to world-historical significance. For the bourgeois
class, heroism becomes private. Thus, the models of heroism presented
in these novels are often reactionary. Yet it should be stressed, too, that
they are frequently undermined; that certain unexpected, radical forces
erupt in them; or when texts dwell on more reactionary forms, they
are shown to be abject failures. This stems from the fact that these
models are based on the examples of Byron and Napoleon, who are
made bourgeois but can never be fully extracted from their radical and
revolutionary histories.

The widespread cultural influence of Byron and Napoleon in the early to mid-nineteenth century emerges in the Byronic and Napoleonic costumes that are frequently donned by the heroes of the novels of the period, though both are frequently figured as obsolete. Whilst I discuss this in detail in relation to the particular texts I am discussing, it is worth also noting examples from the cultural milieu which immediately follows the period examined in this book, which attests to the longevity of the influence of these two figures. Looking at two examples of this can help to illuminate some of the issues around Byron and Napoleon as simultaneously anachronistic and haunting figures throughout the nineteenth century. In Matthew Arnold's poem 'Stanzas from the Grand Chartreuse' (1855), for example, Arnold writes,

> What helps it now, that Byron bore,
> With haughty scorn which mock'd the smart,
> Through Europe to the Ætolian shore
> The pageant of his bleeding heart?
> That thousands counted every groan,
> And Europe made his woe her own?[3]
>
> (ll. 133–138)

Here, Byron's imputed, seemingly superhuman, ability to figure an entire European experience in his own subjectivity is seen as obsolete: 'What helps it now' that Byron 'bore,' 'scorned' and 'mocked'? Yet, although Byron is claimed to be obsolete, he still clearly represents a powerful cultural figure who must be come to terms with.[4]

Similarly, Marx writes in the 1869 preface to 'The Eighteenth Brumaire' that 'particularly in the last few years, French literature has knocked the Napoleonic legend on the head with the weapons of historical research, criticism, satire and wit' (p. 144). Nonetheless, his text still spirals insistently around Napoleon, both in terms of Napoleon III's imitation of him, and the ongoing influence of Napoleon's own superhuman force and ability in the period following the French Revolution. For all that Napoleon is a myth that has been shattered, for all that Byron no longer matters to the prophets of the Victorian bourgeoisie, they still weigh on the minds of the nineteenth century. These accounts of Byron and Napoleon suggest the massive pan-European importance of these figures in the later nineteenth century. Even as they began to be seen as anachronistic, they remained insistent reference points, especially for understanding heroism.

III

No discussion of heroism in the nineteenth century would be complete without a discussion of Thomas Carlyle's book *On Heroes, Hero-Worship and the Heroic in History* (1841). Carlyle undertakes a similar process to that described by Marx in 'The Eighteenth Brumaire.' Believing that there is a lack of heroes in an essentially unheroic society, he turns to history in order to construct forms of modern heroism: 'could we see them well, we should get some glimpses into the very marrow of the world's history.'[5]

Particularly relevant for this study is the discussion of 'The Hero as King' since Carlyle's 'second modern King' is Napoleon (p. 191). Carlyle cleverly and ironically pairs Napoleon with Cromwell as his two examples of the hero as king: two revolutionaries who make themselves kings rather than inheriting a crown. For Carlyle, kingship is defined by a spiritual sense of command: the hero-king

> is practically the *summary* for us of *all* the various figures of Heroism; Priest, Teacher, whatsoever of earthly or of spiritual dignity we can fancy to reside in a man, embodies itself here, to *command* over us, furnish us with constant practical teaching, tell us for the day and hour what we are to *do*.
>
> (p. 161, emphasis in the original)

For Carlyle, Napoleon is much less significant a hero since he does not possess the rich spiritual life of Cromwell. Intriguingly, though, Carlyle does see a sort of spiritual sincerity in Napoleon, and this is based on the idea of democracy:

> Accordingly was there not what we can call a *faith* in him, genuine so far as it went? That this enormous Democracy asserting itself here in the French Revolution is an insuppressible Fact, which the whole world, with its old forces and institutions, cannot put down.

Carlyle continues, 'Napoleon, in his first period, was a true Democrat' (p. 192). Yet, paradoxically, according to Carlyle, for Napoleon being a democrat meant asserting autocratic authority:

> [Napoleon] knew that Democracy, if it were a true thing at all, could not be an anarchy [...]. On that Twentieth of June (1792), Bourrienne and he sat in a coffee-house, as the mob rolled by: Napoleon expresses the deepest contempt for persons in authority that they do not restrain this rabble.
>
> (p. 193)

Raymond Williams observes that the interest in heroes in this period of Carlyle's thinking 'underlines the steady withdrawal from genuinely social thinking into preoccupations with personal power.'[6] In this book, I hope I engage in social thinking on heroism rather than in elevating hero-kings!

The decline of the 'great man' model of heroism after Carlyle, for example, in Marx's particular focus on the historical dynamics of classes rather than individuals in his theory of history, in spite of his interest in heroes in 'The Eighteenth Brumaire,' seems to inform a resistance on the part of modern critics to noticing how the nineteenth-century novel still deploys a discourse of heroism, a resistance I want to counter. Why is it that so little critical attention has recently been given to the concept of the hero? The paucity of attention to the concept of heroism, the displacement of old critical terms such as 'the hero of the novel' by anti-humanist structuralist and post-structuralist theory, the shift to imagining history driven by class struggle that Marx pioneered, and a more general suspicion of deploying the term heroism are all bolstered by a more general sense of the bankruptcy of the concept of the hero in light of the developments of history over the twentieth century. As David R. Sorensen points out in his introduction to Carlyle's book, Carlyle's work has been tarnished, along with Carlyle himself, 'by their association with the authoritarian and totalitarian personality cults that brought European civilization to the brink of destruction in World War II.' Sorensen adds,

> Hero-worship itself has followed a similar downward trajectory. The trend began in the period following the "Great War" [...]. Later in the century, in the way of the catastrophic experiments in human transformation that traumatized societies as politically and culturally diverse as China, Cambodia, Germany, Iraq, Libya, North Korea, Romania and the Soviet Union in the twentieth century – experiments conducted to exalt the supreme wisdom of transcendent leaders – scepticism towards heroic avatars became more deeply entrenched in Western thought.[7]

The politics of this book, of course, do not endorse heroism in general or the 'Great Man' theory of heroism. As Brecht puts it in *The Life of Galileo*, 'Unhappy is the land that is in need of heroes.'[8] Though the hero is, quite rightly, seen as a regressive or even dangerous concept for the twentieth- and twenty-first centuries, this does not mean that analysis of its history and its role in the creation of political and social formations should be overlooked. The fact remains that nineteenth-century novelists deployed and explored questions of heroism insistently. As such, I wish to offer a corrective to the general assumption that the nineteenth century began the historical shift away from heroism per se.

Alongside the excellent introduction to Sorensen and Kinser's new edition of Carlyle's text, other recent studies have revived the concept of the hero for thinking about the culture of the long nineteenth century. The historian John Price, whose work I discuss in more detail below, argues for a study of heroism which thinks about its construction rather than taking for granted received judgements of *who* is heroic.[9] Similarly, Madeleine

Callaghan's work on Byron and Shelley draws attention to the risk of losing sight of 'poetry's own claims for its status as made by a unique individual' under a historicist anxiety to debunk a Romantic ideology of transcendent individualism.[10] In her reading, which I concur with, heroic 'claims should not be understood as egotistical self-aggrandizement on the part of the poets' but rather that 'force a fresh consideration of what the poet is and can become, where heroism is the ultimate aim as well as a dangerous avatar of the poet.'[11] Analysis of the *construction* of heroism, and its effects and meanings, rather than uncritical acceptance of heroism as an ideal category, is central here.

These readings challenge an established critical belief that claims that as the hero disappears from nineteenth-century culture generally, so too does the hero disappear from the nineteenth-century novel. Or so the story goes. To take two widely divergent examples, from two very different points in the history of literary criticism, both Mario Praz and Franco Moretti see the hero disappearing from the nineteenth-century novel. Both of their studies are important for understanding how the bourgeoisie created themselves as a class through their literature, and particularly how the bourgeoisie conceptualised the hero.

Mario Praz's book *The Hero in Eclipse in Victorian Fiction* (1956) makes quite clear the trajectory Praz sees occurring in nineteenth-century literature. Praz's book describes a process whereby 'Romanticism in England gradually turned bourgeois.'[12] The results of this process are explained in his discussion of Dickens, where Praz observes that 'even violent scenes are tempered by humour,' which, he adds, 'is the typical Biedermeier attitude towards sensationalism; the anti-heroic attitude that we shall find in Thackeray, in George Eliot, in those novelists who exerted themselves to look beyond the external aspects of deeds into the souls of their characters.'[13] On the one hand, then, heroism is subordinated to a depiction of everyday life and complex and subtle psychology rather than action. On the other hand, the hero is eclipsed by the democratic impulse of the novel.[14]

Praz also observes that Dickens is more interested in 'action [of the plot at large], gesture, dialogue' than heroism, meaning that the hero is in eclipse because the actual mode of writing intervenes.[15] Sixty years later, this same argument is put forward by Franco Moretti in his book, *The Bourgeois* (2013). Summarising his book, Moretti writes, '[R]eaders of this book know that prose is its only true hero.'[16] In the nineteenth century, prose becomes the hero of the bourgeois too. For Moretti, the hero as protagonist in older forms has been replaced in the bourgeois novel by prose itself.

> A few recurrent traits clustered around [the bourgeois] figure: energy, first of all; self-restraint; intellectual clarity; commercial honesty; a strong sense of goals. All 'good' traits; but not good enough to match

the type of narrative hero – warrior, knight, conqueror, adventurer – on whom Western story-telling had relied for, literally, millennia.[17]

Thus, according to Moretti, to make up for this deficit, 'where capitalistic structures solidify, narrative and stylistic mechanisms replace individuals as the centre of the text.'[18] For Moretti, too, then, the hero is in eclipse, the old forms of heroism that still characterised Byron and Napoleon have disappeared and have been replaced by prose itself.

In this book, I suggest that new mutations of heroism are directly created through new modes of writing, rather than writing displacing heroism. Here I echo recent work by the historian John Price. In *Everyday Heroism: Victorian Constructions of the Heroic Civilian*, Price calls for the creation of 'a new approach to the study of heroism' which will 'encompass all of society rather than simply the great men of history.'[19] In a move which echoes my own, he focuses on the examination of 'how particular models of heroism were constructed, rather than just identifying that certain individuals were viewed as heroic.'[20] Beginning in 1850, prior to which, 'there was little or no recognition or reward for the heroism of the working-class man or woman,'[21] Price seeks to demonstrate that the work of constructing new forms of heroism was a key component of the creation of working-class consciousness in the second half of the nineteenth-century, where 'not only did constructions of heroism originate from within the working classes as readily as those outside them, but also constructions that did not equate with theirs were rejected or at least less enthusiastically embraced.'[22] If this book contributes to the claim that the bourgeoisie produced models of heroism which defined and promulgated a class consciousness, Price's work demonstrates that this process migrated into the analogous formation of working-class consciousness later in the nineteenth century. What these two processes share, strikingly, is a movement from the military-public to the domestic. Whilst Price shows that '[p]olitical and military themes were, then, important driving forces behind the processes of Victorian civic commemoration' and high political discussion of heroism, working-class everyday heroism is characterised by 'ordinary civilian men and women who undertook life-risking heroic acts in the course of their everyday lives.'[23] These acts were in turn commemorated at home, in local newspapers, and in subscription memorials. Similarly, the bourgeois heroism I describe in this study is constructed in the domestic sphere, both in terms of fictional narrative and the domestic form of the novel. The key difference between my bourgeois heroes and Price's working-class heroes is that the acts of heroism that Price rediscovers are genuinely heroic: '[T]he miners, labourers, factory workers, train drivers, domestic servants, stewardesses, housewives and schoolchildren who [...] risked and gave their own lives for others' became heroes 'unselfconsciously because it was thrust upon them suddenly, when it was largely unexpected, rather than them seeking out situations which might offer the opportunity to perform it.'[24]

This book sets out to show that the hero retained some purchase on the nineteenth-century novel, which continued heroising the bourgeois class, who were under the threat of losing their legitimacy if they did not have models of heroism available through which to assert their new social hegemony. Taking into account what I have set out about Marx's theorisation of the unheroic nature of the nineteenth century, the mechanism that I argue is deployed is the appropriation and redeployment of aspects of heroic figures from the recent past, Byron and Napoleon, in order to lend a heroic costume to the prosaic lives of the bourgeoisie. Particularly, the heroic aspect is redirected away from the heroism of being involved in world events and to the heroism of the private sphere, the heroism of engaging in professional work, of shoring up the bourgeois world. Yet, on the other hand, these earlier heroes simultaneously introduce dissonances. Both Byron and Napoleon are linked particularly both to memories of radical politics and revolution and to aristocratic interests that stand outside the bourgeoisie proper. Just as they prop up the bourgeoisie, they subvert it. This double dynamic is central to my claims.

In its attempt to defend the interests of the bourgeois world, the nineteenth-century conception of bourgeois heroism is therefore related, but distinct from, what Robin Gilmour has described as the creation of the idea of the gentleman in the Victorian novel. Gilmour describes this as a 'social and political accommodation between the aristocracy and the middle classes in the period' and connects this to 'the growth of the professions and of a professional class.'[25] However, this idea of the gentleman does not account for the connections between the bourgeois characters of the novels this book discusses and earlier models of revolutionary-aristocratic heroism. This is a matter not of an accommodation but of a bourgeois repurposing of particular forms of aristocracy for the bourgeoisie's ends. Nor is Gilmour's conception of the gentleman internationalist enough. Furthermore, Gilmour, a conservative critic, sees the gentleman himself as conservative, writing of 'the civilising role [the idea of the gentleman] played in the genesis of Victorian Britain.'[26] Whilst some of the characters I discuss play this conservative, bourgeois role, more important to me are the dissonances between conservative appropriations of the hero and the memory of revolutionary disruption. Whilst in the period I discuss those dissonances remain active, I find little to celebrate in the results of bourgeois recuperations of the concept. Gilmour's claims find one of their final Victorian expressions in the bankrupt heroism of the late-Victorian imperial romance, though even here there are the seeds of the anxiety of imperial barbarism and decline.[27]

IV

At this point, it is appropriate to define three of my key terms: Byronic, Napoleonic, and bourgeois.

Peter L. Thorslev, in *The Byronic Hero: Types and Prototypes*,[28] offers a summation of the mode of the Byronic Hero that is established by Byron's poetry:

> [The] agonized Hero of Sensibility was Byron's legacy to the literature of the age which succeeded […]. The agonized Hero of Sensibility appears again and again in the literature of the succeeding age: sometimes morbidly analytic of his own emotional and spiritual states, and in his *Weltschmertz*, longing for some engagement to [sic] absolute truth which will rid him of his painful self-consciousness; longing to "mingle with the universe," but being continually frustrated in this desire by the reassertion of his sceptical, sometimes cynical, and sometimes remorseful ego.[29]

This definition of the Byronic Hero, though I will slightly deviate from it in due course, is most clearly discernible, according to Thorslev, in *Childe Harold's Pilgrimage*, and whilst I discuss this to illustrate some points, the figure is perhaps more visible in Byron's first, and in many ways exemplary, Oriental narrative tale *The Giaour*.[30] This poem narrates the story of a Christian character, the Giaour, in Ottoman Greece, who falls in love with the wife, Leila, of an Ottoman regional ruler, Hassan. She is thrown in the sea for infidelity, and the Giaour kills Hassan in a battle. He then withdraws to a monastery and makes a confession of his life, in which he expresses remorse, not for the death of Hassan but his role in Leila's death. This story illustrates its hero in the middle of the action, in a consciously heroic mode. The poem's preamble, which comments on the contemporary situation of Greece occupied by the Ottoman Empire, asks, referring to Ancient Greece, 'when shall such hero live again?,'[31] which implies that what follows is an illustration of that hero. Furthermore, the Giaour is portrayed in a key scene in battle. He leads his followers 'on with foreign brand, | Far flashing in his red right hand' (ll.608–609), and even when he has withdrawn from the world at the end of the poem, he still imagines his own destiny shaped by action in the world rather than withdrawal from it through suicide. He did not seek 'the self-accorded grave | Of ancient fool, and modern knave' (1006–1007), but rather states, 'I have not quailed to danger's brow – | When high and happy – need I *now*?' (1027–1028). As will be seen shortly, *Childe Harold* frequently portrays its hero as inactive, an observer, and so less easy to characterise as heroic in terms of shaping his own experience. As such, *Childe Harold* already suggests one way in which Byronic heroism mutates into what I will suggest is a bourgeois form of subjectivity. Thorslev suggests that the Byronic

Hero attempts to escape his subjectivity, that his is a heroic quest to go beyond individuated subjectivity. Bourgeois heroism stresses dwelling in this subjectivity, a characteristic that is stressed both by Thorslev's observation that the Byronic Hero returns to his own 'remorseful ego' and by Childe Harold's relative inaction.

My definition of Byronic heroism centres on four key aspects: the image of the Byronic Hero as a cynical, isolated, melancholy outsider (often an observer); the Byronic Hero as aristocratic; the Byronic Hero as a heroic, individual revolutionary; and the Byronic Hero as a narrator of his own heroic life and subjectivity. There are other aspects of the Byronic Hero which are present in *Childe Harold*, *The Giaour*, and in other Byron texts, but these four have the most bearing on my argument about the mutations of heroism in the nineteenth century from Byronic to bourgeois heroism.

The key form of the Byronic Hero which is described by Thorslev is the cynical, detached, melancholy outsider, who in *Childe Harold* is an observer that views what he sees but does not engage in it, suggesting instead a sense of superiority or hauteur. He is visible in such stanzas as the following:

> But where is Harold? Shall I then forget
> To urge the gloomy wanderer o'er the wave?
> Little reck'd he of all that men regret;
> No lov'd-one now in feign'd lament could rave;
> No friend the parting hand extended gave,
> Ere the cold stranger pass'd to other climes:
> Hard is his heart whom charms may not enslave;
> But Harold felt not as in other times,
> And left without a sigh the land of war and crimes.
>
> (II.16)

Here there is an individualistic detachment from the quotidian world and its concerns. Elsewhere, this figure may also be engaged in action, such as the battle in *The Giaour*, but still retains a detached, melancholy sense of isolation – an isolation he must heroically survive. At the beginning of the poem, the Giaour is described as stopping within his action in order to brood on melancholy: '[H]e restrained | That fiery barb so sternly reined' (257–258) and 'in that instant, o'er his soul | Winters of Memory seemed to roll, [...]. A life of pain, an age of crime.' (261–264). In this passage, even in action, he is presented as driven by this melancholy recollection of 'pain' and 'crime' – he 'sped as if by death pursued' (260). After he has killed Hassan, he states, 'I go – but go alone' (688) and, in the monastery, a space of detachment anyway, his detachment from the world is emphasised: '[H]e broods within his cell alone' (806). Even at a moment which brings him together with Leila and shows him in action, the narration offers an element of uncertainty that stresses his isolation. The narrator at this point (there are several), states that Leila escaped to the Giaour dressed 'in likeness of a Georgian page' (456), but when the Giaour is seen to leave, 'Nor maid nor page behind him bore' (472).

Within this isolation, his love is depicted as a self-destructive intensity. It is 'The cherished madness of my heart!' (1191). Elsewhere, though, the Byronic Hero is presented as formerly having been licentious and something of a sexual libertine, though this has been renounced in favour of gloomy detachment:

> Little knew she that seeming marble-heart,
> Now mask'd in silence or withheld by pride,
> Was not unskilful in the spoiler's art,
> And spread its snares licentious far and wide;
> Nor from the base pursuit had turn'd aside,
> But Harold on such arts no more relied;
> And had he doted on those eyes so blue,
> Yet never would he join the lover's whining crew.
>
> (II.33)

Born of a sense of superiority and 'pride,' the Byronic Hero's isolation is a self-imposed discipline, a determinedly sustained holding back ('never would') heroically suffered alone ('mask'd in silence'). And though this is ironised in *Childe Harold*, it is presented in an entirely earnest, heroic poetic mode in poems such as *The Giaour*.

Furthermore, the Byronic Hero, not least in his silent suffering, is frequently conflated with both some of Byron's narrators and particularly with Byron himself. As Jerome McGann observes, 'Byron of course disclaimed the identification even as his life and works repeatedly encouraged it.'[32] This blurring of characters with biography is visible in the reception of Byron where the ambiguous difference between his biography, characters, and narratorial personae is often not maintained. For example, the travels of Childe Harold directly follow the same travels Byron made, which are recounted in Byron's own notes to the poem. The poem maps Harold's travels in Albania:

> He pass'd bleak Pindus, Acherusia's lake,
> And left the primal city of the land,
> And onwards did his further journey take
> To greet Albania's chief, whose dread command
> Is lawless law
>
> (II.47)

This chief is Ali Pacha. Byron recounts in his own notes to the poem, 'we were invited to Tepaleni, his Highness's [Ali Pacha's] birth-place, and favourite Seraid [...]. After some stay in the capital, we accordingly followed' (p. 87). The Byronic Hero, the Byronic narrator (who is often more reflective and more ironical), and Byron himself are not easily separable here when it comes to the figure of the Byronic Hero. It is telling that Byron displaces Harold in the final canto of the poem, 'But where is he, the Pilgrim of my song? [...] He is no more [...]. And he himself as nothing: – if he was | Aught but a phantasy' (IV.164). Yet whilst he replaces Harold with his own lyric self-projection, that self-projection is in many fundamental ways a more articulate amplification of the state of mind represented in the earlier stages of the poem by Harold. This is not to say Harold is simply Byron – rather, *Childe Harold* sees Byron progressively transform his lyric self into another version of Harold, into another Byronic Hero as outlined by Thorslev: agonised, heroically bearing his solitude in magnificent isolation, and seeking but failing to find self-transcendence.

The next aspect of the Byronic Hero relevant here is the aristocratic. Again, this is evident in the figure of Byron himself, who is known as a writer by his aristocratic title, and is, as Newey states, 'an exponent of aristocratic high culture [...] especially in Canto IV of *Childe Harold*.'[33] Again, turning to *The Giaour*, which depicts a Byronic Hero characterised by action, rather than the inaction of *Childe Harold*, the Giaour is 'a noble soul' with 'lineage high' (869), and this is also stressed by his material wealth since he has brought to the monastery 'great largess' (816), and by his 'haughty mien' (256). This has political implications. Malcolm Kelsall has described Byron's politics as the combination of aristocratic and liberal associated with the Whig party.[34] This manifests itself in Byron's poetry as an aristocratic stance which is also socially liberal. For Kelsall, socially liberal tradition is not a revolutionary one: '[T]he Whig aristocracy was to act as "friends of the people", and to redress the balance between the extremes; the Crown and the people' (p. 9). In this characterisation of Byron's Whig politics, the stress of aristocracy is important since it separates Byron from bourgeois values and identifications despite the development of Whig politics towards bourgeois liberalism during and beyond Byron's lifetime. Alongside the mediating tradition of Whig politics, Kelsall stresses the Whig tradition of opposition to autocracy and the party's commitment to 'liberty' (pp. 9–10). This ideological background helps to explain Byron's support of nationalist independence movements such as that of Greece, where Byron's politics are taken to the heroic lengths of fighting for freedom but also his opposition to the French Revolution. Nonetheless, Kelsall's approach is notably stringent on two points: his desire to extrapolate the historical Byron and his work from the Byronic legacy, and an insistence on valuing Byron's concrete political achievements. In this sense, Byron's own views and behaviour are related to, but not fully analogous with, the way Byronism was perceived after Byron's death. Thus, Kelsall states that he is 'cynical about Byronism – a Romantic phenomenon constructed by revolutionary enthusiasm' (p. 2) since, according to him, Byronism cannot be attributed to Byron's own politics. Byronism then stresses the transformative political pole of Byron's politics on the basis of Byron's commitment to the freedom of oppressed people, rather than his party politics, and informs the more extreme revolutionary enthusiasm of parts of the Byronic tradition. I show in this book that Byron's political legacy is tripartite: aristocratic liberalism, a more far-reaching revolutionary imperative, and, ultimately, the creation of a conservative bourgeoisie.

The Byronism Kelsall is sceptical of is a posthumous creation. Thus, whilst Kelsall dismisses Delacroix's depiction of Byron in 'Greece on the Ruins of Missolonghi,' with its celebration of 'the artist who died that men might be free' and 'the mourning female figure of Greece [which] suggests analogy with the familiar image of revolutionary France' (p. 1), these depictions inform this book. The posthumous (mis)understanding of Byron's poetic and personal politics counts for just as much in the construction of Byronic heroism as the more clear-eyed, historical assessment that Kelsall offers.

Moreover, the impossibility of differentiating between Byron the poet and the Byronic Hero is part of what Jerome Christensen describes as Byron's aristocratic 'strength,' a political intervention which forecloses on the possibility of separating the private and individual from the public and textual which the bourgeois world seeks to demand:

> Byron announces his decision to desist from drawing the line between himself and Harold [...]. We might take that announcement as an example of the problem of drawing a line, in public or in private, between the public and the private.[35]

This results in the problematising of liberal discourse in favour of the aristocratic-revolutionary command 'past all the criteria of liberal reason.'[36] Whilst I am sceptical of Christensen's emphasis on the predominantly textual basis of political intervention, the problems of differentiating between Byron's politics and the political demands of his texts reiterates the impossibility of separating Byron the man from his texts' posthumous critical work. Moreover, where Christensen does discuss the material implications of the politics of Byronism, he notes that the aristocratic strength of Byronism ultimately inaugurates its bourgeois reappropriations in the act of their refusal. For Christensen, by playing on the line between public and private, biographical and textual, Byron both refuses differentiation between his own public and private *and* introduces the critical discourse that seeks to accurately return the public text to the private self and reinstate the separating line by establishing accurate, parallel correspondence: '[T]he poems are imagined as an elaborate code that, by way of a handily metamorphic secret [...] can be brought into some determinate relation with a singular circumstance of Byron's life.'[37] This in turn allows the private reader to imagine him or herself as Byronic within the confines of the private bourgeois space and life: 'It also tempts a reader to make application to him- or herself: Why not my life as well as Byron's? Why not this moment as well as that?'[38]

For Christensen, this problematic emanates from the problematic of aristocracy, which vacillates between 'imperial ambition and a public regimen answerable to a republican ethic.'[39] Similarly, in his historical account, Kelsall identifies similar complexities in the Whig tradition. For all its liberal rhetoric, material conditions indicate its claims to political power: 'Remove the ideological rhetoric which sought to divide Whig from Tory, and one has in reality a self-perpetuating aristocratic oligarchy' (p. 9). Kelsall hints that the Whig admiration of Napoleon also stemmed from an aristocratic-Whig solidarity with his actions, which vacillates between the imperial and republican: 'There were many Whig sympathisers for the new force in Europe which shook despots from their thrones, and established liberal constitutions among the freed nations' (p. 3). The obverse and disavowed imperialism evident in this admiration is stressed by Byron's later disillusionment with Napoleon, in whom, 'turbulent republican liberty was involved with a corrupting monarchical ambition' (p. 69). Byron's ambivalence towards Napoleon can be seen in his 'Ode to Napoleon Buonaparte,' where he writes, 'Oh! ne'er may tyrant leave behind | A brighter name to lure mankind' (ll. 89–90).

Yet before Napoleon's fall, Byron was a supporter – there is some suggestion that he was proud to adopt Napoleon's initials as his own in later life when obliged to add 'Noel' to his name – and Byron's Whig ideology actively came into contact with the revolutionary in his work in other ways too. Aristocratic liberalism itself, according to Whig tradition, issues in a particular kind of politically radical heroic action.[40] Alan Rawes connects this to the Whig politics that Malcolm Kelsall describes, characterised by an 'aristocratic revolt against corruption and tyranny' – that is, 'a noble acting nobly on behalf of the oppressed population.'[41] But Byron's poetic Whiggism also 'flirts dangerously with "Jacobinism."'[42] It is easy to see how a broad sense of Byron's politics could become connected with a broad sense of revolutionary activity. This revolutionary aspect to the Byronic legacy is easily established in his biographical associations with the Carbonari in Italy and in the Greek War of Independence but is most recognisable in his poetry. The revolutionary aspect of Byron's politics is stressed in *The Giaour* by Byron's commitment to freedom for oppressed people. As I have said, *The Giaour* begins with a call for a hero in the face of 'Tyranny' and to win 'Freedom's battle,' both marked with capital letters (120, 123). These figures then have an allegorical resonance for the tale of the Giaour itself. During the Giaour's confession at the end of the poem, when he speaks of Leila, he states, 'To me she gave her heart, that all | Which tyranny can ne'er enthrall' (1069–1070). Thus, the story of the Giaour killing Hassan seems to suggest a parallel with the Greek struggle against the Ottomans. It should be stressed that this is a political struggle for freedom, rather than a clash of Christian and Islamic civilisations. In this respect, it is telling that the poem essentially takes an Islamic and Turkish stance, evident in the fact that its protagonist, the Giaour, is given the Ottoman name for an infidel. When this is added to Byron's obvious respect for and interest in Islamic culture in the poem's notes, where, for example, he states that the Islamic call to prayer is 'solemn and beautiful beyond all the bells in Christendom' (p. 244), the relative status of the religions is problematised. What comes through is a noble commitment to freedom.[43] Similarly, in *Childe Harold's Pilgrimage*, Byron calls on the people of Spain and Greece to rise up against oppressors. Of the Spanish, he writes, 'Such be the sons of Spain, and strange her fate! | They fight for freedom who were never free' (I.86). Similarly, he advises the Greek 'hereditary bondsmen' that, 'Who would be free themselves must strike the blow' (II.76).

The final aspect of Byronic heroism I want to stress here is Byronic self-narration. In order to read this alongside the nineteenth-century novel, it is useful to clarify self-narration in relation to the conceptualisation of literary subjectivity set out by Georg Lukács in *The Theory of the Novel*. In this respect, the Byronic stands between two forms which represent subjectivity. Lukács writes that in the epic, 'subjectivity gave rise to the heroism of militant interiority.'[44] That is to say, epic writing depicts a conception of subjectivity where subjectivity extends far beyond the bounds of the individual body in order to heroically conquer the world with that subjectivity. In the novel, on the contrary, subjectivity does not fill the world, is not expansive, but rather uses its materials in order to create the private subject, which, I will argue in the chapters of this book, is characteristic of the bourgeoisie. Byronic self-narration draws on both of these ways of depicting selfhood.

An illustration of the heroism of militant interiority can be seen in the Colosseum scene towards the end of *Childe Harold* Canto IV (IV.128–145). In this long sequence, in which the Byronic persona stands in the Colosseum, there is an interlacing and expansion of subjectivity through the reflection on memory in relation to the space in which it finds itself. First, the arena reminds the Byronic persona of his own sufferings, and subjectivity is made small and individual by the size of the place: 'Amidst this wreck [...] Among thy mightier offerings here is mine' (IV.131), which are compared to the heroism of the gladiators, 'Have I not had to wrestle with my lot? | Have I not suffered things to be forgiven?' (IV.135). This exploration of subjectivity is directly related to the consolidation of memory, with the Byronic persona adding, 'But in this page a record will I seek' (IV.134). The comparisons of self with the space of the Colosseum and the gladiator are already grandiose but memory remains largely individualised, despite the intermingling of Byron's and the gladiator's subjectivity in the comparison, which is brought to bear through the reference to Janus, which gradually begins to transport the Byronic persona into the past (IV.136). This is eventually made explicit by the observation, 'That we become a part of what has been I And grow unto the spot, all-seeing but unseen' (IV.138), and this opens on to the vision of the gladiator in the arena. Byron's own process of reflecting on memory in the Colosseum is transferred to that of the gladiator, who is also seen engaged in constructing his subjectivity, elsewhere, through memory: '[H]is eyes I Were with his heart, and that was far away [...] where his rude hut by the Danube lay I *There* were his young barbarians all at play I *There* was their Dacian mother' (IV.141). Memory gathers up things far beyond itself, and this does not stop here. The Byronic persona asks, 'What matters where we fall to fill the maws I Of worms – on battle-plains or listed spot?' (IV.139). 'Listed' is used adjectivally here to give the sense of an enclosed ground for combat, like the lists that knights would joust in. With this question, the comparison between the Byronic persona and the dying gladiator connects both to the history of war in general and, particularly, the battles of the Napoleonic Wars that all of *Childe Harold's Pilgrimage* has been concerned with and thus the references to 'imperial pleasure' (IV.139) and the injunction, 'Arise! ye Goths, and glut your ire!' (IV.141), recalls Byron's defence of freedom against Napoleon in Canto I. This is not the consolidation of memory in order to create a self-contained individuated subject, but rather the recall of memory in order to open subjectivity up to all of European history, from the Classical world to the moment at which it is written. And yet it is still absorbed and reconfigured through 'militant subjectivity,' and it is from the individual subject that it begins. This subject is both vast and all-encompassing and small and alone in the world, made both large and small specifically in relation to the vastness of the Classical world (via the Colosseum). The subjectivity of the Byronic Hero as narrated in the Byronic mode stands between two forms of subjectivity: that of the small, enclosed subject alone in the world, that becomes even more developed and marked in the bourgeois novel, and the expansive, militant, heroic subjectivity of the epic, as Lukács defines it.

The contradictions in Byron's poetic heroism, between the rebel and reactionary, aristocratic and bourgeois, individual and collective have been taken up in more detail within his poetry by Madeleine Callaghan. For Callaghan, Byron '[l]iberat[es] heroes from their conventional epic context' but is also 'alive to the dangerous slippage possible from the solitary poet- hero's self-mastery and its tyrannous possibilities.' He 'exposed his poet-heroes to his audience's doubt, courting both the reader's enchantment by such power and rejection of its misuse.'[45] These contradictions continue to play out in his novelistic afterlife. Thus, the connection between the Byronic and the transcendental homelessness of the novel in Lukács's *Theory of the Novel* is stressed by Deborah Lutz in her wonderful book *The Dangerous Lover: Gothic Villains, Byronism, and the Nineteenth-Century Seduction Narrative.*[46] However, whereas I read the Byronic Hero's novelistic afterlife as essentially negative, the prototype for a hollowed-out bourgeois subjectivity, Lutz argues for the character's redemptive potential: the

> possibility of redemption for Byronic dislocation is, of course, finding a home in the beloved. Byron's unique manifestation of the myth of the wandering and outcast hero brings homelessness into a narrative of love by delineating it as a melancholy chaos that might possibly be ordered or bounded through a second self.[47]

Strikingly, Lutz traces this redemptive capacity through the work of the Brontë sisters, and into the mass-market romance novel. There is a 'much-hidden dialogue that exists between the most difficult and important continental philosophers and the most formulaic of female-coded genres,' which produces 'an aesthetic based on women's desires and pleasures [...] as a basis for understanding contemporary constructions of subjectivity.'[48] Lutz's sees this as a process of liberation. The romance novel does not simply maintain and reproduce an oppressive gender system but rather opens onto 'an outside that holds the possibility of freedom, of death, of an infinite mourning or an entering into transcendent meaning.'[49]

Susan Wolfson also stresses the creative and liberating potential of the Byronic for women writers, particularly those of the late Romantic period. Wolfson adopts a similar definition of the Byronic to my own, 'not so much the historical referent as the multiple, various, conflicted radiations into a hot zone of interaction.'[50] Like Lutz, she stresses the possibility of the Byronic for the articulation of women's desire, 'a potent language for gender investments' which 'gave ears to rapture.'[51] In addition, she stresses the importance of parodies, rewritings, and intimate rejections of the Byronic, 'by which women aspiring to fame could show their credentials and, in the venture, discover a lively authority.'[52] The Byronic here, as in Lutz, does not impose upon the women who respond to it a preordained, hierarchical active-passive model through which to experience desire but the possibility of creative negotiations and reimaginings.

The production of gender in Byronic afterlives, from Austen, Eliot, and Gaskell, and in popular film and television adaptations, is also the topic of Sarah Wootton's *Byronic Heroes in Nineteenth-Century Women's Writing and Screen Adaptation.* Whilst more cautious than Lutz and Wolfson, perhaps because she deals with more cautious material, Wootton's book also argues for the productive possibilities of the Byronic Hero for the articulation of women's social status and desire: 'His presence, under various guises, is persistent if changeable in novels that dramatise his shortcomings and profit from a regenerative potential that destabilises sexual mores and probes the political status quo.'[53]

These readings of the Byronic draw attention to one of the decisions I made about omissions in this book: the absence of the novels of the Brontë sisters. These novels represent one of the major engagements with the legacy of the Byronic. Whilst the critics discussed previously recognise liberating energies in a range of women writers' responses to the Byronic, my reading focuses on writing by canonical men and predominantly advances a particular delineation of bourgeois masculine. It implies a pessimistic historical process, a subjectivity closed upon itself as the bulwark of an oppressive gender hierarchy. The Brontë sisters stand outside this narrative. Their novels are not located in the same urban bourgeois cultural milieu but on geographical borderlines on which they develop bold experiments in subjectivity. Whilst there are dissonances in their experiments, including conservative reterritorialisations, the specificity and complexity of their different approaches deserve their own unfoldings, such as that developed so compellingly by Lutz, rather than being hastily shoehorned into a different sort of argument as a clumsy counterweight. Lutz's, Wolfson's, and Wootton's books offer essential alternative readings to the entire historical trajectory which I unfold below.

Napoleon, as Simon Bainbridge observes in his study of his influence on English Romantic literature, 'was the supreme embodiment of the hero in an age in which the artist was increasingly seen as heroic, but his career raised numerous questions about the nature of heroism itself.'[54] Through textual representation, Napoleon's own heroism asks questions about the meaning of the writer-as-hero, be that Byron the heroic poet or the hero as author of novels, as well as of the hero of the novel. Napoleon is harder to define in literary terms, but is, perhaps more than Byron, deployed as a sort of generalised cultural idea rather than in historical or textual specificity. As Molly Wesling puts it in her detailed study of the importance of Napoleon to Russian literary and cultural life in the nineteenth century, 'Napoleon wielded iconic power unrivalled in the Western world.'[55] Napoleon's influence on the texts discussed by this book comes from this iconic power rather than the complex combination of authored texts and biographical influence that Byron exerted as a literary figure. Wesling's summary of the iconic power of Napoleon for the Russian Romantics holds for his influence in Western Europe too. Indeed, she directly compares the Russian writers with Western European writers. Thus, Alexander Nikitenko, whose words began this introduction, is 'like Julien Sorel in Stendhal's novel *The Red and the Black*,'[56] insofar as he comes from peasant origins (in Nikitenko's case, he was a serf who, after involvement in the Decembrist revolution, became a prominent government censor) but rises, if not as far as Napoleon, into the world of the ruling classes.

Wesling's description of the Napoleon myth in Russia offers a useful definition for what Napoleonic heroism also signifies in the texts of

Western Europe and, in particular, *The Red and the Black* and *Vanity Fair*, which I discuss in later chapters. She stresses the 'dramatic elements from his life story – a rise from supposedly humble origins, the accumulation of heroic feats,' Napoleon's meteoric rise to power.[57] Wesling lingers particularly on the frequency with which Napoleon is attached to metaphors of comets: '[Napoleon] was no doubt aware of the tradition wherein comets were associated with kings and great rulers. By quickly adopting comet symbolism, Napoleon gave his reign a traditional resonance and legitimacy.'[58] Napoleon, as far as the mythology goes, comes from humble origins but becomes a figure of heroic power. He even assumes an air of aristocratic legitimacy associated with the divine right of kings. This echoes Carlyle's description of Napoleon as acceding to kingship because of inherent virtues. Napoleon is meritocratic, aristocratic, and monarchical. This contradictory character is stressed by a further aspect of Napoleon, the way he is 'symbolically imbued with the democratic ideals of the French Revolution.'[59] Wesling discusses this in relation to the 'increasingly conservative' Russian regime that followed the Napoleonic Wars, but conservatism was the post-Napoleonic order of the day in France and Britain too.

Bainbridge, in his study, suggests that English Romantic writers recognised similar qualities in Napoleon, 'genius, energy, imagination and daring.'[60] However, he also offers a persuasive theoretical framework for thinking about Napoleon in literature. Discussing Richard Whatley's *Historic Doubts Relative to Napoleon Bonaparte* (1819), Bainbridge observes that in the culture of the Romantic period, Napoleon is presented 'on the one hand, [as] a real historical personage and, on the other, [as] a "fabrication" or "imaginary figure". As such Napoleon is a textual construction: '[T]hen, as now, of course, there was no definitive or stable "Napoleon" but innumerable and varied accounts of him, themselves available for interpretation.'[61] Napoleon, then, represents a contradictory complex of various values that defy logic but are frequently mobilised simultaneously in the texts I discuss, and which vary according to their literary context. Both Julien Sorel's and Becky Sharpe's social climbing and revolutionary insurrections are against a hybrid aristocratic-bourgeois social order that they attempt to integrate themselves into. They are revolutionaries who look for aristocratic legitimacy at the same time as ripping it to pieces. In the contradictory nature of the Napoleonic, there is a sense that this form of heroism is the necessary precondition of a historical movement which, as it emerges, erases its origins. Nevertheless, the aristocratic aspects of Napoleon are, paradoxically, a key part of the insurrection against the aristocratic which marks the bourgeois, even whilst, simultaneously, Napoleon offers a bourgeois dream of meritocracy which is mobilised against the aristocracy in the form of revolution. Napoleonic heroism gives birth to, but also subverts, the bourgeois.

In the context of Russian literary culture, Wesling observes that Belinsky saw Napoleon ushering in 'an original literary tradition in Russia,' 'the dawn of Romanticism, when Russians finally overcame their slavish dependence on the French by literally and figuratively driving them from Russia.'[62] It requires the intervention of the French Napoleon to usher in a new Russian tradition that paradoxically destroys the French tradition, and yet, as Wesling's book attests in its exploration of Russian literature's obsession with Napoleon, the destruction of that French tradition is never complete. As in the texts I discuss, despite the obsolescence of Napoleon, he remains an insistent spectral presence that haunts the texts that insist on his anachronism.

If, as this book argues, Byron and Napoleon help to define the bourgeois, even whilst they subvert it, I next need to define what I mean when I use the word 'bourgeois.' At its most basic level, as defined by Marx, the bourgeoisie are simply the owners of the means of production. However, in *The Communist Manifesto*, Marx and Engels ascribe a whole series of cultural values to them, most of which centre around progress, contradiction, and the destruction of old values.[63]

Marx and Engels's description of bourgeois values, whilst capturing the radical side of the bourgeoisie, a side which they frequently describe in heroic terms, does not capture the other side, famously recognised by Max Weber as the *spirit of capitalism*, of conservatism, the home, stability, professionalism, and the pleasures of everyday life, which are the ideological supports to the endless economic progress and contradiction of the bourgeois era, and which tend to be celebrated in its literature: 'not simply a means of making one's way in the world, but a peculiar ethic.'[64] It is the features of this ideological 'spirit' which I argue in various ways are consolidated by heroism in the nineteenth-century novels I discuss, consolidated at the expense of the idea of revolutionary heroism.

In *The New Spirit of Capitalism*, Luc Boltanski and Ève Chiapello set out a succinct definition of this Weberian spirit of capitalism. Boltanski and Chiapello are sociologists, and, for them, ideology is defined as 'a set of shared beliefs inscribed in institutions, bound up with actions, and hence anchored in reality,' rather than what they deem a vulgar Marxist definition of ideology as 'moralizing discourse, intended to conceal material interests, which is constantly contradicted in practice.'[65] Particularly, they define the 'spirit of capitalism' as 'the ideology that justifies engagement in capitalism.'[66] Moreover, Boltanski and Chiapello particularly link the configuration and establishment of the spirit of capitalism as it is manifested in the nineteenth century to the novel as form (as do so many Marxist critics). They identify both the 'heroic' risk taking associated with Marx and Engels's bourgeoisie *and* the parsimonious conservatism associated with Weber's:

[The description of the spirit of capitalism] undertaken at the end
of the nineteenth century – in novels as much as the social sciences
proper – is focused on the person of the bourgeois entrepreneur [...]
stressing gambles, speculation, risk, innovation. [...] [Providing an
element of stability to counterbalance this risk], the figure of the
bourgeois, and bourgeois morality, afford elements of security in an
original combination, combining novel economic propensities (ava-
rice of parsimony, the spirit of saving, a tendency to rationalize daily
life in all its aspects, the development of capacities for book-keeping,
calculation, prediction) with traditional domestic predispositions:
the importance attached to the family, lineage, inheritance, the chas-
tity of daughters in order to avoid misalliances and the squandering
of capital; the familial or patriarchal nature of relations with employ-
ees – what will subsequently be denounced as paternalism – whose
forms of subordination remained largely personal in firms that were
generally small in size; the role accorded charity in relieving the sufferings of the poor.

For them, the *spirit* of capitalism actually puts checks on capitalism in
its rawest form of pure accumulation, in order to maintain the acquies-
cence of non-capitalists to it. Bourgeois ideology provides the feelings of
engagement and safety that encourage wage labourers to work under the
capitalists. Hence the ideology that Boltanski and Chiapello describe is
grafted on to the economic definition of the bourgeoisie that Marx and
Engels give, which essentially colours the Marxist definition of bourgeois
values. It is the consolidation of these bourgeois values, how they are
woven into ideas about subjectivity, and how they are heroised, as well as
how they are subverted, that I am particularly interested in, though they
are never separable from the economic status of the bourgeoisie.

V

Having offered these definitions, and before giving a chapter-by-chapter
outline of the book, I want to address one major methodological issue,
that of translation. Throughout this work, I look at English literature
alongside Russian and French literature, which I have predominantly
read and refer to in translation, though with reference to the original
languages where this is necessary or appropriate. Though there are limitations to this approach, I believe it justifiable. Throughout the book, the
pan-European stature of Napoleon and Byron is at the forefront. With
Napoleon, translation is less of a problem since his importance stems
from his status as a cultural icon rather than from texts he wrote. Byron,
on the other hand, was known not just as a cultural icon but as a poet.
His pan-European fame came from the circulation of his texts in translation. To take an example that directly bears on what follows, Diakonova

and Vatsuro twice state that Pushkin read Byron 'mainly in French translations.'[67] Pushkin was also familiar with Russian translations of Byron. For example, the journal *Vestnik Evropy* published 'papers on Byron's work, derived mainly from French but also partly from German magazines.'[68] Similarly, Lermontov's early contact with Byron came through various forms of translation, 'between 1828 and 1829 the young Lermontov became acquainted with Byron in translation,' and 'it was Pushkin who became the principal intermediary between Byron and Lermontov.' Lermontov translated Byron himself.[69] The French translations which Pushkin and Lermontov were familiar with were produced by Amédée Pichot who translated most of the major works between 1819 and 1821.[70] As Joanne Wilkes points out, these translations of Byron, which would also have been familiar to Stendhal, were all in prose.[71] Wilkes attributes this to two factors. In the first place,

> Translators evidently found it difficult to render into French verse Byron's various metrical forms and rhyme schemes [...] French poetry was, in the early nineteenth century, still very much affected by neo-classical conventions of metre and diction in a way that would have made Byron's writings seem, in their form alone, more daring than they appeared to English readers.[72]

Moreover, secondly, it seems that to French readers Byron's ideas seemed more important than his poetry: '[H]e was perceived as expressing the mood of the age [...] a confused time of transition.'[73] In my discussion of Byron in Chapters 1 and 2, I suggest that Byron's poetry points towards a formal transition to the novel. In this respect, the prose translations of Byron's poetry point towards the novelistic transformations the Byronic was to undergo with its readers.

The notion that the importance of Byron's poetry lay in its ideas which could be circulated in translation challenged an important dogma of some Romantic writers: untranslatability. Famously, for Percy Shelley, translation is 'vanity' since 'it were as wise to cast a violet into a crucible that you might discover the formal principle of its colour and odour, as seek to transfuse from one language into another the creations of a poet.'[74] As Timothy Webb observes, this theory of translation owes much to a Platonic idealism. The poem is a transcendent ideal form, and the translation a shadowy copy.[75] It takes little imagination to connect this to the various theories of the transcendent, ideal, original, individual-ised theories of poetry and the poet which are expressed by Wordsworth, Coleridge, and Keats. As my later discussion of the dialogism and disen-chantment of Pushkin, Lermontov, and Dickens demonstrates, the circu-lation of Byron's texts in translation and prose, which disassociated them from an aesthetic theory of idealist individualism, finds its echo in the form of the novel in its transition from Romanticism.

Where there are limitations, these are most pronounced in relation to the Russian texts. In relation to Stendhal, I have tried to indicate the original French where this is relevant to the reading I am positing. My lack of knowledge of the Russian language has meant that I have had to rely much more heavily on translations and have approached this by comparing multiple translations as much as possible and taking advice from Russian speakers.[76] Language difficulties are particularly a risk in relation to *Eugene Onegin* whose complex poetic form and the marked difference between English and Russian means that it is particularly resistant to translation. On the other hand, certain formal features of *Eugene Onegin*, particularly its status as a transitional text between epic poem and novel, are comparable to English texts like the long poems of Byron and remain discernible in translation, as they were to those who read Byron in translation. My focus elsewhere in the book on the status of the novel as a vehicle for the depiction of heroism, and as a privileged example of the art of the bourgeoisie under high capitalism, means that it is these latter features of *Eugene Onegin* that I am concerned with here, rather than particular issues of local prosody or diction.

In order to address these difficulties as fully as possible, I have used the most recent verse translation of *Eugene Onegin*, by Stanley Mitchell, which had the benefit of the most recent scholarship and critiques of previous translations and seeks to emulate Pushkin's distinctive verse form; he is undoubtedly successful in translating Pushkin's poetry into convincing English verse.[77] I also compared this to Vladimir Nabokov's translation and voluminous commentary, which entirely dispenses readability and seeks as far as possible to render Russian syntax and diction as literally as possible in another language, and offers detailed explanations of etymology, context, and nuance.[78] I also compared the translations of Roger Clarke, James E. Falen, and Charles Johnston.[79]

In Nabokov's wonderful poem 'On Translating "Eugene Onegin,"' he laments that 'Reflected words can only shiver | Like elongated lines that twist | In the black mirror of a river | Better the city and the mist.' Ultimately, and sadly, I am confined to what Nabokov describes as the 'shadow' of Pushkin's monument.'[80] But, though I acknowledge the limitations of working with translations, I believe that what can be gained by this sort of comparative work, which would always be dogged by questions of cultural difference, far outweighs the limitations, particularly in an academic environment which under neoliberalism pushes towards extreme specialisation in favour of broader cultural comparison. As will be seen, though my contribution is far more modest than these great thinkers, my theoretical references throughout this book, Marx, Freud, Nietzsche, Benjamin, Auerbach, Foucault, and Rancière, highlight the immense gains to be had working across cultures and in translations, even at the risk of blind spots and oversights.

Equally, however, by working across languages and national traditions like this, I hope to illustrate connections that would have otherwise gone unnoticed and also to allow a recognition of the transnational circulation of Byron and Napoleon rather than their being bound to 'original,' national contexts. Indeed, whilst neither figure is unambiguously radical, one way in which both emerge as radical figures is in the way they confuse questions of nationalism and allow one to imagine what Nietzsche describes as a Europe-to-come which asserts itself against nationalism. Nietzsche lambasts nationalist politicians, claiming that 'Europe wants to be one,' and that 'all of this century's deeper and more generous individuals have actually directed their souls towards preparing a path to a new *synthesis* and experimentally anticipating the European of the future.' These figures are 'people like Napoleon, Goethe, Beethoven, Stendhal, Heinrich Heine, Schopenhauer,' to which this book adds Byron, Pushkin, Lermontov, Dickens, and Thackeray.[81]

VI

I wish now to turn to explain how I approach the ideas of the hero and heroism and set out a more detailed summary of each chapter of the book.

That a narrative interest in the hero is still insisted upon in the texts I am discussing is signalled by the ways in which they all broach the topic of the hero from the very outset. In the cases of *A Hero of Our Time* and *Vanity Fair*, which is subtitled *A Novel Without a Hero*, this is signalled in the titles themselves. In the other texts, questions of heroism are approached very early on in the text, establishing them as key concerns that each novel addresses. Given that I am addressing the *mutations* of heroism, rather than having a fixed definition of the term, I will, rather, examine the specific ways in which the term is deployed through the Byronic, Napoleonic, and bourgeois.

Each chapter, however, follows the same basic structural principle. It shows how Byronic or Napoleonic heroism has informed the creation of a new form of bourgeois heroism and how each has in turn rendered Byronic or Napoleonic heroism obsolete. It then shows the continuing, disruptive, influence of Byronic and Napoleonic heroism on bourgeois heroism as a memory of non-bourgeois origins of bourgeois heroism. The Byron theme has chapters on the influence of Byron on Pushkin's *Eugene Onegin* and Lermontov's *A Hero of Our Time*, and on Dickens's *David Copperfield*. The Napoleon theme has chapters on Stendhal's *The Red and the Black* and Thackeray's *Vanity Fair*. However, as I will show, the influences of Byron and Napoleon often go hand-in-hand and a division into either/or is not always possible.

In the first chapter on Pushkin and Lermontov, I track the influence of Byron in *Eugene Onegin* and *A Hero of Our Time* and suggest that

Byronic heroism informs a depiction of nascent-bourgeois values and subjectivities in both writers, whilst also stressing the particular economic and political situation in Russia in the early nineteenth century, which saw a development of modernity alongside much less industrial development than in Western Europe and a very different set of political institutions. I argue that both writers imagine new forms of bourgeois individualism that are a product of the aristocratic, revolutionary heroism of Byron and Byronism, and illustrate this with an analysis of Pushkin and Lermontov's depictions of the aristocratic, but individualist, Decembrist Revolt. I suggest that Lermontov shows a greater movement towards bourgeois values than Pushkin since his work represents a pessimistic view of the possibilities for Romantic individualism, encapsulated by Byronic self-narration, after the failure of the Decembrist Revolt and a concomitant movement towards a sense of professionalism. In short, the Byronic directly informs the creation of bourgeois values, a nascent form of bourgeois hero is imagined, even as the Byronic is shown to be obsolete. In spite of this, the Byronic is still troublingly visible in the bourgeois hero insofar as the bourgeois hero still describes himself in reference to the Byronic. This happens to a differing extent in *Eugene Onegin* and *A Hero of Our Time*, with *Eugene Onegin* being much more positive about the possibilities of Byronic heroism and revolution than *A Hero of Our Time*.

The chapter on Dickens traces the influence of Byron on Dickens in some detail. It suggests a contrast between Byronic heroism, as embodied by Steerforth and conceived simultaneously as aristocratic and revolutionary, and bourgeois, professional heroism, as embodied by David Copperfield, and conceived in terms of duty, professionalism, and the celebration of the self-contained, private subject. I pay particular attention to the way in which both Byron and David Copperfield are concerned with acts of self-narration, but whereas Byron's is deployed both to create a sense of Romantic individualism which partakes in an idea of nature and a world that goes far beyond the individual subject and to suggest a wide political consciousness, David's is deployed to imagine himself as a private subject, which I argue by drawing attention to similarities between Dickens's writing and Freud's theories and the experiences of his patient in the 'Rat Man' case study. I put this into relation to the accent on Steerforth as both revolutionary and aristocratic in order to draw a contrast, but Steerforth in my account, whilst a Byronic revolutionary figure who represents the obverse of David's bourgeois conformism, is also the precondition of it. I argue that bourgeois subjectivity is explicitly modelled on a Byronic narration of the self which is echoed in both Steerforth and David. The novel disavows this connection by killing him off. However, I suggest through a careful reading of images of revolution in the text, that the bourgeois subject still bears the disruptive traces of his revolutionary past.

The chapter on Stendhal's *The Red and the Black* considers what it means for Julien Sorel to imagine himself as Napoleonic in relationship to the 1830 revolution in France which installed the 'bourgeois king' Louis-Philippe and saw the economic ascendancy of the French bourgeoisie. It dwells on the fact that Julien imagines himself to be a Napoleonic figure but the novel ends with him being executed. Similar to the way in which Steerforth is killed at the end of *David Copperfield*, this novel eventually erases the heroic figure of the past who acts as a precondition to – the model for – the creation of its bourgeois heroism of the present. Equally, however, this chapter stresses the way in which Julien's sense of himself as Napoleonic is absorbed into the bourgeois ideological demands of professionalism and the accumulation of capital, even though the novel does not always depict Julien as aware of this himself. This means that Julien imagines himself as a Napoleonic heroic figure, but, with characteristic irony, the novel reveals how he is actually a vanguard of a militantly unheroic bourgeois class. I argue that this transference of the Napoleonic into the bourgeois sphere is part of a more general change in the aesthetics of the period. I take up Jacques Rancière's suggestion that the novel is pioneering a new form of representation that he calls 'the aesthetic regime of the arts,' the philosophical term that he applies to the distinct democratising effects of literary realism. I argue that the aesthetic regime of the arts is not congruent with a notion of heroism, and alongside the satirising of Julien's Napoleonic heroism at the level of plot and novelistic discourse, the form of the novel demands that Napoleon must be figuratively executed in the literal execution of Julien. Yet Napoleon still suffuses the novel in complex and destabilising ways, in spite of its final attempt to remove him.

Finally, in the chapter on Thackeray's *Vanity Fair*, I argue that Napoleon, rather than being rejected, is integrated into the novel, within the bourgeois domestic sphere and that, significantly, it is a woman, Becky Sharp, who becomes the new Napoleonic hero for the new age. I demonstrate the historical influence of Napoleon on Thackeray's work. On the one hand, in the post-Napoleonic world, Napoleon has become an object of parody for Thackeray, where possibilities of heroism have been exhausted for the bourgeois men who dominate that world. Thus, Thackeray reactivates the disappearance of heroism with memories of Napoleonic heroism, transferring heroism away from the men who could traditionally claim to be heroic. It is Becky who becomes a Napoleonic heroic figure. Napoleon informs the creation of the heroic figure Becky Sharp, but, nonetheless, she is not strictly Napoleonic since she transfers Napoleonic heroism from the world-historical to the domestic stage. She appears as a working-class figure who has a meteoric rise through the haute bourgeoisie and the aristocracy, gains a degree of aristocratic recognition, and then falls away into exile. She is characterised as a force of joyful malignity and as a sort of prostitute figure, and so repeats Napoleon's revolutionary uprising on a domestic scale. Simultaneously she gleefully undermines all bourgeois values whilst aspiring to them. The

Napoleonic in this respect is more completely preserved in the bourgeois context, though, once again, in mutated form, because Becky Sharp does not, like the other figures in the book, become a characteristically bourgeois hero. Rather, Napoleonic heroism informs her revolutionary heroism in a bourgeois setting, a different mutation from the others discussed. She is perhaps the only truly heroic figure in my book and is certainly the most powerful instance of the haunting presence in nineteenth-century bourgeois fiction of the modes of heroism that it worked so hard to displace.

It will be noted that the division of Byron and Napoleon in this structure is to a certain extent arbitrary. Part of my aim is to demonstrate that the reinscriptions of the Byronic and Napoleonic result in similar models of heroism, and as this implies, the two are interlinked from the very outset. Inverting the two terms and their relations to the texts would produce a shadow book to this one on Pushkin, Lermontov, Dickens and Napoleon, and Stendhal, Thackeray, and Byron or would double this book's length. As such, divisions had to be made. I invite the reader to bear in mind that Napoleon and Byron are shadowing each other in all these texts, and they did in literature from the outset as Byron's poetry worked through their identification.[82] I can only hope that this book inspires further work on the presence of Byron, Napoleon, and the complex discourse of heroism in the nineteenth-century novel, which might fill in the gaps I have left. Eugene Onegin's study, with 'Lord Byron's portrait on the wall' and its statue of Napoleon 'on a little column standing [...] with gloomy forehead and a hat,' might symbolise the future work of interlacing these two figures more fully in the literature that responds to them.[83] And with that, I turn to Pushkin's great poem.

Notes

1 Quoted in Molly W. Wesling, *Napoleon in Russian Cultural Mythology* (New York: Peter Lang, 2001), p. 55.

2 Karl Marx, 'The Eighteenth Brumaire of Louis Bonaparte,' trans. Ben Fowkes in *Political Writings*, ed. David Fernbach, 3 vols (Harmondsworth: Penguin/ London: New Left Review, 1973), II, pp. 143–249 (p. 144). Further references to this text will be included parenthetically in the body of the chapter.

3 Matthew Arnold, *Poetical Works*, ed. C. B. Tinker and H. F. Lowry (Oxford: Oxford University Press, 1969), pp. 299–306.

4 For analyses and historical accounts of Byron's enduring influence in contexts beyond the scope of this book, see Frances Wilson (ed.), *Byromania: Portraits of the Artist in Nineteenth- and Twentieth-Century Culture* (Basingstoke: Palgrave, 1999); Ghislaine McDayter, *Byromania and the Birth of Celebrity Culture* (Albany: State University of New York Press, 2009); and Richard Cardwell (ed.), *The Reception of Byron in Europe* 2 vols. (London: Bloomsbury, 2004).

5 Thomas Carlyle, *On Heroes, Hero-Worship, and the Heroic in History*, ed. David R. Sorensen and Brent E. Kinser (New Haven: Yale University Press, 2013), p. 21. Further references to this text will be incorporated parenthetically into the body of the chapter.

6 Raymond Williams, *Culture and Society 1780–1950* (Harmondsworth: Penguin, 1966), p. 95.
7 Sorensen, 'Introduction' to Carlyle, *Heroes*, pp. 1–2.
8 Bertolt Brecht, *The Life of Galileo*, trans. Desmond I. Vesey (London: Methuen, 1971), p. 108.
9 John Price, *Everyday Heroism: Victorian Constructions of the Heroic Civilian* (London: Bloomsbury, 2014).
10 Madeline Callaghan, *The Poet-Hero in the Work of Byron and Shelley* (London: Anthem Press, 2019), p. 6.
11 Callaghan, pp. 6–7.
12 Mario Praz, *The Hero in Eclipse in Victorian Fiction*, trans. Angus Davidson (Oxford: Oxford University Press, 1969), p. 39.
13 Praz, p. 163.
14 This could be compared to Bakhtin's democratic reading of the novel in terms of heteroglossia. For heteroglossia, see Mikhail Bakhtin, *The Dialogic Imagination: Four Essays*, ed. Michael Holquist, trans. Caryl Emerson and Michael Holquist (Austin: University of Texas Press, 2008), and *Problems of Dostoevsky's Poetics*, ed. and trans. Caryl Emerson (Minneapolis: University of Minnesota Press, 1984). For Bakhtin as a theory of democracy in the novel see Roy Hirschkop, *Mikhail Bakhtin: An Aesthetic for Democracy* (Oxford: Oxford University Press, 1999).
15 Praz, p. 163.
16 Franco Moretti, *The Bourgeois: Between History and Literature* (London: Verso, 2014), p. 181.
17 Moretti, p. 16.
18 Moretti, p. 17.
19 Price, p. 15.
20 Price, p. 8.
21 Price, p. 15.
22 Price, p. 13.
23 Price, p. 5; 9.
24 Price, p. 10.
25 Robin Gilmour, *The Idea of the Gentleman in the Victorian Novel* (London: George Allen & Unwin, 1981), p. 2.
26 Gilmour, p. 2.
27 Joseph Bristow, *Empire Boys: Adventures in a Man's World* (Abingdon: Routledge, 2016) is an important foundational study in the conservative recuperation of heroism in the late-Victorian romance. See also Frederic Jameson's celebrated chapter on Conrad in *The Political Unconscious* (Abingdon: Routledge, 2002), pp. 194–270.
28 Peter L. Thorslev, Jr, *The Byronic Hero: Types and Prototypes* (Minneapolis: University of Minnesota Press, 1962).
29 Thorslev, pp. 144–145.
30 This focus on *Childe Harold* and *The Giaour* is not adopted in order to dismiss another of Byron's major poems which remains in the background of this book, *Don Juan*, but to suggest that the form of the Byronic Hero that the texts I discuss depict is the type Thorslev describes. The satirical *Don Juan* does not depict a Byronic Hero according to Thorslev's typology.
31 Lord Byron, 'The Giaour,' in *Major Works*, ed. Jerome J. McGann (Oxford: Oxford University Press, 2008), l. 6. All references to Byron's poetry throughout this book, unless otherwise noted, will be to this edition.
32 Jerome McGann, note in Byron, *Major Works*, p. 1036.
33 Vincent Newey, 'Rival Cultures: Charles Dickens and the Byronic Legacy,' *The Byron Journal* 32 (2004), 85–100 (p. 88).

34 Malcolm Kelsall, *Byron's Politics* (Brighton: Harvester Press, 1987), p. 2. Further references to this text will be included parenthetically in the body of the chapter.

35 Jerome Christensen, *Lord Byron's Strength: Romantic Writing and Commercial Society* (Baltimore: Johns Hopkins University Press, 1993), p. xxiii.

36 Christensen, p. xxiv.

37 Christensen, p. 16.

38 Christensen, p. 16. The interpretation of the politics of Byron's life and work has become a veritable industry, and there are books and essays on every conceivable facet of Byron's politics and in relation to the entire breadth of his oeuvre and afterlife. Since this work focuses on the politics of the Victorian novels which develop their own Byronic configurations for their own political ends, a full discussion of works on Byron's own politics is beyond the scope of this book, but other key moments in the critical debate include Roderick Beaton and Christine Kenyon Jones (eds.), *Byron: The Poetry of Politics and the Politics of Poetry* (Abingdon: Routledge, 2017); James Chandler, *England in 1819: The Politics of Literary Culture and the Case of Romantic Historicism*, (Chicago: University of Chicago Press, 1998); myriad works of Jerome McGann, such as the essays collected in *Byron and Romanticism*, ed. James Soderholm (Cambridge: Cambridge University Press, 2002); and Jane Stabler, *Byron, Poetics and History* (Cambridge: Cambridge Univ. Press, 2002).

39 Christensen, p.12.

40 When Byron adopted the name Noel, he wrote in a letter to Thomas Moore, 'You see the great advantage of my new signature; it may either stand for "Nota Bene" or "Noel Byron." The editor of Byron's letters, Leslie Marchand, quotes from Leigh Hunt in a footnote that Bryon 'delighted, when he took the additional name of Noel...to sign himself N.B.; "because," said he, "Bonaparte and I are the only public persons whose initials are the same."' See, George Gordon, Lord Byron, 'To Thomas Moore' and f.n., in *Letters and Journals*, ed. Leslie A. Marchand, 12 vols. (London: John Murray, 1973–1982), IX, p. 171. Elsewhere, Marchand suggests that Byron's identification of his own initials with Napoleon's is an apocryphal story which he attributes, interestingly for this book, to Stendhal. See, Leslie A. Marchand, *Byron: A Portrait* (London: John Murray, 1971), p. 366.

41 Alan Rawes, 'Marino Faliero: Escaping the Aristocratic,' in *Liberty and Poetic Licence: New Essays on Byron*, eds. Bernard Beatty, Tony Howe and Charles Robinson (Liverpool: Liverpool University Press, 2008), pp. 88–102 (pp. 89–90).

42 Malcolm Kelsall, 'Byron's politics,' in *The Cambridge Companion to Byron*, ed. Drummond Bone (Cambridge: Cambridge University Press, 2004), pp. 44–55 (p. 48).

43 However, the poem itself, in a cynical, melancholy mode, seems to question the possibility of that freedom (which is not the same as denying a commitment to it). If within the allegorical schema of the poem, Leila is Greece, then her death and the Giaour's subsequent withdrawal from the world are sceptical about the possibility of freedom, a thought emphasised by the narrator of the preamble on contemporary Greece blaming the Greeks for their own subjection: 'Self-abasement pav'd the way | To villain-bonds and despot sway' (140–141).

44 Georg Lukács, *The Theory of the Novel*, trans. Anna Bostock (London: Merlin, 2006), pp. 117–118.

45 Callaghan, pp. 4; 2.

46 Deborah Lutz, *The Dangerous Lover: Gothic Villains, Byronism, and the Nineteenth-Century Seduction Narrative* (Columbus: Ohio State University Press, 2006), pp. 49–52.

47 Lutz, p. 50.

48 Lutz, p. 88.

49 Lutz, p. 89.

50 Susan J. Wolfson, *Romantic Interactions: Social Being and the Turns of Literary Action* (Baltimore: Johns Hopkins University Press, 2010), p. 213.

51 Wolfson, p. 213.

52 Wolfson, p. 252.

53 Sarah Wootton, *Byronic Heroes in Nineteenth-Century Women's Writing and Screen Adaptation* (Basingstoke: Palgrave Macmillan, 2016), p. 182.

54 Simon Bainbridge, *Napoleon and English Romanticism* (Cambridge: Cambridge University Press, 1995), p. 2.

55 Wesling, p. 35.

56 Wesling, p. 35.

57 Wesling, p. 55.

58 Wesling, p. 55.

59 Wesling, p. 36.

60 Bainbridge, p. 2.

61 Bainbridge, p. 4.

62 Wesling, p. 36.

63 Karl Marx and Friedrich Engels, 'Manifesto of the Communist Party,' in *Political Writings*, ed. David Fernbach, 3 vols (Harmondsworth: Penguin/ London: New Left Review, 1973), I, pp. 62–98.

64 Max Weber, *The Protestant Ethic and the Spirit of Capitalism*, trans. Talcott Parsons (London: Routledge, 2001), p. 17.

65 Luc Boltanski and Ève Chiapello, *The New Spirit of Capitalism*, trans. Gregory Elliott (London: Verso, 2007), p. 3.

66 Boltanski and Chiapello, p. 8.

67 Nina Diakonova and Vadim Vatsuro, '"No Great Mind and Generous Heart Could Avoid Byronism": Russia and Byron,' in *The Reception of Byron in Europe*, ed. Richard Cardwell, 2 vols. (London: Thoemmes Continuum, 2004), II, pp. 333–352 (pp. 336–337).

68 Diakonova and Vatsuro, p. 334.

69 Diakonova and Vatsuro, p. 342.

70 All information on French translations of Byron is taken from the invaluable chapter by Joanne Wilks, '"Infernal Magnetism": Byron and Nineteenth-Century French Readers,' in *The Reception of Byron in Europe*, ed. Richard Cardwell, 2 vols. (London: Thoemmes Continuum, 2004), I, pp. 11–31 (p. 15).

71 Wilkes, p. 16. On Stendhal and Byron, see Peter Cochran, 'From Pichot to Stendhal to Musset: Byron's Progress Through Early Nineteenth-Century French Literature,' in *The Reception of Byron in Europe*, ed. Richard Cardwell, 2 vols. (London: Thoemmes Continuum, 2004), I, pp. 32–70.

72 Wilkes, p. 16.

73 Wilkes, p. 17.

74 Percy Bysshe Shelley, 'A Defence of Poetry,' in *Poetry and Prose*, 2nd edn., ed. Donald H. Reiman and Neil Fraistat (New York: W.W. Norton, 2002), pp. 509–535 (p. 514).

75 Timothy Webb, *The Violet in the Crucible: Shelley and Translation* (Oxford: Clarendon Press, 1976), pp. 27–29.

76 I take this opportunity to reiterate my thanks to Rachel Platonov and Dan Kennedy for their advice on the Russian language. Any mistakes or errors are, of course, my own.

77 Alexander Pushkin, *Eugene Onegin: A Novel in Verse*, trans. Stanley Mitchell (London: Penguin, 2008).

78 Aleksandr Pushkin, *Eugene Onegin*, trans. Vladimir Nabokov, 2 vols. (Princeton: Princeton University Press, 1990)

79 Alexander Pushkin, *Eugene Onegin*, trans. Roger Clarke (Richmond: Alma, 2015); Alexander Pushkin, *Eugene Onegin: A Novel in Verse*, trans. James E. Falen (Oxford: Oxford University Press, 1998); Alexander Pushkin, *Eugene Onegin: A Novel in Verse*, Rev. edn., trans. Charles Johnston (London: Penguin, 2003).

80 Vladimir Nabokov, 'On Translating "Eugene Onegin,"' *New Yorker*, 8 January 1955, p. 34.

81 Friedrich Nietzsche, *Beyond Good and Evil: Prelude to a Philosophy of the Future*, trans. Marion Faber (Oxford: Oxford University Press, 2008), p. 148.

82 See Jerome J. McGann's detailed explication of the Byron-Napoleon doublet in *"Don Juan" in Context* (London: John Murray, 1976).

83 *Eugene Onegin*, trans. Stanley Mitchell, p. 151.

1 Byronism, Revolution, and the Birth of Bourgeois Individualism

Heroism in Pushkin and Lermontov

I

Georges Bataille describes the fate of the heroic in modernity: 'Reason subordinates the heroic moment to services rendered.'[1] Under capitalism, argues Bataille, heroism is no longer free to exist for itself but instead is chained to demands made upon it from outside: the demands of capitalism to render services, in the form of wage labour, or to accrue capital. This is parallel to Lukács's argument, which I set out in the introduction, that subjectivity and heroism undergo fundamental changes under the rise of capitalism: from a subjectivity that expands and asserts itself in the world to one that is self-contained within the private individual. Bataille's formulation adds that the private individual's heroism not only no longer exists in epic self-assertion, but rather in his or her ability to render services to capitalism. In either wage labour or the accruing of capital, Bataille argues, the demand of capitalism is the demand of self-interest: '[T]he form that material interest has actually taken today [is …] personal interest, precisely under the form of self-interest, within capitalist society.'[2] What Bataille describes, then, is a becoming-professional of the hero and a subordination of the heroic to private interests. This is part of a more general turning inwards of subjectivity, which I have suggested in my introduction is the fate of heroism in the nineteenth century. Heroism under capitalism takes the form of being a professional. As I discussed in the introduction, the spirit that justifies engagement with capitalism combines a heroisation of the bourgeois figure as risk-taker and speculator, along with a valourisation of the safe, stable values of professionalism and integration into the bourgeois social world. With the rise of high capitalism, a system that dominates and defines all social relations in society, the only position available to heroism is as an appendage to the dominance of capital, and, if the bourgeois class ultimately only has an interest in the accumulation of capital, then the mode of heroism valourised can only be one that tends towards this.[3] The heroic assertive pole of bourgeois identity, then, must necessarily inhabit an increasingly small niche in the global smooth running of a dominant capitalist system.

DOI: 10.4324/9781003160168-2

In this chapter, I argue that the production of the professional hero is evident in two important early Russian novels by Alexander Pushkin and Mikhail Lermontov, but that, in their Russian context, where bourgeois capitalism was not as advanced as in Western Europe, this remains connected to the heroic efforts of the new bourgeoisie to assert their own values, as the bourgeoisie in Western Europe did several decades earlier. Heroic efforts which Pushkin and Lermontov show, will themselves pass away, to leave a bourgeois conformity to the reign of high capitalism. I particularly demonstrate how both the heroic, revolutionary efforts to assert subjectivity and the shift to bourgeois, professional heroism, as depicted in these writers' works, are, in part, the results of the Europewide influence of Byron. In Pushkin and Lermontov, a shift occurs, from the Byronic heroic subject of revolution to the 'heroic' subject of capitalism.[4] This shift is also a move away from the aristocratic salon culture towards a peculiarly Russian, and very nascent, form of bourgeois capitalism, centred on the cosmopolitan cities of Moscow and Saint Petersburg, as well as on imperialist conquest in the Caucasus.

Marx and Engels write in *The Communist Manifesto* that, under bourgeois capitalism, 'all fixed, fast-frozen relations, with their train of venerable prejudices and opinions, are swept away [...] and man is at last compelled to face with sober senses, his real conditions of life, and his relations with his kind.'[5] In the novels I discuss in this chapter, it is the formally regulated relations of society embodied by the aristocratic social code and the salon that are 'swept away,' and instead heroism becomes an expression of the 'real conditions' of nineteenth-century 'life' – integration and success in capitalism. This process is informed, in Russia, by the consumption of Western literature: '[T]he bourgeoisie has through its exploitation of the world-market given a cosmopolitan character to production and consumption in every country [...] from the numerous national and local literatures, there arises a world literature.'[6] It is important that Marx and Engels particularly note the creation of world literature as an important aspect of the bourgeois upheaval of society. Key to this development of world literature is Byron, who, as I have shown in the introduction, exerted a broad influence over so much European literature and was read avidly in translation by Pushkin and Lermontov. For these two writers, Byron, I argue, is a model for revolutionary thought but also informs the integration into professionalised heroism which marks the stability of the bourgeoisie. The Byronic informs this through a revolutionary ideology that overturns the aristocratic world in favour of a heroic individualism, which then mutates into bourgeois individualism and defines itself against the Byronic. The Byronic is rejected by the bourgeois subjectivity that it has historically informed, though the traces of the Byronic remain.

I will explain how a cosmopolitan literary taste amongst the Russian intelligentsia in which Pushkin and Lermontov moved provided the raw materials from which to fashion the nascent bourgeois hero, particularly through the writings and cultural image of Byron. My case studies are the two major novels of the period: Pushkin's 'novel-in-verse' *Eugene Onegin* (*Yevgeniy Onegin*, 1825–1832, published in one volume 1833) and Lermontov's *A Hero of Our Time* (*Geroy nashego vremeni*, 1840).[7] The analogous birth of the bourgeois hero took place much earlier in Western European literature. Marx begins *Grundrisse* with a discussion of 'Robinsonades,' the Robinson Crusoe conceits of classical economics which imagine the point of departure of 'socially determined individual production,' which is to say a conception of economic production based around the unit of the individuated subject. [8] For Marx, the individual, 'heroic' production of the Robinson Crusoe figure becomes a privileged starting point for Western capitalism.[9] Crusoe as a character is a new hero for the new bourgeois class and is an origin point for the bourgeois individual. As Franco Moretti puts it, 'Robinson Crusoe is the genuine beginning of the world today.'[10] Russia, which developed capitalism later than Western Europe, and which developed it from different forms of social organisation – for example, serfdom and absolutism – which persisted into its nascent capitalist period, sees a different version of the single individual becoming heroic in relation to capitalism. Particularly notable, from this global perspective, is the increased speed with which bourgeois heroism is produced and dissolved. In English literature, the heroism which is produced in *Robinson Crusoe* is clearly decaying in Dickens and Thackeray a little less than a century and a half later, in spite of Byronic and Napoleonic revitalisation. In Russian literature, according to this reading, the process occurs across two texts in some 15 years.

The distinct economic, ideological, and cultural trajectory of capitalism in the Russia of the nineteenth century is described by Marshall Berman as the 'modernism of underdevelopment.'[11] Russia did not have the advanced capitalist economy of Western Europe, and yet, particularly amongst the metropolitan elite (in whose social sphere these novels are both set), elements of advanced modernity were active within the culture and society, alongside the emergence of the nascent bourgeois class. This is reflected in the two novels not least in their depictions of the shift from older models of heroism towards a professional, bourgeois notion of the hero. Such elements were given cultural shape via Western literature, and whilst both Pushkin and Lermontov explicitly name their protagonists as new models of heroism, that heroism is created and situated in relationship to the cultural legacy of Byron.

As such, these works are transitional in terms of form and allusion: both mutate Byronic poetry towards the novel and mutate Byronic forms of heroism into bourgeois forms of heroism. In this chapter, I suggest some contextual and ideological explanations for this by relating both the content of the works and the contexts in which they are written to the Byronic Hero as revolutionary and to the Decembrist Revolt in Russia. I also argue that *A Hero of Our Time* is a much more pessimistic, post-revolutionary, and post-Romantic text than *Eugene Onegin. A Hero of Our Time* attempts to lay the revolutionary possibilities of Byron to rest and substitutes them with a model of purified bourgeois professionalism. In this situation, Byron remains a more generalised cultural memory rather than a model for heroism. *Eugene Onegin,* on the other hand, is more Byronic and more positive about the liberating effects of revolution. This is in part because *Eugene Onegin* is related specifically to the context of the Decembrist Revolt of 1825 – in terms of its ideology of subjectivity, an aristocratic revolution with features of the bourgeois revolutions of Western Europe – whereas *A Hero of Our Time* is written with a greater distance and disenchantment. Yet even in *A Hero of Our Time*, the radical possibilities of the Byronic Hero are not fully exhausted, and elements of dissonance enter into the seemingly stable construction of the bourgeois hero. The contradictory revolutionary aristocracy of the Byronic Hero, which I discussed in the introduction, haunts these texts.

   Some of the ideas of cultural transition that I address in this chapter, particularly in relationship to Lermontov, are dealt with in Elizabeth Cheresh Allen's book *A Fallen Idol Is Still a God: Lermontov and the Quandaries of Cultural Transition.* However, useful as her work is, and I will be referring to it in the chapter, my interpretation differs importantly from hers. Allen rejects big theories of cultural transition, including Marxism, preferring instead to think about cultural transition in terms of 'the lives of individuals,' as though large-scale models of cultural change and localised occurrences are opposed.[12] It seems evident to me that in Marx's writings, and later Marxian readings of both literature and history, claims of large-scale change can only be made through minute readings of particular historical incidences. There is no contradiction there. Indeed, Allen's work is particularly problematic because it presupposes a notion of the 'life of the individual' in trans-historical terms. Rather, I am interested in how the very notion of 'the life of the individual' is historically mutable precisely because it changes in different historical, economic, and cultural situations. Similarly, her rejection of social and material conditions in defining culture is so total as to look reactionary: '[T]he ideals and norms, the values and beliefs, of a historical period [...] might have little to do with the social system or material conditions.'[13] It is precisely part of the aim of this chapter to show how the discourse of heroism posits models of individuality linked to the specific historico-cultural circumstances in which they exist. The lives of individuals cannot be presupposed, but rather must emerge from a more historically inflected reading.

   Most important to this study though is Allen's carefully argued contention, drawing on many previous critics and theorists of Romanticism, that Romanticism aspired to 'values of integrity and its offspring integration.'[14] Allen singles out subjectivity as an area where Romanticism aspired to integrity:

[T]he Romantic ideal of the self presupposed a psychological core of human identity that always had the potential to become fully integrated and whole, even if divided by conflicting attributes of human nature and the complex conditions of contemporary existence.

Furthermore,

while striving to unite the divergent parts of the self into a whole, Romanticists also often assumed that such a whole self could never exist in mere 'sensible people' [...]. Individuals possessing an overarching wholeness would be 'geniuses' or 'heroes.'

Allen observes that the Romantic 'period faded and passed away, leaving behind members of a younger generation, including Lermontov, as they floated in a sea of cultural transition during a time bereft of Romanticism's cultural integrity and integration.'[15] Allen suggests that whilst Lermontov registers this in *A Hero of Our Time*, he still 'had an implicit vision of cultural health, even while representing cultural malaise.'[16] However, I see Lermontov's post-Romanticism as being essentially pessimistic. The valorisation of a subjectivity based on the Romantic idea of an integral, psychological core is transferred under capitalism to the private individual rather than being the special attribute of geniuses or heroes; any old bourgeois can feel heroically self-contained (though of course often still marked with repressed contradictions). Thus, on the one hand, what is heroic in Romanticism, integrated subjectivity, becomes a general delusion of the bourgeois way of life, captured in the idea of the private individual. On the other hand, and to complicate this further, the possibilities of self-contained subjectivity no longer exist in the face of the material contradictions of capitalism. Allen calls this post-Romantic anomie, 'a sense of loss of cultural integration and integrity' but does not link this specifically to the rise of high capitalism.[17] I argue that the tensions between integrity and capitalist individuation on the one hand, and the breaking down of self-contained subjectivity on the other, are already found in Byron and Pushkin, who are generally accepted as Romantic writers, and that these tensions only become more marked in Lermontov.

II

I turn now to briefly establishing the ways in which both authors conceive of their protagonists as heroes and the way in which this differs from the conventional notions of heroism that one may find in any standard dictionary. These conceptualisations of the hero are specifically modern and related to questions of textuality.

It is evident that both *Eugene Onegin* and *A Hero of Our Time* conceive of their protagonists as heroes. Onegin is introduced specifically as 'the hero of my novel' (I.2) and the title *A Hero of Our Time* refers to Pechorin: as the 'travelling narrator' of the first sections of the novel puts it, 'Perhaps some readers will want to know my opinion of Pechorin's character. My answer is the title of this book' (p. 54).

Dictionary heroism is broadly associated with the 'active,' the 'courageous,' and the 'noble.' On the other hand, Lermontov's 'Author's Introduction' to *A Hero of Our Time*, states that he has depicted 'the vices of our generation in the fullness of their development' (p. 2). Similarly, Onegin is, from the outset, written in contradiction to these received notions of heroism. The opening stanza depicts the death of Onegin's uncle, 'a man of honour' (I.1), whilst the narrator comments on Onegin's notably unheroic attitude towards his uncle: '[S]hameful cunning to be cheerful | With someone who is halfway dead [...]. To sigh – while inwardly you think: | When will the devil let him sink?' (I.1).[18] Nonetheless, Onegin is still named the hero of the novel and shows heroism both in terms of a Byronic heroism and in his offhand courage in the duel that forms the centrepiece of the novel-in-verse, where the 'dormant hero' (VI.24) is so relaxed that he oversleeps.

Why this difference between the two heroes presented here and the received dictionary definitions of heroism? One way to explain this is to shift attention to explanatory potential of the word 'time' in the Lermontov's title. In his typically opinionated way, Vladimir Nabokov states in his introduction to *A Hero of Our Time*:

> The point to be marked in a study of *A Hero of Our Time*, is that, though of tremendous and at times somewhat morbid interest to the sociologist, the 'time' is of less interest to the student of literature than the 'hero.'
>
> (p. xvii)

What Nabokov misses here is that the two are fused quite deliberately in the title, and that fusion is reiterated in the novel itself. Likewise in *Eugene Onegin*, for both are about the particular historical contexts that they are set in. The notion of heroism must be placed into a conception of 'our time,' then, that is the time of nascent capitalism, of modernity, in order for us to understand why the heroes are constructed as they are. This modernity, whilst part of wider European shifts, also has manifestations specific to Russia between the 1820s and 1840. 'The Author's Introduction' states that for the Russian public, 'in decent company as in a decent book open abuse cannot occur' (p. 1), however, the introduction goes on, 'people have been fed enough sweet-meats [...] they need some bitter medicine, some caustic truths' (p. 2). This reflects a movement away from the codified life and language of aristocratic society, and it also reflects the cultural condition of capitalist modernity that Marx and Engels describe in *The Communist Manifesto*. What the introduction

describes here is the process of confronting society with the 'real conditions of life,'[19] rather than mediating these through an aristocratic milieu,
a social formation of highly regulated speech. As such, whilst the novel
addresses its specific context, it is also symptomatic of the cultural shift
towards bourgeois society. The term 'real' is, of course, problematic, but
in both Lermontov and Marx and Engels, there is the desire to attempt
to describe the world without the dominant ideological forms of expression. In Lermontov's case, this is by describing the world unencumbered
by the regulated speech of 'sweet-meats.' Lermontov's novel thus asserts
itself as dealing in unregulated linguistic truth. In Marx and Engels's case,
it is by describing the material conditions of production unencumbered
by the ideological assumptions of the capitalists. In both cases, the notion
of 'our time,' allows new perspectives to be asserted which destabilise old
values and modes of representation.

The opening of *Eugene Onegin* also presents its hero in rejection of
the prevailing values of the previous generation. The epigraph to Chapter
I, 'And it hurries to live and it hastens to feel' (p. 7), refers to 'youthful ardour' (Mitchell's note, p. 215). The novel begins with the ushering in of a new generation, the same generation which, in the 'Author's
Introduction' to *A Hero of Our Time* is, '*our* generation' (p. 2, italics
mine). These are two novels about now, about newness, about the nineteenth century and the effects of emerging capitalism on heroism and
subjectivity. What is at issue here is not just the hero conceived in the
abstract, as Nabokov would have it, but a mutation or manifestation of
the hero in a changed social situation that is specific to the social, economic, and political situation of Russia (or at least the Russian capital
cities and the upper echelons of its society) in the early to mid-nineteenth
century. On the other hand, this is also an example of general currents in
the cultural expression of the rise of high capitalism. This is evident both
from the influence of Western European ideologies, particularly from the
work of Byron, on a changing Russia, but also in the possibilities of plac-
ing the Russian experience alongside that of Western Europe and showing analogous patterns at work. The shift in the economic base of society
was a pan-European one. The move towards high capitalism, and its concomitant cultural formations, produced a subjectivity that is valorised
and heroised for its submission to instrumentality for capital, as part of
both a pan-European process and one that is dependant simultaneously
on local economic and cultural formations.

Pushkin and Lermontov do not actually name this new historical experience capitalism or the bourgeois epoch but speak in broader generalities
of 'our time' or the 'modern.' This experience of modernity is nevertheless
particularly marked by capitalism and shows both a move towards forms
of subjectivity developed in the rise of bourgeois culture and a move
towards the hero as a professional. To examine these new forms of heroism and their development into something new, a further examination of

their antecedents is needed. Thus, I wish to turn to the use of the Byronic in both these novels to show that the Byronic is a template through which these two Russian writers construct the idea of the hero but, simultaneously, a model of heroism which is subsequently rejected as outdated for the heroism.

III

Biographically speaking, both writers were strongly influenced by Byron. In their detailed survey of the influence of Byron on Russian literature, Nina Diakonova and Vadim Vatsuro observe that, in the early 1820s, 'Pushkin turned to Byron,' and they list in detail a number of his poems which deploy 'problems and stylistic devices similar to those of *Childe Harold's Pilgrimage* and the Oriental tales.' Similarly, they describe Lermontov's work as 'the fullest and deepest expression of Russian Byronism' and trace a series of mutating responses to Byron through Lermontov's short career, including translations and imitations.[20] Nonetheless, they suggest that both poets, to varying extents, abandoned Byron. As a prelude to writing *Eugene Onegin*, Pushkin broke 'loose from the spell of Byron,' whilst they see Lermontov as reading Byron to surpass him.[21] I wish to trace the continuing influence of Byron in both *Eugene Onegin* and Lermontov's late work *A Hero of Our Time*, but to show that rather than being abandoned, Byron is modified in the face of a new historical and social context. This is, in part, the mutation that Diakonova and Vatsuro recognise – Byronic heroes become 'objects of parody' – however, I will show how the relationship between parody and the serious deployment of the Byronic Hero is much more complex than their survey suggests.[22]

Onegin is presented specifically to the reader in the context of Pushkin's previous work: 'Friends of Ruslan and of Lyudmila | Let me acquaint you with this fellow' (I.2), in reference to his early major poem *Ruslan and Lyudmila* (1820). Furthermore, Onegin is defined by the novels that he reads, which also stress his modernity; the narrator of *Eugene Onegin* describes Byron's poems *Don Juan* (1819–1824) and *The Giaour* (1813), as well as 'two, three novels of the hour,' as works of modernity where, 'the epoch was displayed | And modern man put on parade [...] with his depraved, immoral soul, | Dried up and egotistical' (VII.22).[23] These allusions establish Onegin as a textual construct, which is then made specifically Byronic. Stressed here, again, are the importance of self-interest and the atrophy of traditional moral values. Similarly, the 'Author's Introduction' to *A Hero of Our Time*, states that the author 'merely found it amusing to draw modern man such as he understood him' (p. 1). It then asks, '[Y]ou have believed in the possibility of so many tragic and romantic villains having existed, why can you not believe in the reality of Pechorin?' (p. 2). In the context of the more sustained set of allusions to

Byron, which I discuss in just a moment, this gestures towards the tragic and Romantic Byronic Hero, whilst suggesting Pechorin, in his *reality*, goes beyond them. Nevertheless, in both *Eugene Onegin* and *A Hero of Our Time*, modernity is stressed as being a function of certain types of literary allusion, and, in the case of *A Hero of Our Time*, the literary allusion is to *Eugene Onegin* itself, as well as to Byron.[24]

Byron's *Don Juan* begins with the demand, 'I want a hero,' a demand that Hadley J. Mozer describes as an 'advert' for a hero that stresses the '"lack" or "desire" [...] of and for a hero.'[25] Pushkin's and Lermontov's texts could be said to respond to this Byronic advert and suggest new models of the hero for nineteenth-century literature, and for Russia particularly. The fact that this is put in relation to advertising suggests the new exigencies of the market on formations of heroism. These writers respond to Byron's advert at the beginning of *Don Juan* by adjusting Byron to the new demands of capitalism, though along Russian lines.

In *Eugene Onegin*, Onegin is repeatedly compared to Childe Harold, who has been shown in the introduction to be perhaps the most important source of the Byronic Hero for European culture. Whilst these two texts can be seen as responding to the demand that begins *Don Juan*, the actual models of heroism they deploy to produce their protagonists come clearly from the Byronic Hero figures, which derive from *Childe Harold* and narrative poems such as *The Giaour*.[26] In Chapter I, Onegin's boredom at the ballet is described in an authorial note as 'a trait of chilled sentiment worthy of Childe Harold,' and he arrives at an aristocratic salon 'like Childe Harold' (I.38).[27] Later, the narrator suggests that Onegin is 'A Muscovite in Harold's cloak' (VII.24), and observes that he keeps a portrait of Byron on his study wall (VII.19), and has a particular liking for *The Giaour* (VII.22). As well as the references that explicitly connect Onegin with Byron's heroes, a more general engagement with Byron's texts and the Byronic is prevalent throughout. This takes the form of reflections on the reading habits of young Russian women who are 'ready to adore' the 'pensive vampire' (III.12), who Pushkin notes is 'incorrectly attributed to Lord Byron,' and 'the Corsair' (III.12).[28]

This dialogue with Byron is carried out in other ways too. The narrator distances himself from Byron at one point, saying that, unlike Byron, he does not write himself into poems:

> I always note with satisfaction
> Onegin's difference from me,
> Lest somewhere a sarcastic reader
> Or publisher or such-like breeder
> Of complicated calumny
> Discerns my physiognomy
> And shamelessly repeats the fable
> That I have crudely versified

Myself like Byron, bard of pride,
As if we were no longer able
To write a poem and discuss
A subject not concerning us.
                    (I.56)

Here, the narrator resists a comparison between himself and Byron, the implications of that comparison being that Onegin is an autobiographical depiction of Pushkin himself, as it is supposed that the Byronic Hero is an autobiographical depiction of Byron. However, whilst Pushkin and Onegin are supposedly not similar, the narrator acknowledges his association with Pushkin whilst separating Pushkin from Onegin. Similarly, Byron actually insists on a difference between himself and his heroes but includes himself as an ironic, and quite different, commentator on the action alongside Childe Harold. There is, therefore, a disavowed parallel between Byron and Pushkin even as Pushkin differentiates himself from Byron that actually strengthens the notion of Onegin being a Byronic Hero since he occupies a similar position in relation to Pushkin/the narrator that the Byronic Hero does to Byron/the narrator. This stanza suggests that whilst the narrator (who seems to be speaking in a version of Pushkin's voice here) does not resemble Onegin or Byron, the similarities between Onegin and the Byronic Hero remain. This is made more complex by the collapse of the narrator and Onegin into a single figure in the final lines of the stanza, where the separation between 'I' and 'Onegin' is collapsed into an 'us,'[29] which implies that the narrator is in some way a Byronic Hero too.

These similarities between Byron's and Pushkin's writing practices take place at a formal level. Pushkin's writing seems to rewrite Byron's. For example, in the allusions to his own poetic works, Pushkin calls his readers 'Friends of Ruslan and of Lyudmila' (I.2), echoing the manner in which Byron reflects on his own work and the work of his contemporaries, such as when the narrator describes the early Cantos of *Don Juan* and *Cain* as failures like Napoleon's disastrous battles: 'Juan was my Moscow, and Faliero | My Leipsic, and my Mont Saint Jean seems Cain' (XI.56). Pushkin also imitates Byron even more closely than this. Nabokov draws attention to the similarity between a passage in *Don Juan* and a passage in *Eugene Onegin* on ennui and spleen.[30] In *Don Juan*, the narrator discusses ennui:

For *ennui* is a growth of English root,
Though nameless in our language: – we retort
The fact for words, and let the French translate
That awful yawn which sleep can not abate.
                    (XIII.101)

A passage on melancholy in *Eugene Onegin* is remarkably similar:

> A malady, whose explanation
> Is overdue, and similar
> To English spleen – the Russian version,
> In short is what we call *khandra*.
>
> (I.38)

In both cases, the condition that signals the hero's alienation is both rooted by the narrator in a national tradition and signified by a word from another European language. These are cosmopolitan conditions. Furthermore, both these passages are stylistically similar, stressing the interplay between the origin of and word for ennui and spleen. Pushkin takes his stylistic cues from Byron, as well as making explicit allusions.

Similarly to Pushkin, Lermontov has a complex attitude towards comparisons of himself with Byron. Laurence Kelly quotes two passages from Lermontov's poetry, both from 1830, where he writes both, 'I wish to emulate Byron | Our souls are one,' and 'No, I am not Byron but another as yet unknown | Chosen as he to be exiled.'[31] Like Pushkin, even when Lermontov distances himself from Byron, this is a sort of disavowal which makes evident their similarities. *A Hero of Our Time* still engages closely with the Byronic, however, the explicit allusions are not nearly so frequent. Princess Mary 'has read Byron in English' (p. 80). Elsewhere, there is an allusion to Polidori's 'The Vampyre' where Pechorin states that 'there are moments when I understand the vampire' (p. 119).[32]

References to Byron in Lermontov tend instead to be more generalised, more a mood of the Byronic than specific quotations and direct allusions. For example, the character Grushnitsky, is a slightly comic Byronic Hero figure, who has come to the Caucasus as 'a consequence of his fanatic romanticism'; Pechorin parodies Grushnitsky's Byronic speech, amplifying the popular image of the Byronic Hero as melancholy outsider, imagining him saying to a

> pretty neighbour, with a gloomy air, that he was going to the Caucasus not merely to serve there, but that he was seeking death because…and here, probably, he would cover his eyes with his hand and continue thus: "No, you must not know this! Your pure soul would shudder! And what for? What am I to you? Would you understand me?" and so forth.
>
> (p. 71. Ellipsis Lermontov's)

This appears as a comic exaggeration of Childe Harold who leaves his home because he 'almost long'd for woe' (I.6), and who is 'self-exiled' through his alienation from the human society around him (III.16).

Nabokov observes that later in the novel, Pechorin, in an address to Princess Mary, uses a very similar formulation to that attributed in parody to Grushnitsky: 'Why must you know what, up to now, has been taking place in my soul? You will never learn it, and so much the better for you' (pp. 113–114, see note on p. 174). Pechorin's quotation is threefold. He repeats the words attributed earlier to Grushnitsky; their general parody of R/romantic passion, and echoes Byronic passages such as this in *Childe Harold's Pilgrimage*:

> Could I embody and unbosom now
> That which is most within me, – could I wreak
> My thoughts upon expression, and thus throw
> Soul, heart, mind, passions, feelings, strong or weak,
> All that I would have sought, and all I seek,
> Bear, know, feel, and yet breathe – into *one* word,
> And that one word were Lightning, I would speak;
> But as it is, I live and die unheard,
> With a most voiceless thought, sheathing it as a sword.
>
> (III.97)

Pechorin's speech recalls his own scathing parody of Grushnitsky's speech, and so parody is no longer reserved for Pechorin to direct towards Grushnitsky from a position outside that which he parodies. Pechorin, the hero himself, has become a parody of the Byronic too. Furthermore, this parodic Byronic speech is reminiscent of the bourgeois discourse of private, self-contained subjectivity.[33] Thus, Pechorin simultaneously remains 'a hero of our time,' a hero of the new capitalist world and a Byronic figure, and the two become intimately linked. Byronism and its parody are difficult to disentangle, pointing towards Byron's obsolescence and cultural staying power. The Byronic remains as a force that causes dissonance within the bourgeois world that follows it. For example, Pechorin's identification with Byronism is strengthened by his claim that he understands the vampire, a figure that I have shown is connected to Byron through the references in *The Giaour* which compare to the Byronic Hero to the vampire, and through Pushkin's observation of the inaccurate attribution of 'The Vampyre' to Byron. The vampire's sexual and life-draining force could not be tied to bourgeois morality, but nonetheless, as an exemplary transgression of it, seems to be a bourgeois fantasy, though one that is also rooted in Byronic identification.

This swerve into the Byronic as parody occurs, in a slightly modified form, in other references to Byron. Elsewhere in 'Princess Mary,' the question of the Byronic as heroic is raised: 'How many people, in the beginning of life, think they will finish it as Alexander the Great or Lord Byron, and instead, retain for the whole of their existence, the rank of titulary counsellor' (p. 110).[34] Again here, the idea of the Byronic no longer seems to function in modern society and is instead replaced with the consolation of becoming a middle-ranking civil servant in the huge state bureaucracy. In later Russian literature, with its relentless, nightmarish focus on the experience of urban, bureaucratic modernity, particularly the work of Dostoevsky and in Gogol, the question of this figure, the titular counsellor, sometimes very poor and at other times in a threshold space between the proletariat and the bourgeoisie, becomes the pressing concern of the novel.

Nonetheless, the simple rejection of the Byronic Hero in favour of the bourgeois professional is not occurring here. Walter Benjamin states, boldly, that the 'hero is the true subject of modernism. In other words, it takes a heroic constitution to live modernism.'[35] He makes this comment in a discussion of Balzac and Baudelaire, whose characters, Benjamin argues, have the ability to face, as poor people, the pressures of modern, high capitalist urban life. This has an obvious counterpart in the writings of Gogol and Dostoevsky. Benjamin puts this model of heroism 'in opposition to Romanticism.'[36] However, what is occurring in Pushkin and Lermontov seems to be rather a transition between a Romantic form of heroism and the modern form of heroism that Benjamin describes, and is directly connected to the transitional figure of Byron, transitional both in his own writings and the way they are deployed, and also in the way he is imagined and deployed as a cultural figure after his death. The Byronic informs the creation of the bourgeois hero and becomes obsolete in the bourgeois hero, whilst lingering as a cultural memory that can introduce dissonances.

IV

This mutation of the Byronic into the bourgeois, with a lingering memory of the Byronic Hero, is most evident in *A Hero of Our Time*. Allusions to Byron and the bourgeois professional become fused in the character of Dr Werner. Werner is an altogether fascinating, and transitional character. Everything about him is contradictory, he is ugly but physically attractive, he makes fun of his patients but is moved to tears by death, and 'the bumps of his skull [...] would have amazed a phrenologist by their bizarre interplay of contradictory inclinations' (p. 75).[37] Particularly relevant in this catalogue of contradictions with which Werner is introduced is that 'his surname is Werner, but he is Russian' (p. 75). In this sense, he represents a fusing of the Western European and Russian in the figure of the bourgeois professional.[38] And, furthermore, he is 'a sceptic and materialist...but he is also a poet' (pp. 75–76), representing both Romanticism and the rationality of bourgeois life. Most curiously of all, 'Werner was of small stature, thin and frail like a child. One of his legs was shorter than the other, as in the case of Byron' (p. 76). Werner then is an explicitly Byronic figure, but he is a child-like Byron in the role of a bourgeois professional, a doctor. Pechorin tells us that Werner 'dreamt of becoming a millionaire,' recalling the bourgeois desire to accumulate capital above all else, and though the text suggests that he is poor, it is clear that he has a successful practice with 'all the really decent people serving in the Caucasus' (p. 76). He is every inch the respectable bourgeois.

Werner, then, though certainly not the hero of the novel, seems to embody the traits towards which the hero, as envisaged by Pushkin and Lermontov, is moving. Finally, though, it is the doctor who loads the pistol that kills Grushnitsky and covers up the duel for Pechorin (pp. 140–141) as though he is both undertaker to the old, stereotypical Byronic Hero, who has been parodied by and in Pechorin and represented more clearly by Grushnitsky, and protector of the mutated bourgeois-Byronic hybrid hero Pechorin. Indeed, the duel itself has a quality of mutated Byronism to it. When Pechorin challenges Grushnitsky, he describes his challenge as an 'awful [...] vengeance' (p. 127) for Grushnitsky's slander of Princess Mary, recalling the vengeance that drives each of the heroes of Byron's tales, but here the vengeance is not for murder (as in *The Giaour*) but for social disgrace in aristocratic polite society.

Pechorin, however, dies at the end of the text, and it seems that the Byronic can ultimately continue to exist in this world only in the figure of a disabled, child-like doctor, both Byronic and bourgeois, whose poetry is subordinated to 'his actions, and frequently his utterings, although in all his life he never wrote two lines of verse' (p. 76). Byronic poetry can only exist if it is expressed by a stolid, solid professionalism. Indeed, this Byronic professionalism, though Werner is its most advanced representative, emerges elsewhere in the novel. So, whilst Werner represents certain traits of the fully professionalised bourgeois hero, of a type that I will discuss at more length in later chapters, my attention must remain with the characters who are explicitly described as heroes in this text and who are more obviously Byronic figures. They become professionalised in notably different ways from the bourgeois figure of the doctor.

In contrast to the bourgeois-Byronic doctor whose poetry is expressed in his bourgeois actions, it is notable that, despite the many allusions to Byron, the only character in either the Pushkin or Lermontov novels who actually writes poetry is Lensky, who is killed by Onegin. It is made clear that Lensky is a traditional Romantic character, who with his 'curling, shoulder-length black hair' (II.6) believes that 'he should be united | With a congenial soul' (II.8). His poetry too is specifically in the Romantic tradition; it is made clear he reads Schiller and Goethe (II.9).

Lensky is more a generic Romantic poet than a Byronic Hero. He writes poems about 'love obedient' and 'romantic roses' (II.10). These images are part of what Mikhail Bakhtin calls 'Lensky's song.' Bakhtin observes that the poetic images (specifically the metaphoric comparisons) representing Lensky's 'song' do not here have any direct poetic significance at all. They cannot be understood as the direct poetic images of Pushkin himself (although formally, of course, the characterisation is that of the author).[39]

Rather, Bakhtin argues, what is depicted here is a stylised image of Romantic poetry:

> What we have before us is in fact an *image* of Lensky's song, but not an image in the narrow sense; it is rather a *novelistic* image; the image of another's language, in the given instance the image of another's poetic style (sentimental and romantic).[40]

The implication here is that as Pushkin's work becomes more like a novel, he becomes less Romantic since Romanticism becomes incorporated into the novel as an image of another style of writing in a parody of Romanticism, which is now obsolete. Bakhtin drives this point home:

> [T]he poetic metaphors in these lines [...] in no way function here as the *primary means of representation* (as they would function in a direct, "serious" song written by Lensky himself); rather they themselves have become the object of representation, or more precisely of representation that is parodied and stylised.[41]

That is to say that in a novel-in-verse, such as *Eugene Onegin*, the insertion of a poem within it must be taken at a point removed from the inserted poem itself. Rather than the poetic metaphors signifying anything themselves, the *idea* of the poetic metaphor is the primary object of representation and with this distance becomes the object of parody in the novelistic discourse of the work. Romantic poetry is being rejected in favour of novelistic prose, which sees Romanticism as one of many images in circulation, one which can be laughed at, and which recalls Benjamin's characterisation of the heroism of modernity in 'opposition to Romanticism.'[42] This is bolstered by the narrator's claim that Lensky and Onegin are more different from each other than 'verse and prose are from each other' (II.13) and the final mocking of the Romantic aspirations of Lensky:

> Of poetry he might have wearied,
> And, parting from the Muses, married;
> A happy squire, with cuckold's crown,
> Wearing a quilted dressing gown;
> He might have learned life's true dimension,
> At forty he'd have had the gout,

Drunk, eaten, moped, declined, got stout
And died according to convention
As children thronged and women cried
And village quacks stood by his side.

(VI.39)

As though to stress the anachronism of Lensky's form of poetry, his decline into prosperous old age does not follow the trajectory of the metropolitan elite or the nascent bourgeoisie, but rather that of the country gentry of a time prior to the nascent modernity of the novel-in-verse. The death of Lensky the poet, then, suggests the passing away of both a form of heroism and a literary form.

As Lensky, the Romantic hero, is replaced by Byronically inflected bourgeois Onegin, the literary form moves towards the bourgeois novel. Byron's *Don Juan* is quite evidently a precursor to *Onegin* as a novel-in-verse. This is important insofar as both works are transitional, somewhere between novel and poem. Whilst they are written in poetic forms at least connected to standard and widely used historical forms: ottava rima and stanzas based on a modification of the sonnet form, respectively, their structure as long works, and their concerns, pre-empt the nineteenth-century novel. Richard Lansdown has noted how *Don Juan* forms a transition between the Romantic poem and the nineteenth-century novel.[43] Similarly, *Eugene Onegin* represents the inauguration of the nineteenth-century Russian novel. I mentioned in my introduction that Boltanski and Chiapello note the importance of the novel in shoring up new bourgeois values that justify a participation in capitalism. Since the nineteenth-century novel particularly concerns complex elaborations of the individuated, bourgeois subject, the importance of this similarity in transitional genre should not go unnoticed, but part of this transition is the eventual rejection of the Byronic model, though its memory lingers on. The discussion of the complex interplay of author-narrator-character in Pushkin above, though it actually demonstrates a concordance with Byron, also reveals the tensions in moving away from Byron, as though he must be adopted as a model only in order to be rejected. This may explain the need of Lermontov and Pushkin to move towards prose. I will discuss Lermontov's novel shortly below, but it is worth mentioning that Pushkin's later writing tended towards prose fiction too: *Tales of Belkin* was written in 1830, *The Queen of Spades* in 1833, and *The Captain's Daughter* was completed in 1836 before his death in early 1837. Capitalism sees a simultaneous dismissal of previous models of heroism, and a shift from poetry to prose, and this occurs in *Don Juan* and in Pushkin and Lermontov's responses to it. In advertising for a hero at the outset of *Don Juan*, and in Pushkin and Lermontov's responses, new models of heroism and new ways of writing heroism are being formed, adequate to the conditions of the time in which they are being written – a heroism that is able to 'render services to capitalism' and a literary form designed to depict the private inwardness of it doing so.

Byron himself, of course, registered the capitalist nature of this change. Mozer observes that at the beginning of *Don Juan*, Byron presents an 'an epic *catalog* [...] from which Byron may order a protagonist for his poem.'[44] This returns to the idea of the hero fulfilling the demands of the market, becoming a professional, being put to work in a capitalist economy in order to glorify that economy and make its resolutely unheroic world look heroic. Following Mozer, then, according to the rhetoric of the opening of the poem, even in Byron's work, the hero is selected for his suitability in fulfilling an economic function. Byron rejects all of the 'heroes' he names at the beginning of the poem as unsuitable for the purposes of his poem and the world it depicts. These form three loose groups, the first made up of 'Vernon, the butcher Cumberland, Wolfe, Hawke, | Prince Ferdinand, Granby, Burgoyne, Keppel, Howe, [...] Wellesley' (I.2). These are all military figures,[45] with the suggestion in this selection of figures representing reactionary political positions. Wellesley is the most obvious figure in this respect, but many of the other figures were actively engaged in British militarism, such as Howe or Wolfe, and Byron's use of the epithet 'butcher' signifies sympathy with the Jacobite cause and the colonial repression of the Highlands that followed it.

The second group is composed of 'Buonaparté and Dumourier [...] Barnave, Brissot, Condorcet, Mirabeau, | Petion, Clootz, Danton, Marat, La Fayette, [...] Joubert, Hoche, Marceau, Lannes, Dessaix, Moreau' (I.3). These figures are of the revolutionary period in France. However, in 1819, when Byron is writing, in the relative stability of the Bourbon Restoration, their figures are also outdated, 'Exceedingly remarkable at times, | But not at all adapted to my rhymes' (I.3). In this sense, they represent failed revolution, a revolution that was unable to sustain itself into the now of the modern. Both conservative and revolutionary figures of the past are rejected.

The final group is composed of 'Duncan, Nelson, Howe, and Jervis' (I.4). These are all naval heroes and rejected on the grounds that 'the army's grown more popular' (I.4). Hence there is an historical trajectory in these stanzas in the move away from the navy to the army, which is led by conservative high society, since 'the Prince is all for land-service' (I.4). The Byronic model pre-empts both the relationship of heroism to failed revolution discussed below and the weakening of the military hero, which is evident in Pushkin choosing an avowedly non-military figure and the weak militarism of Pechorin in *A Hero of Our Time*, who, I will argue, comes to look more like a bourgeois government official. Similarly, *Don Juan* selects a non-military hero who takes part in military action but in the course of the narrative becomes more at home in fashionable society of a sort similar to that depicted in *Eugene Onegin* and *A Hero of Our Time* and familiar to the nineteenth-century novel in general.[46]

Just as *Don Quixote* depicts the rejection of the hero of chivalry and a new formulation of heroism, and does so through a concomitant shift in form, away from poetry and to the creation of the novel, the works in this chapter represent a similar shift, to new forms of heroism suitable for high capitalism and, again, away from poetry to prose.[47] The transitional status of *Eugene Onegin* and *Don Juan*, as novels-in-verse, are testament to this, and *A Hero of Our Time* is a novel by a writer until then known as a poet, set in the transitional borderlands of the Russian empire and reflecting a movement away from aristocratic to bourgeois models of subjectivity.[48]

However, if Byron announced this historical shift, its progress required that he be left behind. I suggested in the introduction to this book that Lukács posits a form of heroism proper to the epic which passes away in the novel. I have detailed here with more local focus the transition between the Byronic and its Russian champions. The latter are transitional figures between old and new forms of heroism, poetry, and prose. But Byron remains more deeply rooted in the epic tradition, whilst Pushkin and Lermontov more fully make the transition over to the novel tradition, so it is worth looking at the new formal mode through which the new bourgeois heroism is depicted, the novel, before finally discussing the mutations of the Byronic Hero this new form demands.

As the hero becomes subordinated to the logic of capitalism and the market, so too, these novels suggest, poetry comes to be viewed as a sort of non-productive activity that cannot co-exist with nascent capitalism. Hence it is subordinated in Werner's life and is structurally dispensed of in the parody and death of Lensky. Of course, *Onegin* is itself in verse, but this is a transitional verse that is deployed for narrative ends akin to those of the novel, and, as I keep stressing, Pushkin called *Onegin* 'a novel-in-verse.' Pushkin states explicitly that the work is 'not a novel' and that between a novel and a novel-in-verse, there is 'a devil of a difference.'[49] However, if there is a marked difference between a novel-in-verse and a novel, there must also be one between a novel-in-verse and poetry itself. Nearly a decade later in *A Hero of Our Time*, the transition away from poetry is further advanced, the novel-in-verse has inspired a novel-in-prose. The diminishing importance of poetry in the form of these works is echoed by their content. This is particularly so in the case of Werner, whose Byronism and more general Romanticism now feed into what makes him a popular doctor, a competent professional: '[H]e has studied all the live strings of the human heart in the same way as one studies the veins of a dead body' (p. 76). This is in stark contrast to Lensky's studies, 'the fruits of learning | From mist-enveloped Germany' (II.6), which consist of 'Kant and rhyme' (II.6).[50] It also strongly contrasts with the strings of the 'lyre' that Lensky is twice metaphorically depicted with (II.9 and VI.37). The deep knowledge Pechorin imputes to Werner of human psychology here is in contrast to Lensky's naivety: 'He sang of life's decaying scene, | While he was not yet quite eighteen' (II.10). Lensky acts, speaks, and writes in broad poetic generalities, whilst Werner's poetic interest is channelled into a useful knowledge of the psychology and physiology of the individuated subject.

The diminished importance of poetry is repeated at the level of allusion in *A Hero of Our Time*. All the references to Byron appear in the 'Princess Mary' section, which comes early in the novel's complex internal chronology, and the narrative then drops the relation between the hero and Byron at the level of allusion. I have already observed how Werner modifies the Byronic. Elsewhere, Grushnitsky, whose Byronism is parodied, is killed, and Princess Mary, who reads Byron, is abandoned and forgotten. It must be admitted that there is a return to a parodied image of Romanticism on the part of Pechorin at the end of 'Princess Mary,' but something rather curious occurs there. Pechorin states, 'I am like a sailor born and bred on the deck of a pirate brig' (p. 148). The reference to a pirate inevitably glances back to Byron's *The Corsair*, whose epic 'soul' is, like the Pechorin's sailor's, 'used to storms and battles' (p. 148). And, just as Childe Harold sets sail to leave 'his native home' at the beginning of *Childe Harold* (I.12), so Pechorin is moving into exile at this point in the internal chronology of the novel. Pechorin further imagines the pirate 'haunt[ing] the sand of the shore, hearken[ing] to the monotonous murmur of the surf' (p. 148).

The tone here is one of Byronic reverie, very different from the levity of *Eugene Onegin*, or the spleen displayed elsewhere in *A Hero of Our Time*. However, Pechorin describes himself as 'like' a sailor, and in the Byronic reverie that follows, it is no longer 'I' the sailor, but 'he' the sailor: 'I am like a sailor born and bred on the deck of a pirate brig. His soul is used to storms and battles' (p. 148). The Byronic sailor, at the moment that Pechorin identifies with him, ceases to be Pechorin and becomes someone else. The identification between Pechorin and the Byronic is broken. The Byronic reverie also includes the word 'separating' twice: 'Will there not appear there, glimpsed on the pale line separating the blue main from the grey cloudlets, the longed-for sail, at first like the wing of a sea gull, but gradually separating itself' (p. 148). The entire passage stresses the idea of separation, just as Pechorin is separated from the sailors in the opening segment of his narration, 'Taman,' where the other characters are Byronic figures, whilst Pechorin, far from being a sailor, is nearly drowned (p. 65).

This shift away from poetry and the Byronic begins in 'Taman,' which is the first section in the novel's internal chronology. Pechorin sees the young smuggler woman in Taman as like 'Goethe's Mignon' (p. 62). It is in 'Princess Mary,' however, that the importance of the bourgeois novel is especially clear. In 'Princess Mary,' as Pechorin reflects on how many people have believed themselves destined to be like Lord Byron, he wonders whether fate 'had designated me to become the author of bourgeois tragedies and family novels, or the collaborator of some purveyor of stories for the "Library for Reading"?' (p. 110).[51] The movement from poetry to novel, and from heroic Byronic self-assertion to heroic bourgeois self-exertion, is not yet complete here but manifestly very much underway.

V

I have shown how these texts distance themselves from Byronic heroism in terms of content and form. Now I turn to the ways in which Byronic heroism nevertheless continues to haunt them.

I argue that, on the one hand, *Eugene Onegin* combines Byronism with revolution in a way that retains the Byronic as a source of energy. *A Hero of Our Time*, on the other hand, is more melancholy since it depicts the mutation of the Byronic Hero into the bourgeois professional. Nonetheless, this bourgeois professional is marked with the disruptive, obsolete remnants of Byronic heroism. This is signalled by the two texts' differing attitudes to revolution: Onegin's heroism combines the bourgeois and Byronic in a moment of positive hope for the future. *A Hero of Our Time*, whilst it still offers disruptive forms of heroism, is much less positive about revolution than *Eugene Onegin*, and even its disruptive forms of heroism are worn out, jaundiced, and bitter.

In his *Fiction and Society in the Age of Pushkin: Ideology, Institutions, and Narrative*, William Mills Todd compares the way that Byron and Byronism are depicted in *Eugene Onegin* and *A Hero of Our Time*. He contends that in *A Hero of Our Time*, the Byronic has become so normalised that it has entered the fabric of everyday life:

> Byron appears in [*A Hero of Our Time*] less as an aesthetic phenomenon [...] than as a phenomenon of everyday life, a pose long familiar in Russian society: 'I replied that...disenchantment, like all fashions that had begun with the highest layers of society had descended to the lowest, which were wearing it out.'[52]

On the other hand, in *Eugene Onegin*, Byronism is something more striking, that stands out from quotidian discourse. This is evident from the way that the allusions to Byron occur in the two novels. In *A Hero of Our Time*, there are passing references to Byron as a shared cultural reference point and a sort of generic Byronic discourse characterised by the passage about the sea and pirates at the end of 'Princess Mary.' On the other hand, in *Onegin*, there is a more complex situation:

> What is he then? An imitation,
> A paltry phantom or a joke,
> A Muscovite in Harold's cloak,
> Of alien fads an explication,

Of modish words a lexicon,
A parody, when said and done?

                          (VII.24)

What is so strange about this is the way in which Onegin, in his
Byronic aspect, in 'Harold's cloak' is both inside and outside fashionable
Russian society. He stands far outside the normal discourse of society,
'of alien fads an explication,' but this difference is also incorporated into
fashionable society if he is a lexicon of 'modish words.' Furthermore, his
originality is recognised as not being universally original; he is 'an imitation,' a 'phantom,' which suggests the return of the past, and a 'parody,'
which is reminiscent of Marx's observations on history as parody in *The
Eighteen Brumaire of Louis Bonaparte*. For example, Marx suggests that
'the revolution of 1848 knew no better than to parody at some points
1789.' Intriguingly, this observation is coupled with an analogy between
revolution and the explication of foreign languages. Revolution parodies
the revolutions that came before, 'in the same way [that] the beginner
who has learned a new language always retranslates it into his mother
tongue.'[53] The description of Onegin as a Muscovite is particularly puz-
zling since the entire novel has associated him with Petersburg; he was
'begotten | By the Neva' (I.2.9–10) and is shown in the sparkling social
life of the capital. By making him a Muscovite here, he is both a reminder
of the past, of the old capital, but, also, stands outside the Petersburg
society that, it is stressed, he is part of.

   Onegin's Byronism, then, is composed of Western European elements
which are incorporated into Russian fashion and also a coming together
of new and old trends within Russian culture and society. Thus, his
alienation as a Byronic figure is both a repetition of something past
in Western Europe, something which seems startlingly different from
Russian society, and something newly characteristic of modern Russian
society. His alienation represents a complicated mixture of inside and
out, present and past. It is untimely: belated, and old, and simultaneously
modern and strikingly new. It is outside the normal purview of Russian
high society and incorporated into it. Thus, the narrator describes his
melancholy as a 'malady, whose explanation | Is overdue, and similar
| To English spleen' (I.38). It is both old by Western standards and yet
ahead of his own society's tastes, as when he comments on the fashion-
able ballet master Didelot: 'I've suffered ballets long enough, | And even
Didelot's boring stuff' (I.21).

   Onegin's disenchantment though is strangely productive of enchantment, which again is emphasised by this inside-outside dichotomy, which
runs over both the spatial and the temporal since it is old in England, new
in Petersburg, and yet somehow old in Petersburg too since disenchantment seems to be fashionable in Russia, as well as in Western Europe.

Indeed, Tatiana is enchanted by the marker of Onegin's disenchantment, his Byronism:

> With melting gaze Tatiana measures
> The objects that surround her here,
> All seem to her like priceless treasures,
> All set her languid soul astir
> With feelings joyful and half-anguished:
> The desk, the lamp there, now extinguished,
> The carpet-covered bed, the books,
> The window over them that looks
> Out on the moonlit dark unending,
> And that pale half-light over all,
> Lord Byron's portrait on the wall.
>
> (VII.19)

For provincial, sheltered Tatiana, the presence of Byron does not only demark a fashion that Onegin conforms to but also aestheticises the entire room so that everyday objects begin to take on an enchanted Byronic quality. According to Todd, in *A Hero of Our Time*, Byron is an ordinary part of everyday life, in the same semantic world as everyday objects and behaviours. A little earlier in *Eugene Onegin*, Byron is something that transforms everyday life into something other and directed towards the future. The sight of Onegin's room sets Tatiana's soul astir, in an echo of the opening epigraph: 'It hurries to live, and it hastens to feel.' I have stressed in the introduction that the militant subjectivity of Byronic heroism fills and alters the world outside itself, and here that occurs through the enchantment of the world. However, in the cities of Russia, whose modernity is in advance of the provinces, it is just beginning to look old. This is the fundamental difference between the narrator's ironic comments on Onegin as a 'lexicon' of 'modish words' and a 'Muscovite in Harold's cloak,' and Tatiana's enchantment with Onegin's library and Byronic persona.

This points to a fundamental difference between *Eugene Onegin* and *A Hero of Our Time*, which Todd also recognises but does not put into such sharp comparative contrast as he could. In *Eugene Onegin*, Tatiana's response to Byron offers an opening up of possibility, of potentiality. Todd finishes his discussion of *Eugene Onegin* by convincingly arguing that 'life and the novel come to share a common "reality."'[54] Thus the novel opens up myriad possibilities of seeing the world; the novel enchants the world, and the world gives back to the novel reality. On the other hand, Todd sees *A Hero of Our Time* as more constricting: 'Its success, in its own time and subsequently, rests on its power simultaneously to constrict both hero and world and to intimate that each might surpass the other and surpass itself,' insofar as Pechorin both 'fits into the novel's polite society' and constantly challenges it.[55] Todd makes clear that his reference to this dialectic of the constriction of the hero in the social world of the novel and the possibility of the hero surpassing it is itself gesturing towards Lukács's distinction between the epic and bourgeois hero, which I have discussed in the introduction. The former has a militant subjectivity that fills the world, whereas the latter is defined by the world. Here Todd suggests that *A Hero of Our Time* is on the threshold between the epic and the bourgeois novel, between what I have called militant subjectivity, associated with the epic, and bourgeois subjectivity. Ultimately, in a slight modification of Todd's position, I argue here that militant subjectivity is subordinated to the bourgeois in Lermontov's novel and appears only in the occasional flash of Byronic memory. In this movement between two types of heroism, bourgeois heroism eventually gains the upper hand.

The openness of *Eugene Onegin* in comparison to *A Hero of Our Time* can be explicitly linked to the depictions of the failed revolution of the Decembrist Revolt. Byron was important to the leaders of the Decembrists and also to the dramatist Griboedov, a Decembrist whose murder as a diplomat in Tehran informs Pushkin's and Lermontov's conceptions of the East and who will be discussed in more detail later in the chapter.[56] Diakonova and Vatsuro state that the Decembrists 'were devout readers of Byron' and add that the 'poet who had so openly stood up against the victory of reaction in Europe, who had sung the liberation movements in Spain, Italy and Greece [...] meant more to the Decembrists than any other European writer.'[57] Attention to the importance of the Decembrists to Pushkin and Lermontov can illuminate a socio-historical and materialist backdrop to the mutation of the Byronic Hero into nascent bourgeois professionalism in the two texts. *Eugene Onegin*'s more positive attitude towards the possibilities of revolution is paralleled by a more positive depiction of Byronic heroism, whereas *A Hero of Our Time*'s more disaffected attitude to revolution is paralleled by a decline in Byronic heroism in favour of bourgeois heroism. In tracing this through *Eugene Onegin*, it becomes clear that Onegin prefigures the idea of the hero subordinated to professionalism, which is repeated in the more prosaic use of Byron in *A Hero of Our Time*, where, ultimately, rather than being a revolutionary, Pechorin's Byronism is subordinated to the bourgeois work of a government official who actually ensures the smooth running of the imperial system. Nonetheless, disruptive Byronic elements remain and confuse any stable claim about Pechorin's bourgeois professionalism.

Onegin can most readily be conceived as a revolutionary in a section of the novel-in-verse that was not published in Pushkin's lifetime and which refers to contemporary political events more explicitly than any other part of the work. The fragmentary Chapter X was never part of the published novel as Pushkin's contemporaries knew it; it is unfinished and yet is published in modern 'Classics' editions as an important part of it.

It is both inside and outside the text we call *Eugene Onegin*. Similarly, its chronology cannot be easily mapped onto the chronology of the novel. It is clear that it refers in some way to the Decembrist Revolt of 1825 and yet begins with discussions of the Napoleonic campaign in Russia in 1812 as a historical context for the Decembrist Revolt. As a continuation of the novel, it seems to occur after the events described in the novel, however, the events in the novel proper seem to also begin after the Decembrist Revolt. Chapter I begins with an allusion to the narrator's (and by extension to Pushkin's) involvement in the Decembrist Revolt, and subsequent exile, when he says that, 'now the North's unsafe for me' (I.2), which is combined with Pushkin's note 'Written in Bessarabia,' his 'initial place of exile' (see Mitchell's notes, p. 216). This confusion in temporal scheme makes the dating of the plot in Chapter X perplexing. The chronology of the novel *Eugene Onegin* seems to take place both before and after the Decembrist Revolt simultaneously. Onegin does not appear in the fragmentary Chapter X, but there is 'evidence to suggest that Onegin might turn up' as a revolutionary (Mitchell's notes, p. 240). Mitchell does not elaborate on what this evidence is, though perhaps the way in which Onegin has been shown as admiring the revolutionary Byron is one piece of evidence.

As well as by his admiration for Byron, the possibility of Onegin becoming a revolutionary can be corroborated by the way in which Chapter X, even in its fragmentary form, seems to be repeating images from the opening chapter, as though the novel-in-verse is constructing a revolutionary new beginning for itself. Onegin as a 'London *dandy*' (I.4) has been replaced by the authoritarian Alexander I who is presented as 'a balding fop' (X.I).[58] Chapter I obliquely refers to Pushkin's own separation from the world of the novel as a result of his political activities when he makes reference to his exile, 'But now the North's unsafe for me' (I.2), but in Chapter X, images which juxtapose Onegin himself (and the Decembrists more generally) to the forces of reaction are deployed. Even Onegin's dandyism is significant here. Ellen Moers, in what is still the only good general study of dandyism, connects dandyism with an assertion of the self, 'the dandy's achievement is simply to be himself.'[59] As will be seen, this is in some ways analogous with the revolutionary assertion of self-practiced by the Decembrists. The original dandy, Beau Brummell, though in a very different (and less dangerous social situation), asserted himself against the monarchy:

> The extent to which Brummell had made himself an independent somebody was demonstrated at the start of the second decade of the century when the Prince suddenly withdrew his favour [...] the break came, it was said, because Brummell ordered the Prince to ring the bell; because he commented once too often on the Prince's increasing corpulence.[60]

Byron also associated himself with dandyism. The narrator of *Beppo* describes himself as a 'broken dandy' (l. 410), whilst Byron himself was 'one of the few literary men admitted' to Waiter's Club, one of the major gathering places of dandies in London.[61] Byron also met the quintessential dandy, Beau Brummell, in the latter's exile in Calais.[62] This same assertion of independence can be traced in *Eugene Onegin*. Thus, the individualist and revolutionary dandy is placed against the autocratic monarchical fop, the former is independent and asserts freedom and the other the slavish follower of society, an impression strengthened by the description of Alexander I as a 'minion' (X.1) and a frequenter of parties (X.12).

The novel has shown Onegin as a frequenter of parties, but in Chapter X, these images of parties are reworked from Chapter I. High society social life is reimagined as gatherings at which Decembrists' conspiracies are organised:

> Foregathering at private meetings, | Over Russian vodka, wine, | They would, reciprocating greetings [...]. Grandiloquent and trenchant pleaders, | This group of friends would congregate | At either turbulent Nikita's | Or cautious Ilya's to debate.[63]
>
> (X.13–14)

In this respect, there is a dialectical tension between the society which is depicted in Chapter I and the repetition of Chapter I in Chapter X, where society is radically reimagined, a tension that is between conservative monarchical society and the revolutionary individualist society of the Decembrists. The 'social hubbub' that leaves Onegin 'bored' (I.37) creates both the extremely reactionary form of itself in Alexander I and the possibility of its own destruction through revolution.

William Mills Todd describes this aristocratic society, and the art it produced, as being 'dedicated to social harmony and the amelioration of manners.'[64] Nonetheless, Todd suggests that the existence of this society was integral to the Decembrists rejection of it:

> The Decembrists in the capital needed the social conventions and ideology of polite society in order to mount challenges [...]. After all, they had to appear at balls in order not to dance at them, take cognizance of social fashions in order to oppose them diametrically.[65]

And, indeed, they seem, in Chapter X, to repeat the life of aristocratic society, the public gatherings of the aristocracy regulated by strict social codes of behaviour: 'reciprocating greetings,' drinking, and engaging in the polite form of political discourse known as debate, which were other conventions of society as much as they were rejections of it. Nonetheless, society was fragmented, like Pushkin's Chapter X, between authoritarian and liberal positions, which were difficult to be reconciled in polite conversation due to their political incompatibility. Five Decembrists were hanged, and many others were subjected to 'ruthless sentences to hard labor and suicidal military missions.'[66] As Todd stresses, aristocratic society and its social codes continued to occupy a major role in Russian cultural life long afterwards, though he also concedes the shift in Russian literature towards the nascent middle class:

> [T]he ideology of polite society would be challenged [...] as it failed to answer the cultural needs of a new generation of Russian intellectuals: aspiring professional writers, university students, low-ranking civil servants, and children of the clergy [...]. Nevertheless, the ideology embedded in the language, behaviour, self-image, art, and ethics of Russia's cultural elite could not be eradicated overnight.[67]

Chapter X of *Eugene Onegin* suggests a revolutionary individualism in the face of the 'ideology of polite society,' which can be discerned both through dandyism's assertion of individualised subjectivity and the manipulation and partial rejection of the conformist codes of aristocratic social regulations. Onegin threatens society by refusing it and is thus a threat to a social organisation that is based on a certain level of conformity. He embodies a concomitant shift towards the Western European bourgeois values of individualism. Pushkin's novel-in-verse, even in the 'finished' versions published in Pushkin's lifetime, which did not include Chapter X, does not then abandon the legacy of the Decembrists, even if they are not visible in the novel. It is haunted with the memories of the hanged Decembrists who decorate the margins of his manuscript.[68] The fragmentary nature of Chapter X is a testament to Pushkin's attempt to represent a new form of social relations outside that dominant in Russian aristocratic society. This is a form of Byronic heroism, where Onegin's subjectivity stands for a whole movement of social potential that goes far beyond him, a militant subjectivity that associates itself with revolution, which is celebrated in the text's revolutionary unfinishedness, not unlike Byron's *Don Juan*. Onegin, at least to an extent, is a positive hero, after the model of Byron, who can carry the possibilities of the Decembrist revolution in literature even after it has been crushed in reality.

Nonetheless, this chapter stands in complex relation to the rest of the text. It was not published in Pushkin's lifetime, and it does not clearly relate to the narrative of the rest of the work. The transition between Onegin's rejection by Tatiana and his becoming a Decembrist is not entirely clear. Furthermore, the chapter was written in 1830 in the full knowledge that the Decembrist Revolt was a failure. Onegin's absence in this chapter then seems to point to fruitful speculations that cannot be realised by the text of the chapter itself, which speak to my wider argument about the status of heroism after the failure of revolution. It is implied that the hero becomes a revolutionary after the failure of his phallic sexuality – that is, after Tatiana rejects him – but this is in the full knowledge that the revolution too will fail. Thus, at the end of *Eugene Onegin*, the hero attempts twice to assert his presence as an active force by trying again to seduce Tatiana and twice fails. Furthermore, the novel leaves it entirely unclear as to whether these are even attempts at seduction or rooted in the desire to settle down into the structure of the bourgeois family with her. The fragmentary nature of the chapter seems to point to the knowledge that the revolution will fail – not only is the political content of the chapter impossible to publish in its historical context but also whilst there is the potential for the revolutionary Byronic Hero to appear in Chapter X, Onegin never does appear. The chapter seems to speak of the ultimate failure of Byronic heroism in relation to revolution. Yet Pushkin does not foreclose on Byronic possibilities. Rather, the fragmentary Chapter X leaves the hero absent, in abeyance or dormant, but implies the possibility that he may still emerge. The failure of revolution haunts Pushkin's text, evidenced by his compulsively repeated drawings of the hanged Decembrists in the margins of the manuscript. Byron, like these revolutionaries, also haunts the text, disrupting the new order it helps to usher in with other possibilities.

In Lermontov, on the other hand, Decembrists are significantly less visible. The images of the death of the Decembrists in the manuscript of *Eugene Onegin* seem to pre-empt their relative absence from *A Hero of Our Time*. Aside from the five Decembrists who were hanged, and who adorn the margins of Pushkin's manuscripts, the other participants were 'sentenced to hard labor, reduced in rank, and stripped of nobility. The once-dashing guards officers found themselves in the mines of Siberia in horrible conditions.'[69] Pechorin is in a similar, though less severe, condition at the chronological beginning of *A Hero of Our Time*. In 'Taman,' he has been exiled to the Caucasus, and in 'Princess Mary,' he is shown stripped of rank, in the 'epaulets of a mere army officer' (p. 69), rather than from an elite guard or cavalry regiment. However, this is in the early 1830s (see Nabokov's introduction, p. ix), and, as Nabokov's note makes clear,

> a deleted passage in the draft corroborates one's suspicion that Pechorin in 1833 [...] was expelled to the Caucasus because of a duel. Officers of the Guard were demoted to low ranks in the Army [...] for escapades of that kind.
>
> (p. 171)

Duelling may seem an archaic and somewhat useless practice for revolutionary modernisers. However, duelling was particularly associated with the Decembrists. Irina Reyfman describes the 'prevalence of senseless duelling among the intellectual elite, the future Decembrists in particular.'

She notes that this was 'especially bewildering' given that they 'wanted to be seen as a group of people who meant serious business.'[70] Thus, on the face of it, duelling seems in conflict with the revolutionary aspirations of Decembrists.

However, in a society marked by a different trajectory of development, the bourgeois epoch, in this case, used an old cultural form to assert new values, and duels such as Pechorin's can be seen as revolutionary insofar as they are an assertion of individuated subjectivity. Reyfman observes that under the increased absolutism of the later part of the reign of Alexander I (r. 1801–1825), 'dueling (as well as some other types of unruly behaviour, such as reckless gambling, heavy drinking, and dangerous mischief) began to serve as a statement of protest against perceived constrictions of personal freedom.'[71] If duelling was a method of asserting personal autonomy under a despotic regime, then it takes on the character of a minor revolutionary practice here. Moreover, it takes on special significance in a nascent bourgeois society where personal subjectivity is particularly valued, and though seemingly an archaic form, it actually implies a shift away from aristocratic values to bourgeois values. Duelling was subsequently taken up in Russia by the bourgeoisie to assert their status as private, individuated subjects. Reyfman also demonstrates how the Decembrists connected the practice of duelling to the rise of the bourgeoisie. She discusses in detail a duel between a minor aristocrat and a highly influential aristocrat and observes how Decembrists reimagined the minor aristocrat as middle class:

> Casting themselves as representatives of the Russian 'middle class' [...] the Decembrists managed to formulate their conflict with the new aristocracy in nationalistic, patriotic and even populist terms. Dueling is more dramatic and thus potentially more heroic action than a political debate. Substituting the former for the latter, the Decembrists elevated the duel to a form of political protest.[72]

In this respect, the disappearance of the Decembrists in *A Hero of Our Time*, along with the continuation of the practice of duelling, suggests, paradoxically, the success of the Decembrist project. The Decembrist Revolt was precisely a demand for individual rights for aristocratic and nascent middle-class fractions relative to royal power. This revolutionary attitude actually mirrors, or is a nascent form of, the bourgeois consciousness of Western Europe in a mutated form due to the different economic circumstances. The historical tendency of duelling to become a bourgeois pursuit corroborates this. Duelling operated analogously to, and alongside, the importance of Byronism, for the Decembrists. It produced forms of individuated subjectivity that were militant in asserting the status of the subject but which ultimately tended towards the atomisation of society in myriad private individuals.

Pechorin himself begins to look more and more like a bourgeois sub-ject. In 'Taman,' which is, in the internal chronology of the novel, the first episode, Pechorin reminds us at the very beginning that he is 'an officer going on official business' (p. 55) and at the end of the same nar-rative stresses his bureaucratic status even more strongly: '[W]hat do I care about human joys and sorrows – I, a military man on the move, and holder, moreover, of a road-pass issued to those on official business?' (p. 67). In this respect, Pechorin seems like a bourgeois professional but through the prism of the military. This is much less the individual asserted through revolutionary action, related to the Byronic model that Pushkin deploys, and more individualism established by professionalism, part of the bourgeois identity I established in the introduction to the book. However, the influence of the Byronic is still here as a remnant since it has formed a backdrop, which, I have shown, is still visible to the ideo-logical changes which are sweeping the Byronic away. I suggested in the introduction to this book that the Byronic, in asserting militant subjec-tivity, paves the way for the creation of bourgeois private subjectivity. In *A Hero of Our Time*, the weak revolutionary potentiality which is still held by Onegin in Pushkin seems to have been subsumed into a nascent form of bourgeois consciousness. This is paralleled by the weakening of the Byronic Hero and the importance of Byron. This is stressed by the fact that the narration itself is in the first person and that Pechorin's individualistic pose, stressed by his lack of a fashionable uniform, is actu-ally a general one. Grushnitsky, the parodied Byronic figure, also wears, 'following a peculiar kind of foppishness, a soldier's thick coat' (p. 70). Dandyism, which was seen as a heroic trait in *Eugene Onegin*, is here no longer about establishing oneself as an individual outside the social body but about showing yourself to be part of a society composed of autonomous individuals who are not of the very highest social class. This is a small but important distinction and emphasises that *A Hero of Our Time*, though haunted by the Byronic and clearly in conversation with it, increasingly loses touch with Byronic heroism; the Byronic becomes a much more commonplace backdrop to life. Nonetheless, Byronic ele-ments in this backdrop come to disrupt the increasing bourgeois ideology of the world that *A Hero of Our Time* depicts.

Bourgeois ideology is seen very clearly at the very end of the novel, according to its internal chronology, in the section 'Maksim Maksimych,' where there is a general atmosphere of bureaucratic business. It is set in Ekaterinograd, a colonial outpost, where Maksim Maksimych has some 'government property [...] to hand over' to the commandant (p. 51).[73] Furthermore, Maksim Maksimych mistakes the carriage that Pechorin arrives in as that of 'some functionary going to an inquest in Tiflis' (p. 44). Pechorin is actually travelling to Persia, and this retains some traces of the Byronic; when asked if he will return, Pechorin 'made a sign with his hand which might have been interpreted as most likely never' (p. 50), however, it is revealed that Pechorin 'died on his way back' (p. 53). This trip to Persia also fits into the impression of heroes no longer standing apart from society but conducting professional work within it since it brings to mind the death of the playwright Griboedov in 1829, on a diplomatic trip to Persia, whose body was brought back to Tiflis.[74] Indeed, in Pushkin's *A Journey to Arzrum*, an account of travels in the Caucasus, based on a diary Pushkin kept in 1829 and published in full in 1836, a few years before the publication of *A Hero of Our Time*, alongside which it is translated in a recent edition, Pushkin records seeing Griboedov's body on its journey back to Russia. Pushkin reflects on Griboedov's character in a way that stresses that his heroism is private:

> His gifts as a statesman remained unused; his talent as a poet was unrecognized [...] a few friends appreciated him at his true worth [...]. People only believe in fame; they do not realize there may be amongst them some Napoleon who has never commanded a single company of chasseurs, or another Descartes who has never published a single line in the *Moscow Telegraph*.

Pushkin stresses that this is part of a disappearance of heroism which is directly linked to writing as a transcription of subjectivity that retains the traces of the subject: 'What a pity that Griboedov has not left us his memoirs. It should be up to his friends to write his biography; but nowadays our remarkable men vanish and leave no trace behind them.'[75]

It should be noted, though, that this professionalism is not some sort of return to a lack of individualism within the social body, or an absorption, post-Decembrists, of any individualism, back into service of the tsar. Rather, Pechorin's stress on not caring about human joys and sorrows when on official business provides the key to what is really going on here. These imperial workers are now professionals, and the split is no longer between the social body and individuated subject, but rather a work subjectivity and a private subjectivity. Hence, Pechorin does not care about personal matters when on imperial official business, as he says when he leaves Taman. Curiously, when Pechorin arrives in Pyatigorsk, in 'Princess Mary,' he says something very similar: '[W]ho, here, needs passions, desires, regrets?' (p. 68), but this is not because he is on official business, but rather because he is on holiday, away from official business. Holiday is just the obverse of work and in this respect is very different from the Byronic journey, which implies an expansion of subjectivity.[76] In both cases, an abandonment of Romantic and Byronic poses to do with passion are evident.

Yet there is also irony in what Pechorin says since, of course, 'passion, desire and regrets' will be the very business of his holiday; they are what are indulged in during moments of private subjectivity, away from work.

A sincere sort of Byronism, marked by the passage I have discussed about the dream of the pirate ship, is re-enacted at the end of this section when things have gone beyond the standard limits of bourgeois life, defined by duty and the family.

At the moment Pechorin seems to have become most bourgeois, his class status is disrupted by traces of Byronism that intimate a more radical form of modern heroism in opposition to the bourgeoisie. The association between Pechorin and the bourgeois novel is most marked in the section 'Maksim Maksimych,' which is placed earlier in the novel than 'Princess Mary,' but which, within the novel's internal chronology, comes later. Indeed, this is the very final section of the novel's internal chronology. Pechorin leaves for Persia, a last act that both represents the last trace of his Byronism and its disappearance, where he will die. This is Byronic in terms of experience exile, like the Byronic Hero, and in terms of travelling to the East. He has also become a 'dandy' (p. 50), which, whilst not truly Byronic, has already been associated with Byron-influenced revolution in *Eugene Onegin*. Like a Regency dandy, Pechorin has 'dazzling clean linen which bespeaks the habits of a gentleman' and, like the Byronic Hero, is 'undefeated either by the dissolution of city life or by the tempests of the soul' (pp. 46–47). These 'tempests of the soul' recall the heroic challenges of subjectivity that the Byronic Hero experiences, as does the triumph over the 'dissolution' of city life, which recalls the Byronic Hero's sexual libertinism and heroic excess, where the dissolution of the immoral echoes the dissolution of subjectivity implied by a heroic subjectivity that exceeds subjectivity itself. Simultaneously, the tenacity in the face of city life recalls the heroism of the hero of modern life discussed by Walter Benjamin. Benjamin suggests that the subject who is able to survive the city is like an Apache in the forest of the city and rejects bourgeois life: 'The apache abjures virtues and laws [...] he believes that a world separates him from the bourgeois.'[77] The Byronic Hero comes together with the Benjaminian hero – past and future forms of heroism swirl and gather beneath the bourgeois surface of the present.

Pechorin seems to resemble the Byronic Eugene Onegin here, whose heroism is stressed by the narrator's observations that one 'can still be a man of action | And mind the beauty of one's nails' (I.25). However, whereas the narrator of *Onegin* suggests that this is to do with being modern, 'Why fight the age's predilection?' (I.25), in Pechorin's case, he seems strangely worn out, anachronistic, and faded. At the moment when bourgeois heroism seems to have cast Pechorin in its own mould, it seems as though bourgeois heroism is itself worn out, disrupted by a combination of the traces of Byronic heroism and the intimations of the more radical form of heroism that Walter Benjamin identifies in the work of Baudelaire. Pechorin's loves are 'soiled,' and 'after a first glance at his face, I would not have given him more than twenty-three years, though later I was ready to give him thirty' (p. 47). Other aspects of his appearance contribute to this: 'the traces of intersecting wrinkles' on his forehead, and eyes which 'never laughed when he was laughing [...] the sign of a deep and constant melancholy' (p. 47), another Byronic trait. This is somewhat more Byronic than Onegin's 'English spleen' (I.37), which associates him with Byron's Childe Harold since this is treated with a lightness of touch by Pushkin, whereas Pechorin's Byronism is treated more seriously, as less of a parody. Nonetheless, both figures are Byronic. Onegin's melancholy, Pushkin's narrator suggests, is caused by the sight of women 'Elucidating Say and Bentham' (I.42), and so whilst, as a Byronic figure, he resists bourgeois utilitarianism, this is still treated with humour, whereas Pechorin's melancholy is far more disturbing, 'akin to the gleam of smooth steel, dazzling but cold' (p. 47).

The Pechorin that is described as 'undefeated by the dissolution of city life' looks not only Byron but also towards Benjamin's description of the city melancholy of Baudelaire, whose heroism, it is worth remembering, is defined by his ability to negotiate the experiences of city life undefeated. But, in fact, looking forward to Baudelaire is an indirect way of looking back at Byron too: after the publication of *Fleurs du Mal*, Baudelaire told his mother that he wrote 'under Byronic signs.'[78] Thus, as Benjamin points out, 'Baudelaire's genius, [...] drew its nourishment from melancholy, was an allegorical one [...] the allegorist's gaze which falls upon the city is rather the gaze of alienated man.'[79] Behind Baudelaire's 'alienated man' is the alienated Byronic Hero. And if Baudelaire's 'Byronic' alienation in the city represents an apex of literature depicting nineteenth-century modernity, Pechorin moves towards this. His melancholy, his exhaustion, and his exile represent profound alienation. This same sort of sexual exhaustion and cultural alienation is present from the very outset of *Fleurs du Mal*:

> Like a poor profligate who sucks and bites
> the withered breast of some well-seasoned trull
> we snatch in passing at clandestine joys
> and squeeze the oldest orange harder yet.[80]

Pechorin is, too, an allegory. As the 'Author's Introduction' puts it, '*A Hero of Our Time* [...] is indeed a portrait, but not of a single individual; it is a portrait composed of all the vices of our generation in the fullness of their development' (pp. 1–2). Benjamin associates Baudelaire's heroism, under high capitalism, with 'the image of fencing' as a metaphor for 'a continuous series of tiny improvisations' which allow the hero to withstand the 'shocks' of city life.[81] Furthermore, this series of improvisations is then tied up with the image of the gladiator, who Benjamin refers to as 'the fencing slave' and who is the professional who withstands the city: '[W]hat the man working for wages achieves in his daily work is no less than what in ancient times helped a gladiator win applause and fame.' This image, of course, recalls Byron's identification with the ancient gladiator which I discussed in the introduction, and gnomically reinforces Byron's modernity, showing once again the continuing survival of the Byronic presence in later nineteenth-century culture. One way in which Byronic heroism survives intact, rather than being subsumed by bourgeois heroism, is by mutating in Baudelaire's heroism of modern life. And in this context, Pechorin is a transitional figure, carrying the Byronic forward and foreshadowing the Baudelairean. Whereas the Baudelairean-Benjaminian hero of modernity can survive the shocks of the city, Pechorin has survived it but is exhausted by it.

This impression of Pechorin's mutation into a bourgeois subject and the simultaneous sense of dissonance introduced by the traces of the Byronic Hero is extended by the final reference to Pechorin as a character from the bourgeois novel, which occurs at the chronological end of the narrative, but not at the end of the novel as it is constructed, in 'Maksim Maksimych.'

In the transition from the Byronic to the bourgeois novel, the exhaustion and feminisation associated with the continuing presence of the Byronic Hero begins to become a key, disruptive element in bourgeois characterisation. Paradoxically, exhaustion and feminisation in a patriarchal society remain subversively powerful remnants of Byronism. The travelling narrator describes Pechorin as 'sat there as a thirty-year-old coquette of Balzac's would sit after a fatiguing ball, in her armchair stuffed with down' (p. 47), the implication being that at thirty he is worn out and past it. Here, at the very end of the novel's chronology, Pechorin is very explicitly no longer like Byron but like a woman in the novels of one of the greatest chroniclers of the nineteenth-century bourgeoisie.[82] Pechorin, over the course of the novel's chronology, has moved from masculine Byronic Hero to woman in a French bourgeois novel. The fact that Pechorin is so heavily feminised here should not be ignored. This kind of feminisation of the hero is strengthened in *Eugene Onegin* and particularly *A Hero of Our Time* where the masculine sexual drive is made more and more contradictory.

Onegin is feminised, but this is integrated into his Byronic heroism. When he is fully dressed to go out in the evening, he '[l]ooked like a giddy Venus wearing | A man's attire' (I.25.12–13), and yet for Onegin, the feminine and masculine are combined: 'One can still be a man of action | And mind the beauty of one's nails' (I.25). Furthermore, Onegin is both more explicitly Byronic, and the text is less disillusioned about the possibilities of Byronic heroism. Thus, Onegin's feminisation is not at the expense of his phallic masculinity: 'How soon he knew how to bedevil | The heart of a professed coquette! | Or, to annihilate a rival' (I.12). Here sexual conquest is related explicitly to an image of masculine, military triumph, as though Onegin is invading society, his sexual libertinage becoming a militant assertion of his subjectivity.

Pechorin succeeds in pursuing women, but it leads simultaneously to a greater draining of his masculinity and a greater feminising. However, in both Onegin's and Pechorin's cases, this feminisation, which is linked to the Byronic, could hardly be called bourgeois since it inaugurates the confusion of gender roles and a lack of constraint by sexual morality that stand in opposition to the celebration of the family. After the death of Bela, Pechorin 'was ill for a long time, and he lost weight' (p. 40), and this emptiness continues beyond the limits of the episode and seems to be reflected in his travel to Persia. '"And remember Bela?"' Pechorin is asked in 'Maksim Maksimych.' The response: 'Pechorin paled slightly and turned away' (p. 49), before leaving almost immediately afterwards.

Pechorin's feminisation is connected to his exhaustion. He is worn out, and this part of the novel stresses the failure of his masculine sexuality. It is true that the narrator also states that 'he was rather handsome and had one of those original faces which especially appeal to women of fashion' (p.48), but in the novel, Pechorin is gradually removed from the sphere of fashion. It is only, it seems, in aristocratic society that he can maintain this sort of phallic sexuality. His move to the provinces is part of the decomposition of his Byronic potency, and it is concomitant with the decline of his phallic sexuality in the Caucasian setting. Maksim Maksimych attempts to revive Pechorin's memories of a more active, heroic, masculine past, 'Remember our days at the fort? Fine country for hunting! You used to be a passionate sportsman' (p. 49). But at this end point of Pechorin's life, the phallic side of his Byronic heroism is nothing but a memory, faint traces on a drained and devalued body. But the exhausted feminisation that is the legacy of the Byronic is still paradoxically active. This is echoed in the contrasting ways in which he responds to the loss of the women he encounters who populate the novel. In 'Taman' he is simply angry that he 'had almost been drowned by an eighteen-year-old girl' (p. 67). In 'Princess Mary,' there is an air of melancholy exhaustion in the Byronic reverie about the pirate ship. Pechorin 'wonder[s] why I had not wanted to tread that path, which fate had opened for me, where quiet joys and peace of mind awaited me? No, I would not have got used to such an existence' (p. 148). And in 'Bela,' he marries Bela and when she dies, he is 'ill for a long time, and he lost weight, poor fellow' (p. 40). Whilst it is heavily mediated through the orientalised, Byronic setting, Pechorin here is in mourning for the loss of a wife. It would not however be satisfactory here to say that Pechorin is mourning for the bourgeois family. After all, his marriage has been one of racial and religious mixing and sexual intensity rather than familial duty. Not all marriages can be subsumed into the bourgeois model.

Thus, though the novel hints at Pechorin becoming bourgeois through his similarity to government officials, a number of dissonances are introduced that prevent him from being seen solely as a bourgeois hero and mark the continuing importance of Byronic heroism. He has begun to resemble the anti-bourgeois heroism of Baudelaire, which has stemmed from the legacy of Byronic heroism, and his feminisation also stands in opposition to bourgeois ideology and may also stem from Byronic roots. Perhaps one could even say that in Pechorin's exhausted, feminised heroism, he begins to resemble the prostitutes who Baudelaire makes the heroines of his own work.

In this discussion of Lermontov's novel, I have suggested that Byronism becomes a disruptive cultural memory, associated with exhaustion and feminisation, rather than a phallic active force. Byronism has rather become an off-duty pose which is contrasted with the work of the (nascent bourgeois) professional, who has emerged as a hero of our time. The hero is subordinated to services rendered. A key part of this shift, in Russia, was the failure of revolution. The failure of the Decembrist Revolt, rather than strengthening the aristocracy in relation to the autocratic monarchy, is instead expressed in a weakening of aristocratic characters, who instead come to look like government officials, subordinate to the autocratic monarch, but also, strangely enough, looking more and more like the bourgeoisie of Western Europe. Returning to Russia, however, what better example of economic and social stability than the extension of empire? This process is chronicled particularly in *A Hero of Our Time*, where the borderlands of the nation, though orientalised in both Pushkin and Lermontov, are markedly new. In Pushkin, the newly colonised areas are places of Romantic refuge, in the latter, they are the province of military and civil officials who holiday in new colonial resorts. Concomitant with this process is a move towards different modes of writing, a move away from poetry and towards something that might be termed the realist novel. Nonetheless, the traces and remnants of the Byronic are still present and active in *A Hero of Our Time* and disrupt any easy claim that Pechorin becomes a bourgeois figure. Indeed, Pechorin's disruptive Byronism, combined with his more obviously bourgeois elements, suggests the ways in which new forms of heroism are imagined that stand against the bourgeois order. Pechorin still dies, though, suggesting a bleak outlook for the future possibilities of heroism. Perhaps it is only in the hybrid figure of Werner, who combines Byronism and the bourgeois in such a way that he is neither fully subsumed to the bourgeoisie nor a *hero*, that Byronism can sustain itself in the bourgeois world.

In the next chapter, I discuss one of the most important English novelists of the nineteenth century, Charles Dickens, though the concerns of this chapter have not abated. Through an analysis of *David Copperfield*, I will discuss how the cultural memory of Lord Byron still plays on the creation of heroes of modernity who are framed in terms of the bourgeois, professional roles, as seen already in Werner in *A Hero of Our Time*. I show how questions of revolution do not vanish as a key feature of the modernity of texts that attempt to create heroes of modern life through the cultural re-imaging of Byron and Napoleon. Indeed, *David*

Copperfield is written in the shadow of the revolution that heralds the Second Empire in France and is full of references to earlier bourgeois revolutions, the Puritan English Revolution of the seventeenth century, and the 1830 revolution in France in particular. I will show how the concerns of the current chapter are present, but differently developed in English literature, and discuss the relationships between sexuality, Byronism, and revolution in Dickens's text.

Notes

1 Georges Bataille, 'Initial Postulate,' in *The Absence of Myth: Writings of Surrealism*, ed. and trans. Michael Richardson (London: Verso, 2006), pp. 91–94 (p. 92).

2 Georges Bataille, 'The Surrealist Religion,' in *The Absence of Myth*, pp. 71–90 (p. 77).

3 High capitalism [*Hochkapitalismus*] was defined by the Marxist economist and sociologist Werner Sombart in his *Modern Capitalism* (1902, revised 1916) and refers to capitalism between about 1760 and the outbreak of the First World War. It refers to the period during and after the Industrial Revolution where the bourgeoisie are at the height of their power. As Peter Osborne notes, 'Today, Sombart's periodizing scheme continues to circulate mainly through the title of a collection of Benjamin's writings on Baudelaire (*A Lyric Poet in the Era of High Capitalism*), reinforcing the association of the "high" with European capitalism in its mid-nineteenth-century bourgeois form.' See Peter Osborne, 'The Postconceptual Condition, Or, the Cultural Logic of High Capitalism Today,' *Radical Philosophy* 184 (2014), 19–27 (p. 19).

4 The word 'subject' here shifts from asserting subjectivity as a philosophical and political value to becoming subjected to capitalism.

5 Karl Marx and Friedrich Engels, 'Manifesto of the Communist Party,' in *Political Writings*, ed. David Fernbach, 3 vols (Harmondsworth: Penguin/ London: New Left Review, 1973), I, pp. 62–98 (pp. 70–71).

6 Marx and Engels, 'Manifesto of the Communist Party,' p. 71.

7 Alexander Pushkin, *Eugene Onegin: A Novel in Verse*, trans. Stanley Mitchell (London: Penguin, 2008). All references to this text will be incorporated parenthetically into the main body of the chapter, in the form of Roman chapter number and Arabic stanza number. References to Mitchell's notes and introduction will be by page number. Mikhail Lermontov, *A Hero of Our Time*, trans. Vladimir Nabokov and Dmitri Nabokov (Oxford: Oxford University Press, 1984). All references to this text will be incorporated parenthetically into the main body of the chapter.

8 Karl Marx, *Grundrisse: Foundations of the Critique of Political Economy*, trans. Martin Nicolaus (London: Penguin, 1993), p. 83.

9 Marx, *Grundrisse*, p. 83.

10 Franco Moretti, *The Bourgeois: Between History and Literature* (London: Verso, 2014), p. 27.

11 Marshall Berman, *All That Is Solid Melts Into Air: The Experience of Modernity* (London: Verso, 1983), p. 173.

12 Elizabeth Cheresh Allen, *A Fallen Idol Is Still a God: Lermontov and the Quandaries of Cultural Transition* (Stanford: Stanford University Press, 2007), p. 6.

13 Allen, p. 18.

14 Allen, p. 26.
15 Allen p. 27.
16 Allen, p. 141.
17 Allen, p. 140.
18 This is a direct allusion to Byron's *Don Juan*:
> Sweet is a legacy, and passing sweet
> The unexpected death of some old lady
> Or gentleman of seventy years complete,
> Who've made 'us youth' wait too – too long already,
> For an estate, or cash, or country seat.

(I.125)

19 Marx and Engels, 'Manifesto of the Communist Party,' p. 71.
20 Nina Diakonova and Vadim Vatsuro, '"No Great Mind and Generous Heart Could Avoid Byronism": Russia and Byron,' in *The Reception of Byron in Europe*, ed. Richard Cardwell, 2 vols., (London: Thoemmes Continuum, 2004), II, pp. 333–352 (pp. 336, 342–345).
21 Diakonova and Vatsuro, pp. 337, 343–344.
22 Diakonova and Vatsuro, p. 345.
23 Mitchell conjectures, based on drafts of *Eugene Onegin*, that Pushkin is referring to Charles Maturin's *Melmoth the Wanderer* (1820), François-René de Chateaubriand's *René* (1802), and Benjamin Constant's *Adolphe* (1816) here (p. 232).
24 Nabokov catalogues the allusions to *Eugene Onegin* in thorough detail in his notes to his translation *A Hero of Our Time*.
25 Hadley J. Mozer, '"I Want a Hero": Advertising for an Epic Hero in "Don Juan,"' *Studies in Romanticism* 44 (2005), 239–260 (p. 240).
26 Of course, Pushkin's playful, ironic tone and the general structure of the novel in *Eugene Onegin* derive much more obviously from *Don Juan*, but the concepts of heroism are not modelled after Don Juan. Speculatively, one might suggest that the playful, ironic narrator achieves the distinction of heroism as the writer of the modern novel, but this is beyond the scope of this study.
27 For the authorial note, see Pushkin, *Eugene Onegin*, trans. Vladimir Nabokov, I, p. 313. Mitchell's translation, which I use as my primary text, inexplicably fails to print Pushkin's important notes. Vol. II of Nabokov's edition, which includes a commentary and index, has been indispensable throughout the writing of this chapter. Nabokov includes exhaustive background material on such information as which French editions of Byron Pushkin may have read and on his attempts to translate Byron into Russian. Further references to Onegin as like Childe Harold occur at IV.44 and VIII.8, and he recites from *The Corsair* at IV.37.
28 Again, for the authorial note, Pushkin, *Eugene Onegin*, trans. Vladimir Nabokov, I, p. 316. As it happens, there is an earlier reference to the vampire in Byron's *The Giaour* which predates Polidori's story by six years: 'But first, on earth as Vampire sent, | Thy corse shall from its tomb be rent; | Then ghastly haunt thy native place, | And suck the blood of all thy race' (ll. 755–758).
29 This 'us' is corroborated by Nabokov's literal translation, *Eugene Onegin*, I, p. 120. It is not the product of Mitchell searching for a rhyme.
30 Nabokov, *Eugene Onegin*, II, p. 155.
31 Laurence Kelly, *Lermontov: Tragedy in the Caucasus* (London: Constable, 1977), p. 190.
32 Polidori was Byron's personal physician. His story 'The Vampyre' (1819) took its origins from the gathering of Byron, Polidori, Percy Shelley, and Mary

Shelley in the summer of 1816, which also saw the genesis of Mary Shelley's *Frankenstein* (1818).

33 In the next chapter on *David Copperfield*, I discuss how the impossibility of stating how one feels becomes a marker for bourgeois privacy.

34 'Titular Counsellor,' as Nabokov explains, is 'an average rank in the civil service, the ninth in a scale where the lowest rung (fourteenth) is a Collegiate Registrator and the highest (first) a Chancellor (Kantsler)' (Nabokov's note, *A Hero of Our Time*, p. 173). These ranks become extremely important in Dostoyevsky's depictions of the lower-middle class experience in St Petersburg, particularly in *Notes from Underground* (1864), where the idea of government official as hero is entirely drained of positive sense.

35 Walter Benjamin, 'The Paris of the Second Empire in Baudelaire,' in *Charles Baudelaire: A Lyric Poet in the Era of High Capitalism*, trans. Harry Zohn (London: New Left Books, 1973), pp. 9–106 (p. 74).

36 Benjamin, p. 74.

37 Byron himself had his skull examined by a phrenologist who declared his skull rather Byronic. In a letter to Annabella Milbanke on 26 September 1814, he writes, 'I have just been going through a curious scene [.] Sir W. Knighton brought me Spurtzheim (I believe is the name) the *craniologist* to see me – a discoverer of faculties & dispositions from heads. – He passes his hand over the head & then tells you – curious things enough – for I own he has a little astonished me. – He says all mine are strongly marked – but very antithetical for everything developed in & on this same skull of mine has its *opposite* in great force so that to believe him my good & evil are at perpetual war – pray heaven the last don't come off victorious,' George Gordon, Lord Byron, 'To Annabella Milbanke (a),' in *Letters and Journals*, ed. Leslie A. Marchand, 12 vols. (London: John Murray, 1973–82), IV, p. 182.

38 To bolster this impression of the meeting of Western Europe and Russia in *Werner*, it may also be worth observing speculatively and in passing that Byron wrote a play entitled *Werner* in 1822, which was dedicated to Goethe. The name Werner perhaps recalls Goethe's Werther too.

39 Mikhail Bakhtin, 'From the Prehistory of Novelistic Discourse,' in *The Dialogic Imagination: Four Essays*, ed. Michael Holquist, trans. Caryl Emerson and Michael Holquist (Austin: University of Texas Press, 2008), pp. 41–83 (p. 43). Bakhtin's important discussion of the language of *Eugene Onegin* can be found on pp. 41–51 of this essay.

40 Bakhtin, p. 44, his italics.

41 Bakhtin, p. 44.

42 Benjamin, p. 74.

43 Richard Lansdown, 'The Novelized Poem & the Poeticized Novel: Byron's *Don Juan* & Victorian Fiction,' *Critical Review* 39 (1999), 119–141.

44 Mozer, p. 246.

45 The biographical background to these allusions is from the notes to Lord Byron, *Works*, ed. Ernest Hartley Coleridge, 7 vols. (London: John Murray, 1903), VI, p. 12.

46 Richard Lansdown discusses at length *Don Juan*'s legacy to the nineteenth-century novel being depictions of the acculturation of individuals in society in a much more total way than any literary depictions that came before. See particularly Lansdown, pp. 137–138.

47 Byron himself hints at the disappearance of the traditional epic hero:

> Cervantes smiled Spain's Chivalry away;
> A single laugh demolished the right arm
> Of his own country; – seldom since that day
> Has Spain had heroes.
>
> (*Don Juan*, XIII.11)

It is perhaps because Cervantes does not write in poetry but in prose that he is able to 'smile chivalry away.' He makes a mockery of old, poetic forms of heroism by making them prosaic and every day. Already in Cervantes, old models of heroism are giving way to individuated, bourgeois subjectivity. Bakhtin observes that in Cervantes, 'bodies and objects begin to acquire a private, individual nature; they are rendered petty and homely and become immoveable parts of private life, the goal of egotistic lust and possession,' though this is still a process 'only in its initial stage.' Nonetheless, this is a nascent idea of a bourgeois heroism subordinated to capitalist demands. Bakhtin's idea of the carnivalesque body, of bodies that 'could not be considered for themselves [... that] represented a material bodily whole and therefore transgressed the limits of their isolation' and led to a regeneration of the communal life of the community, enjoyed by all, is one model of the heroic body that challenges the model of the heroism of bourgeois individualism. Nonetheless, as the carnivalesque model of the body begins to weaken, in favour of a heroism related to bourgeois individualism and capitalist rationality, simultaneously, poetry gives way to prose. When the narrator says that Spain has no more heroes, he means that the hero of the chivalric romance could no longer exist. See Mikhail Bakhtin, *Rabelais and His World*, trans. Hélène Iswolsky (Bloomington: Indiana University Press, 1984), p. 23.

48 I discuss questions of empire, the East and Orientalism intermittently in these chapters. They are not a primary focus of attention here, but I must note in passing the importance of empire in creating modern nation states where the bourgeoisie are able to thrive. Significant attention has been paid to questions of empire and Orientalism in Pushkin's and Lermontov's work. See Harsha Ram, *The Imperial Sublime: A Russian Poetics of Empire* (Madison: University of Wisconsin Press, 2003); Susan Layton, *Russian Literature and Empire: Conquest of the Caucasus from Pushkin to Tolstoy* (Cambridge: Cambridge University Press, 1994); and Peter Scotto, 'Prisoners of the Caucasus: Ideologies of Imperialism in Lermontov's "Bela,"' *PMLA* 107 (1992), 246–260.

49 Quoted in Mitchell's 'Introduction,' p. xiv.

50 It would be intriguing to know whether Pushkin had enough English to make the pun on Kant and the important Byronic word 'cant.' Sixty years later, Nietzsche makes the pun in *Twilight of the Idols*, IX.I (Friedrich Nietzsche, *Twilight of the Idols, or, How to Philosophize with a Hammer*, trans. Duncan Large (Oxford University Press, 2008), p. 43.

51 The 'Library for Reading' was an extremely popular periodical (it had around 7,000 subscribers in 1837, the same year in which the second edition of *Eugene Onegin* sold 5,000 copies), around whose content a debate about the professionalization of literature, and the idea of literature for commerce, raged. Furthermore, it introduced a generation of Russian readers and writers to the new bourgeois, Western European novels of Balzac, Scott, and Dickens. For a short factual account of 'Library for Reading,' from which I take this information, see William Mills Todd III, 'Dostoevskii as a Professional Writer' in *The Cambridge Companion to Dostoevskii*, ed. W.J. Leatherbarrow (Cambridge: Cambridge University Press, 2002), pp. 66–92 (pp. 68–71). Lermontov himself published *A Hero of Our Time* with Glazunov, a rival to Smirdin, the publisher of 'Library for Reading.' However the novel 'received a warm review from one of Smirdin's periodicals when Glazunov bribed the reviewer.' Lermontov's novel is very definitely in this nascent bourgeois economy of literature in a way that Pushkin's was not. See William Mills Todd III, *Fiction and Society in the Age of Pushkin: Ideology, Institutions, and Narrative* (Cambridge, MA: Harvard University Press, 1986), pp. 93–103, for

another, different, account of the debates around 'Library for Reading' and the commercialisation of Russian literature.

52 Todd, *Fiction and Society in the Age of Pushkin*, p. 144. The equivalent passage from Lermontov appears in Nabokov's translation on p. 34.

53 Karl Marx, 'The Eighteenth Brumaire of Louis Bonaparte,' trans. Ben Fowkes, in *Political Writings*, ed. David Fernbach, 3 vols (Harmondsworth: Penguin/ London: New Left Review, 1973), II, pp. 143–249 (p. 147).

54 Todd, p. 135.

55 Todd, p. 163.

56 Griboedov was a member of the Northern Society of Decembrists. See Ludmilla A. Trigos, *The Decembrist Myth in Russian Culture* (Basingstoke: Palgrave Macmillan, 2009), p. 13.

57 Diakonova and Vatsuro, pp. 335–336.

58 Pushkin's italics. The word is given in English in the Russian text.

59 Ellen Moers, *The Dandy: Brummell to Beerbohm* (London: Secker & Warburg, 1960), p. 18.

60 Moers, p. 26.

61 Moers, p. 43.

62 Fiona MacCarthy, *Byron: Life and Legend* (London: John Murray, 2002), pp. 305–306. Byron also compared Beau Brummell in exile to Napoleon. MacCarthy quotes a letter in which he writes, 'Brummell at *Calais* [...] Buonaparte at St Helena' (p. 378). Finally, MacCarthy notes that Brummell himself compared Byron to Napoleon. During his exile, Brummell 'work[ed] on a decorative screen [...]. The sixth and final fold of the screen represents Napoleon and Byron' (p. x).

63 The ellipsis represents the material missing from the existing texts of this part of the novel.

64 Todd, p. 37.

65 Todd, pp. 40–41.

66 Todd, p. 42.

67 Todd, p. 44.

68 For a discussion of these images, and a further discussion of political violence in Pushkin's work more generally, see Alexander Groce, 'Aleksandr Pushkin's *The Captain's Daughter*: A Poetics of Violence,' *Ulbandus Review* 13 (2010), 64–78.

69 Edvard Radzinsky, *Alexander II: The Last Great Tsar*, trans. Antonia W. Bouis (New York: Free Press, 2005), p. 37.

70 Irina Reyfman, *Ritualized Violence Russian Style: The Duel in Russian Culture and Literature* (Stanford, CA: Stanford University Press, 1999), p. 78.

71 Reyfman, p. 76.

72 Reyfman, pp. 83–84.

73 Incidentally, Ekaterinograd was a very unsuccessful colonial outpost. See, Thomas M. Barrett, 'Lines of Uncertainty: The Frontiers of the North Caucasus,' in *Imperial Russia: New Histories for the Empire*, ed. Jane Burbank and David L. Ransel (Bloomington: Indiana University Press, 1998), pp. 148–173 (pp. 158–159).

74 See Laurence Kelly, *Diplomacy and Murder in Tehran: Alexander Griboyedov and Imperial Russia's Mission to the Shah of Persia* (London: I.B. Tauris, 2006).

75 Alexander Pushkin, *A Journey to Arzrum*, in Mikhail Lermontov, *A Hero of Our Time*, trans. Boris Pasternak Slater (Oxford University Press, 2013), pp. 141–184 (p. 162).

76 On 'free time' mirroring work time, see Theodor W. Adorno, 'Free Time,' in *The Culture Industry: Selected Essays on Mass Culture*, ed. J.M. Bernstein (London: Routledge, 1991), pp. 162–170.

77 Benjamin, pp. 78–79. Similarly to the argument presented in this book, that the oppositional Byronic becomes partially subsumed in the bourgeois that it paves the way for, Benjamin sees the disruptive elements of his modern heroism ultimately entering into league with the bourgeois. For Benjamin, heroism always ultimately fails.

78 Jerome McGann, 'Byron and the Anonymous Lyric,' in *Byron and Romanticism*, ed. James Soderholm (Cambridge: Cambridge University Press, 2002), pp. 93–112 (p. 94). This essay traces in some detail similarities between Byron and Baudelaire.

79 Benjamin, p. 70.

80 Charles Baudelaire, *Les Fleurs du Mal*, trans. Richard Howard (London: Picador, 1987), p. 5.

81 Benjamin, pp. 70–71.

82 There is an extensive study of the influence of the French novel on Lermontov in Priscilla Meyer, *How the Russians Read the French: Lermontov, Dostoevsky, Tolstoy* (Madison: University of Wisconsin Press, 2008), pp. 34–88.

2 *David Copperfield*
Byronic Heroism and Bourgeois Privacy

In the last chapter, I showed bourgeois heroism's nascent form emerging from Byronic heroism in early nineteenth-century Russia. In this chapter, I show the relationship between these two forms of heroism at the centre of global industrial capitalism. The question of heroism is one that orientates Charles Dickens's *David Copperfield* (1849–1850). The novel opens with its titular character wondering, '[w]hether I shall turn out to be the hero of my own life, or whether that station will be held by anybody else, these pages must show.'[1] Thus there is a question about who the hero of the novel might be from the outset. Two key candidates for this are David and Steerforth, who offer two different models of heroism. Steerforth offers a form of Byronic heroism, and David offers a form of bourgeois heroism.

This chapter sets up an opposition between Byronic heroism, as represented by Steerforth, and a new form of bourgeois heroism that is represented by David Copperfield, with bourgeois heroism eventually emerging as the dominant ideological position of the novel. It will, however, also suggest the limitations of this opposition, both in the inability of the novel to leave behind Steerforth's Byronic heroism and in the ways in which the Byronic lays the ground for, but also continues to inform, David's bourgeois heroism. I discuss the general influence of Byron on Dickens before turning to the importance of Byronic self-narration for bourgeois self-narration. Bourgeois self-narration ultimately rejects Byronic heroism, which, thus becomes obsolete and is rejected by the bourgeois novel. Finally, I discuss how Byronic heroism continues to haunt bourgeois heroism with the spectre of revolution.

I

There have been two comprehensive articles on the influence of Byron on Dickens, William R. Harvey's 'Charles Dickens and the Byronic Hero' and Vincent Newey's 'Rival Cultures: Charles Dickens and the Byronic Legacy.'[2] These can be supplemented by Juliet John's chapter

DOI: 10.4324/9781003160168-3

on Byronic characters in her *Dickens's Villains: Melodrama, Character, Popular Culture*; however, this is significantly less attentive to the specificity of Byron's texts. [3]

Harvey traces a series of Byronic characters through Dickens's later fiction: Steerforth in *David Copperfield*, James Harthouse in *Hard Times*, Blandois in *Little Dorrit*, Sydney Carton in *A Tale of Two Cities*, and Eugene Wrayburn in *Our Mutual Friend*, a schema which John broadly reproduces. Newey reflects this whilst also noting more general resonances of *Childe Harold's Pilgrimage* in *David Copperfield* and *Don Juan* in Dickens's later satire, particularly in *Bleak House* and *Our Mutual Friend*. Newey notes that both Harvey and John see Dickens's writing as oppositional to Byron since Dickens's Byronic characters

> represent the kind of 'Romantic individualism', involuted, role-playing, self-destructive, antisocial, careless of the external world [...], that Dickens 'despised', and over against which, either through critique or programmes of redemption, or both, he sets 'models of moral improvement [... and] communality.'
>
> (p. 85)

Instead, Newey argues for a more complex view of Dickens's 'engagement with Byronic romanticism, which, though he must forfeit it in favour of an ethos of solid social virtues, held for him a deep fascination' (p. 85). In this chapter, I will go further by suggesting, firstly, that in Dickens, Byronic heroism paves the way for bourgeois heroism, and, secondly, that even when bourgeois heroism seems to have killed off Byronic heroism and become a hegemonic ideology in *David Copperfield*, the Byronic still disrupts the stability of bourgeois heroism. Particularly in the case of *David Copperfield*, Newey argues that Steerforth is marked as a Byronic Hero by his 'sub-aristocratic hauteur,' a sense of ennui and an attitude towards life in general and women in particular which can be characterised as 'the idea of life as a game [...] the extreme form of playing for thrills' (p. 87). In contrast to this, David installs the 'Victorian domestic ideology, the bourgeois valorization of the family,' and the novel represents a more general shift as 'command of the social hierarchy is transferred from the upper to the middle class' (pp. 89–90). However, Newey is also aware that 'there is always more to David's view of Steerforth, and to Steerforth's status in the novel, than condemnation and deficit' (p. 87). Critically, he enacts this recognition in an intriguing way, through an appeal to the links between aristocracy and the 'Classical body' – that is, the smooth, perfect, united body of Classical and renaissance sculpture, which Mikhail Bakhtin links to aristocratic dominant culture. Newey thus forges a link between the admiration of the Apollo Belvedere in Canto IV of *Childe Harold's Pilgrimage* and David's admiration of Steerforth's body on the beach after the storm in which the latter dies. Thus, Steerforth, the Byronic and the aristocratic retain 'a fallen, though still appealing, hegemony' (pp. 88–89).

Newey's reading is useful for recognising the ways in which Byron is incorporated into rather than rejected by bourgeois ideology. His deployment of Bakhtin draws together the ideological orientation of *Childe Harold* and *David Copperfield*. By registering aristocratic and bourgeois ideologies, Newey is clearly political in his understanding, though I think by focussing largely on the interpersonal relationship of Steerforth and David as characters, on a sort of general attitude to life and on the seduction of Little Em'ly in particular, he sometimes underplays the specifically political aspects of Byronic heroism. Newey portrays Steerforth's Byronism as socially disruptive but not politically revolutionary. Later in this chapter, I argue that Steerforth, as a Byronic Hero, is presented as an explicitly revolutionary figure. Steerforth becomes an intriguingly contradictory character, an aristocratic revolutionary, whose revolutionary act erases him from history in favour of the bourgeois order of things. In this chapter, I connect Steerforth both with the French Revolution of 1830 and the English Revolution of the seventeenth century. Intriguingly, Newey's image of a fallen idol links with that of a headless statue, or even a headless body, an image which recurs again and again in *David Copperfield*. It points to a certain limitation in Newey's Bakhtinian reading: that the Classical body itself, once it falls, necessarily becomes carnivalised since it no longer represents the intact body of the sovereign or aristocrat. Byron himself, in fact, as a fallen figure, represents a disruption to the order that Newey suggests he maintains. This is further emphasised by a complication to Newey's argument that he himself acknowledges. Byronism a transmitter of the aristocratic ideology that is represented in the Classical body, but the 'persona of Lord Byron himself,' complicates the aristocratic and Classical with 'the legendary defects, the club foot, obesity and sexual promiscuity' (Newey, p. 88).

These readings of Byron suggest that Dickens's understanding of Byron conflates aspects of both Byron's writing and his public image into a generalised image of the Byronic, which is often vague and caricatured. In some ways, this explains why Juliet John spends so little time discussing Byron's texts directly in her essay on Byronic villains in Dickens. To some extent, the Byronic has become a set of quite vague signifiers intended to evoke a certain mood and set of expectations, rather than being closely related to Byron's texts, though they are obviously derived from them. On the other hand, in *David Copperfield*, Byron's influence on Dickens is based on an attentive engagement with Byron's writing. *Childe Harold's Pilgrimage* has a privileged status in relation to *David Copperfield*, which it frequently alludes to. It is also the basis on which Dickens develops Steerforth as a paradigmatic Byronic Hero.

II

At the time of the composition of *David Copperfield*, Dickens owned two copies of Byron's *Works*, and at some point, he acquired a separate edition of *Childe Harold's Pilgrimage* (Newey, p. 87).[4] And at a number of key points in the text, *David Copperfield* directly alludes to and engages with Byron. A good place to start, where this engagement directly impinges on my argument, is in an analysis of David's attitude towards self-narration on his journey to the Alps.

As Newey observes, 'David talks of his "pilgrimage" and like Harold repeats the gentleman's Grand Tour among "the abiding places of History and Fancy" as an introspective journey' (p. 89). Certainly, David sees the Alps in a Romantic mode which is also evident in Byron:

> [H]igh above this gentler vegetation, grew forests of dark fir, cleaving the wintry snow-drift, wedge-like, and stemming the avalanche. Above these, were range upon range of craggy steeps, grey rock, bright ice, and smooth verdure specks of pasture, all gradually blending with the crowning snow.
>
> (p. 821)

This is directly comparable to Byron:

> Above me are the Alps,
> The palaces of Nature, whose vast walls
> Have pinnacle in clouds their snowy scalps,
> And throned Eternity in icy halls
> Of cold sublimity, where forms and falls
> The avalanche – the thunderbolt of snow!
> (III.62)

David's language is also similar to Byron's 'Alpine Journal' (1816, and as such contemporaneous with Canto III of *Childe Harold*), where Byron describes the Hockthorn as 'very lofty & craggy – patched with snow only – no Glaciers on it – but some good epaulettes of clouds.'[5] Newey is right, however, to observe the differences here too:

> For David [...] the sublime is something to be left behind *en route* to the beautiful and the humane. 'I had found sublimity and wonder in the dread heights and precipices [...] but as yet, they had taught me nothing else', he records.
>
> (p. 89)

This loosely implies the shift from Byronic to bourgeois values which I argue for in this chapter.

However, Byron's influence might still be felt in David's sense of being 'taught [...] nothing' by the Alps: the very notion of Switzerland being didactic is, for Byron, anathema.[6] In the astonishing closing passage of the 'Alpine Journal,' Byron writes,

> I am a lover of Nature – and an Admirer of Beauty – I can bear fatigue – & welcome privation – and have seen some of the noblest views in the world. – But in all this – the recollections of bitterness – & more especially of recent & more home desolation – which must accompany me through life – have preyed upon me here – and neither the music of the Shepherd – the crashing of the Avalanche – nor the torrent – the mountain – the Glacier – the Forest – nor the Cloud – have for one moment – lightened the weight upon my heart – nor enabled me to lose my own wretched identity in the majesty & the power and the Glory – around – above – & beneath me. – I am past reproaches – and this is a time for all things – I am past the wish of vengeance – and I know of none like for what I have suffered – but the hour will come – when what I feel must be felt – & the – – but enough.[7]

Despite Byron's claim in this passage that he has not been able to lose himself in what he has seen, the passage points to a breakdown in language and subjectivity through its diffuseness, intensity, and, ultimately, the failure of language itself. Thus, rather than the sublime landscapes of the Alps being didactic or healing in any way, rather they represent, in this passage, self-narration itself partaking of that part of the sublime that breaks down subjectivity, with little sense of the subsequent reconstruction of subjectivity that Kant associates with the sublime.[8] Byronic self-narration here results in the breakdown of subjectivity which cannot be contained by the self. Yet this kind of epic, militant, Byronic self-narration paves the way for the self-contained, individualised self-narration that is exemplified by David Copperfield's autobiographical discourse. In contrast to Byron's, David's act of self-narration draws to him bourgeois values: family life and economic success in bourgeois professions. Self-narration here is itself a bourgeois value since it establishes the bourgeois individual as self-sufficient, self-contained, and private.

However, that this kind of self-narration initially shows itself as Byronic discourse, before mutating into David's bourgeois discourse, attests to the fact that Byronism can never be fully erased in *David Copperfield*. Elsewhere, too, Byronic self-narration lays the ground for, and then haunts, the kind of bourgeois subjectivity we see in David's self-narration. Byronic self-narration, as I suggest in the introduction to this book, is epic and involved in the world, whereas bourgeois self-narration is private and inward-looking. Yet Byron can also be retrospectively appropriated for this bourgeois inwardness: Steerforth, the novel's Byronic Hero, is not immune from the type of proto-psychoanalytic experience of subjectivity, memory, and self-narration represented by David. In one very curious passage, he states, 'I have been a nightmare to myself, just now – must have had one, I think. At odd dull times, nursery tales come up into the memory, unrecognised for what they are' (p. 330). In this passage, Steerforth shifts from being a nightmare to himself, which could well characterise the Byronic Hero, plagued by self-remorse and the weight of his own subjectivity, to somebody who has had a nightmare. The person who has had a dream is the analysand in psychoanalysis, that privileged apparatus for producing the bourgeois subject as disciplined, private, secret, and individualised. Furthermore, the contents of this nightmare are childhood memories that have returned to the consciousness in a mutated form. This is the very basis of psychoanalysis. In the dash that separates Steerforth being a nightmare to himself and having had a nightmare the passage from the Byronic Hero to the bourgeois subject of psychoanalysis is enacted, though, curiously, this is dramatised in the Byronic character who must ultimately be erased from the novel in order that its ideology establish itself. If the Byronic is a prefiguring of the bourgeois subject in the novel, it must erase itself (like the dash, which stands for the mutation which is not visible), yet also continues beyond that erasure.

I have suggested that Byronic heroism is defined by a 'militant interiority' where subjectivity imposes itself on the world within which it narrates itself but which nonetheless constructs for itself a sense of interiority. According to Georg Lukács's theorisation of the epic and the novel, militant interiority in Byron stands midway between the epic and the novel. In Byron's experience of the Alps in his 'Alpine Journal,' subjectivity breaks down in relation to the sublimity of the landscape, whereas David Copperfield's experience of the Alps helps him reconstruct an interiorised subjectivity independent of the landscape around him. To take another example and to reiterate my reading of Lukács in more detail, Byron's *Childe Harold* not only paves the way for novelistic, bourgeois self-narration but also retains some features of the epic. Lukács sets out the process by which the epic transitions to the novel. He writes that in the epic, 'subjectivity gave rise to the heroism of militant interiority.' On the other hand, in the transition from the epic to the novel, '[t]he precondition and the price of [the] immoderate [novelistic] elevation of the subject is, however, the abandonment of any claim to participation in the shaping of the outside world.' In the novel, 'a man can become the hero, the central figure of a literary work, because he has the inner possibility of experiencing life as a literary creator.' The Byronic Hero, as I have shown, has a subjectivity which still mingles with the world in which it is set, though it is precisely through becoming the composite writer-hero of literary works that Byron becomes famous. Indeed, Lukács locates the transition from this to novelistic self-narration in Romanticism. He writes, 'In Romanticism, the literary nature of the *a priori* status of the soul vis-à-vis reality, recognises itself as the source of the ideal reality, and, as a necessary consequence, as the only material worthy of self-realisation.'[9] There is the epic form of subjectivity which is in direct contact with the world around it. As the novel develops, this subjectivity, when it narrates itself, develops a militant interiority which asserts itself in the world that lies outside the individual subject. Finally, this militant interiority eventually turns back on itself in bourgeois subjectivity, which celebrates the self-contained and private individual whose consciousness is turned inwards, and which narrates itself in the creation of the individuated subject whose separateness from others and the rest of the world is stressed. Romanticism is, for Lukács, the period in which the first kind of subjectivity turns into the second. Byron is a key figure in this transition.

Byron exists between the bourgeois conception of subjectivity and self-narration, which is evident in the discourse of *David Copperfield* and the epic one. There are moments in Byron where his subjectivity is militantly asserted on the world and fills it. However, there are other moments where the privacy and difficulty in narrating the self characteristic of the bourgeois are stressed, such as that passage I discussed in the previous chapter in *Childe Harold's Pilgrimage*: 'Could I embody and unbosom now I That which is most within me […]. But as it is, I live and die unheard' (III.97). This suggests Byron as a marked case of the transition between the epic and novel.

What, then, are the differences between this transitional Byronic self-narration and bourgeois self-narration proper? Whereas in Byronic self-narration the epic traces of militant interiority mean that the subject opens out onto the world, in bourgeois self-narration, the individual becomes strongly self-contained, discrete, individualised, and interiorised. This conception of subjectivity is given its fullest description, in relation to *David Copperfield*, in D. A. Miller's Foucauldian reading of the novel. Miller argues that David Copperfield 'regularly and almost ritually "secretes" his subjectivity at precisely what would appear its determining moment.'[10] Through a process of self-narration, David creates the notion of his subjectivity as private, individualised, and interiorised, argues Miller, quoting amongst many other examples: 'That I suffered in secret, no one ever knew' (p. 172; Miller truncates the quotation).[11] Where Byron's self-silencings suggest the tortured subjectivity of a man alienated from society, however, David's suggest the creation of a private subjectivity that establishes him as a functioning part of bourgeois society. As Miller points out, this process is part of the establishment of what Foucault calls 'disciplinary society,' which Foucault explicitly formulates in relationship to the same literary history of forms that Lukács describes: '[T]he passage from the epic to the novel, from the noble deed to the secret singularity, from long exiles to the internal search for childhood, from combats to phantasies, is also inscribed in the formation of a disciplinary society.'[12] Just as importantly, though, the early Lukács's

Hegelian and not-yet-materialist theories actually come very close to the materialist arguments of Mary Poovey and D. A. Miller: 'Life becomes a work of literature; but, as a result, man becomes the author of his own life and at the same time the observer of that life as a created work of art.'[13] Thus David Copperfield becomes a novelist who narrates his own life, whereas Byron lyricises his subjectivity.

Whilst the novel explicitly shies away from describing David's own novels, they are one of its secrets, there is a distinct impression that the novel *David Copperfield* is one of David the character's novels within the fiction as well as one of Dickens's. The title page makes clear that this is David's novel. The qualification that his 'personal history,' was 'never meant to [be] published on any account,' stresses the fact that it has been published, that it has entered into David's body of work as a novelist, though simultaneously differentiates it since it is an autobiography, written in the first person. This tension between novel and autobiography is resolved by the relationship between David the novelist and Dickens the novelist. David also famously mirrors Dickens so that Dickens's novels and David's novels become the same thing. Miller points out both the well-known fact that Dickens 'abandoned what remained an autobiographical fragment to write *David Copperfield*,' and that Dickens

> points to the story of the other, in which C. D., authorial signature, will be inverted – or rather, extroverted – into D. C., sign of a character who is also, as though to indicate his purely verbal existence, sign of a book,

and, I might add, in this respect, David Copperfield becomes the sign of an author, any non-specific author, the narrator of one's own subjectivity.[14] Self-narration and the novel become inseparable as the novel stresses David Copperfield not just as the subject of the novel but as the author of it and the self it narrates.

As a self-authoring novelist under capitalism, David also transmits the spirit of capitalism, as Boltanski and Chiapello describe it, and as I have set out in the introduction, in terms of the 'traditional domestic predispositions' of family life and the value of hard work and economic parsimony (David is contrasted with Micawber).[15] This novel also particularly transmits the ideology of the universalised, individuated, private, subject. As Mary Poovey points out, the novel 'constructs the reader as a particular type of subject [...] classed [...] individualized, psychologized, and ahistorical.'[16] This is in contrast to Byronic Hero as a self-conscious representative of aristocratic values and militant subjectivity. It might be added, to stress this, that Byronic Heroes do not work for a living. As Jerome Christensen puts it, key to Byron's upheaval of values is his strength, his refusal to submit to the imperatives of the market: 'Strength does not await the conferral of credit; it commands it.'[17]

David's writing practice is an autobiographical consolidation of memory specifically employed in order to create an interiorised individuated subject. This is clear in the very form of the novel, which presents itself as an autobiography which is engaged in the construction of a sense of identity. The novel specifically places this creation of self in terms of heroics – David's process of self-narration is to discover whether he is the hero of his own life. The novel is an experiment in (self-)narrating bourgeois heroism in contrast to self-asserting Byronic heroism.

Furthermore, as Mary Poovey observes, 'the conditions by which novels were serialized made absolutely clear the extent to which "literature" was part of the market economy and literary work was alienated labor,' and this was the case even with works that were not serially published since they still went out with the expectation of accumulating capital.[18] David's own comments on his writing confirm this. He 'labored hard' at his book, and this is described in a proleptic echo of Weber 'a vocation' (p. 696).[19] He does this against the backdrop of Carlyle's *On Heroes, Hero-Worship and the Heroic in History*, which describes the professional writer, the 'Man of Letters,' as a heroic figure precisely because the writer produces social norms:

> Do not Books still accomplish miracles, as Runes were fabled to do? They persuade men. Not the wretchedest circulating-library novel, which foolish girls thumb and con in remote villages, but will help to regulate the actual practical weddings and households of those foolish girls.[20]

The novelist – David – is an example of the heroic worker under capitalism. This is a long way from Byron's aristocratic disdain for the whole 'business' of writing, for example when he writes,

> [Walter Scott] & Gifford & Moore are the only *regulars* I ever knew who had nothing of the *Garrison* about their manner – no nonsense – no affectations look you! – as for the rest who I have known – there was always more or less of the author about them – the pen peeping from behind the ear – & the thumb a little inky or so.[21]

In David's case, and this may be one of the reasons why the novelist is an exemplary participant as a wage-labourer in the capitalist system, the dissemination of bourgeois values and the creation of an individuated, interiorised bourgeois subjectivity are absolutely interlinked. As I have shown, David's own life-writing is both autobiography and novel and so disseminates the bourgeois values of individualisation which it depicts, and, furthermore, the very process of writing reflexively creates bourgeois individualism. This work of dissemination requires a very bourgeois self-discipline. D. A. Miller observes of the disciplinary nature of writing itself,

> The discipline from which [David] has escaped to become the 'subject of the Novel' reappears as his own self-discipline. 'What I had to do,' he says of the time he labored to win Dora, 'was to turn the painful discipline of my early years to account, by going to work with a steady and resolute heart' [...]. But what seems to ensure this self-discipline most of all is writing itself. 'I could never have done what I have done, without the habits of punctuality, order, and diligence, without the determination to concentrate myself on one object at a time, no matter how quickly its successor should come upon its heels, which I then formed.' Though David is not recalling here his service at Murdstone and Grinby's, but rather his apprenticeship in shorthand, he might well be: minus the value judgments, the habits required are the same.[22]

To make the implicit references to Foucault, which Miller assumes a knowledge of on the part of his reader, absolutely clear here, panopticism, beginning with the prison, puts prisoners in 'so many small theatres, in which each actor is alone, perfectly individualised and constantly visible.'[23] But for Foucault this prison arrangement becomes a generalised mode of life, where this individualised subject 'becomes the principle of his own subjection,' and so can be used as a generalised mode for propagating the dominant order.[24] Lest this seem to mostly refer to disciplining those who work in factories and others who are excluded from the bourgeois order, Miller's account of David's self-discipline stresses the way in which this panoptical mode of power also creates the very values that Boltanski and Chiapello set out as being the comforting props of capitalism for the middle-class wage-labourer: David's skills of self-discipline are 'immediately raised to high moral values – and these values [...] are the very ones that help the characters to box themselves in.'[25]

Psychoanalysis is a key discourse in creating this individualised, private subject. It is a form of a confession that, according to Foucault, is part of the constitution of the individuated subject: '[T]he confession is a ritual of discourse in which the speaking subject is also the subject of the statement,' which 'produces intrinsic modifications in the person who articulates it.'[26] Furthermore, it appropriately situates the individual within the family unit, that privileged social form of bourgeois ideology. Psychoanalysis is also, according to Foucault, one of the main literary ways in which the formation of subjectivity from childhood is articulated:

> The adventure of our childhood no longer finds expression in 'le bon petit Henri', but in the misfortunes of 'little Hans'. The *Romance of*

the Rose is written today by Mary Barnes; in the place of Lancelot, we have Judge Schreber.[27]

In short, the transition from the epic to the novel is a transition into psychoanalysis. *David Copperfield* in particular has a privileged position in Freud's thinking. Steven Marcus points out that Freud may have given his famous patient the pseudonym Dora in reference to the character in *David Copperfield* and adds,

> Freud's favourite novel by Dickens was *David Copperfield*. Like David Freud was born with or in a caul [...] on at least one occasion Freud described his father as a Micawber-like figure. The first book he sent as a gift to Martha Bernays [who became his wife] shortly after they met was a copy of *David Copperfield* [...] one could go on indefinitely with such analogies.[28]

This similarity between David Copperfield and Freud goes as far as scenes in Freud's case studies echoing scenes in Dickens's novel. In his explanatory notes to David Copperfield, Jeremy Tambling suggests that the atmosphere of the scene where David is beaten by Mr Murdstone, his stepfather, is similar to Freud's study of the 'Rat Man,' who is beaten by his father (p. 946). I wish to take this further and suggest there are structural analogies that can further illuminate David as a bourgeois hero.

In this scene, David is beaten by Murdstone for being unable to learn the lessons that Murdstone sets him, and, after the first blow of the cane falls, he bites all the way through Murdstone's hand as he holds him still. These lessons seem not so much about learning, but rather instilling the law of the father:

> They were presided over nominally by my mother, but really by Mr Murdstone and his sister, who were always present, and found them a favourable occasion for giving my mother lessons in that miscalled firmness, which was the bane of both our lives.
>
> (p. 63)

Freud's 'Rat Man' study provides a useful way to think about how David's practices of self-narration create the self through the consolidation of memory and how the subject is integrated into the family. Psychoanalysis provides a theoretical framework through which to analyse bourgeois self-narration. Freud's analysis of the 'Rat Man' in particular helps us to recognise the heroic components of this self-narration. In a footnote in *Notes Upon A Case of Obsessional Neurosis* (1909), to give the 'Rat Man' study its official title, Freud argues that people's 'childhood memories' are only consolidated at a later period, usually at the age of puberty; and that this involves a complicated process of remodelling, analogous in every way to the process by which a nation constructs legends about its early history,

and that

> a deeper interpretation of the patient's dreams in relation to this episode revealed the clearest traces of the presence in his mind of an imaginative production of a positively epic character. In this his sexual desires for his mother and sister and his sister's premature death were linked up with the young hero's chastisement at his father's hand.[29]

Note particularly Freud's characterisation of this process as having an 'epic' character and the protagonist of the process as a 'hero.' For Freud then, autobiographical thought establishes bourgeois integration as heroic. There may have been a transition from the epic to the novel, but in order for bourgeois values to have traction, in order to make them heroic, in order to shore up participation in the bourgeois order, the rhetoric of the epic is still employed. Thus, at a further remove from Byronic self-narration's transitional status between the epic and the bourgeois, bourgeois self-narration recalls the epic but with no actual epic content at all, just a standard family romance.

To appreciate the relationship between bourgeois self-narration and epic rhetoric and establish how a specifically bourgeois form of heroism is established through self-narration, it is worth reiterating that the mechanism by which David consolidates his own is tied up with the dissemination and consolidation of bourgeois values. The idea that *David Copperfield* is about the creation of subjectivity through the consolidation of memory is now a common one. An early influential account is offered by J. Hillis Miller who argues that the novel is the 'recollecting from the point of view of a later time the slow formation of an identity through many experiences and sufferings. As David says: "this narrative is my written memory."'[30]

Freud's argument about the consolidation of memory shares similarities with the process through which David writes his own life, and this is part of the process of him being established as an individuated and private bourgeois subject through writing. Furthermore, sometimes David consolidates his memory in legal terminology, as though he is appealing to the discourse of the state, and which recalls the disciplinary nature of the creation of bourgeois subjectivity. For example, David states, 'If the room to which my bed was removed, were a sentient thing that could give evidence, I might appeal to it at this day [...] to bear witness for me what a heavy heart I carried to it' (p. 55). Here, subjectivity, which is created in line with the ideology of the bourgeois order, is not defined wholly for itself, but rather as subject to the legal instruments of the state. By speaking as though he is giving evidence, David is behaving as though he is directly addressing what Louis Althusser calls the 'ideological state apparatuses' that demand that the subject accounts for himself and so police the subject by making him create himself in their terms.[31] Thus, as David's consolidation of memory dialogically takes part in the discourse of the legal process, his creation of himself as a bourgeois subject takes place under the jurisdiction of the state (as well as the family and the precepts of work) – in sharp contrast to a Byronic subjectivity which is partially constituted in the rejection of power in favour of a militant interiority that asserts its own power on the world around it.

Another key example of David's bourgeois consolidation of his memories in the novel is in Chapter LV, 'Tempest,' which begins,

> I now approach an event in my life, so indelible, so awful, so bound by an infinite variety of ties to all that has preceded it, in these pages, that, from the beginning of my narrative, I have seen it growing larger and larger [...] and throwing its fore-cast shadow even on the incidents of my childish days.

> (p. 790)

Here, too, the 'epic' character of the consolidation of memory that Freud describes, and which establishes the heroism of bourgeois self-narration, becomes visible. In the process of writing autobiography, a consolidation of memory, earlier events with no causal connection come to take on a significance which is both dream-like and epic in its atmosphere of portentousness, of fateful inevitability. However, this is not the epic totality that Lukács describes in contrast to the novel, where 'everything is already homogeneous before it has been contained in forms' and where, 'in the hero who, creating himself, finds himself, pure essence awakens to life, mere life sinks into not-being.'[32] That is to say that for Lukács epic totality occurs where the world is fully integrated and consolidated outside and inside the subject so that the two are not easily distinguishable. Rather, another meaning of epic is in play here, where everything that surrounds the subject contributes to the work of creating that subject as individuated and ultimately negates the world in favour of that subject. Private life, bourgeois life, has become the 'epic' subject of the novel under the bourgeoisie. In what is now commonplace, Hegel observes that the novel is the 'modern bourgeois epic,' precisely because the retrospective act of narrating memory, the bourgeois narration of self which is also the labour of the writer, makes heterogeneous elements cohere in novel form as props for bourgeois subjectivity.[33] Thus, what has been depicted in *David Copperfield* is a series of events which are discrete and serial in their presentation but which are also retrospectively presented as being part of a narrative, the subject David Copperfield, so that they could not exist independently of each other. As Lukács puts it, in the novel, 'reality disintegrates into a series of mutually absolutely heterogeneous fragments which have no independent valency of existence even in isolation.'[34] However, the bourgeois consolidation of memory attempts to make them homogeneous in relation to the individuated subject. This is the 'epic' work of the bourgeois subject.

Writing of this 'event,' David says that 'for years after it occurred, I dreamed of it often' (p. 790), but he may as well say that he dreamt of it for years before it occurred: in Chapter III, he relates that, on his first visit to Yarmouth, 'as slumber gradually stole upon me, I heard the wind howling out at sea and coming across the flat so fiercely, that I had a lazy apprehension of a great deep rising in the night' (p. 46). There is a trace of the old idea of the epic in the fatefulness of this huge event inevitably coming about, as though David's perception and the world in which he lives are inseparable, in the fact that the dramatic central scene near the end of the novel is already presaged in its early stages. However, this portentous scene, as though in parody of the epic, shows David as anything but an epic hero, as he does nothing but stand helpless on the shore as the heroic Steerforth and Ham are out in the sea. Thus, it becomes a personal, traumatic event whose significance is constructed by a consolidation of memory rather than by a porous border between the subject and the world which he inhabits.

If individuation is the defining aspect of bourgeois novelistic heroism, then a Freudian reading can offer more insights into its composition. Following Freud's lead in examining how the consolidation of memory produces bourgeois heroism, we can see in the incident of the beating and biting a particularly strong example of the creation of David Copperfield's individuated subjectivity, as this ultimately connects with the 'Tempest' chapter. The language of the tempest is already faintly traceable in Chapter IV, which features the beating and biting. When David fails at the lessons which lead to his punishment, he takes 'a last drowning look' at the books (p. 64). How David envisages his own heroism in relationship to this climactic incident, which is the keystone of the consolidation of his memories, also comes to the fore in this chapter. David imagines himself as 'Captain Somebody, of the Royal British Navy [...] the Captain was a Captain and a hero' (p. 67). Here, though, heroism is simultaneously established in David and displaced since the heroic figure is replaced by a blank. The hero is both David and somebody else (or nobody) since he does not name himself Captain David Copperfield but Captain Somebody. This is a foreshadowing of David's lack of heroism in the tempest where he can only watch helplessly as the ship goes down and sees Steerforth at sea at his most heroic. In this respect, David imagines his heroism, like Steerforth's, expressed at sea, though whilst at this moment, as shall be seen, Steerforth is a towering, revolutionary

Byronic figure, David's heroism is expressed in terms of patriotic duty. Steerforth stands against the state whilst David stands for it and before it. The anxieties about David's attempt at heroism are stressed by the depiction of him as a subject split between his heroic fantasy and his everyday life: 'The Captain never lost dignity, from having his ears boxed with the Latin Grammar. I did' (p. 67). Yet by the mutual interlacing of the hero and of the abused schoolboy, a certain parody of heroism comes about, the hero is brought to the level of the schoolboy, whilst the schoolboy as hero remains a fantasy. As such, heroism is integrated into the disciplinary order. Even the sufferings that David undergoes are part of the constitution as a bourgeois subject. As Miller puts it, David's 'liberation' into bourgeois subjectivity – a happy, stable family life and a profession as a writer – 'runs parallel to the story of his submission: the chastening of what, with an ambiguous wistfulness, he calls an "undisciplined heart."'[35] Heroism is thus simultaneously a valorisation of bourgeois values and born of suffering; to that extent, it is akin to Byronic heroism, except that, here, suffering is an unRomantic effect of discipline.

Psychoanalytic consolidation of memory, then, runs alongside the Foucauldian discipline which establishes the bourgeois hero; indeed, it is an operative part of it. *David Copperfield* recalls the production of subjectivity, theorised by Foucault, in the family setting, the very setting that psychoanalysis wishes to normalise; it will be remembered that the Rat Man's consolidation of memory is specifically linked by Freud to chastisement for his sexual desires for his mother. Similarly, David has his sexual desires for his mother transferred to Little Em'ly under Murdstone's supervision. This is part of the work of making him a good bourgeois subject, redirecting his desires to an appropriate object. In *David Copperfield*, the stepfather, Mr Murdstone, comes to interpose between David and his sexual attachment to his mother. 'I could not look at her, I could not look at him, I knew quite well that he was looking at us both,' he relates at one point (p. 54). At another, 'he seemed very fond of my mother – I am afraid I liked him none the better for that' (p. 58). In this episode, Murdstone finds David's mother Clara and Pegotty comforting David because he has fled from him after he interposed between David and his mother. It is here that David's desire for his mother is displaced onto Little Em'ly:

> I was crying all the time, but, except that I was conscious of being cold and dejected, I am sure I never thought why I cried. At last, in my desolation I began to consider that I was dreadfully in love with Little Em'ly, and had been torn away from her.
>
> (p. 55)

It is only as a later rationalisation, a consolidation of memory, of a feeling of loss that David attaches himself to a new object of desire, and the previous object of his desire must be his mother. When Murdstone finds Clara comforting David, he tells her that she needs to exercise 'firmness' with David and that 'we shall soon improve our youthful humours' (p. 56–57). Leaving the subject of this 'our' indeterminate, unclear whether it applies to both David or his mother, Murdstone suggests that both David and Clara were involved mutually in a kind of infantile sexuality before Mr Murdstone interposed. The words are addressed to 'Clara, my dear,' though David takes them as referring to himself: 'I might have been improved for my whole life' (p. 57). The implication is that both of them are being 'controul[ed]' (p. 54) by Murdstone. By coming to attach himself to an acceptable object choice, discipline 'liberates' David into a bourgeois subjectivity that is heroised by the novel, comprising of habits of work and a normalised bourgeois family, whilst, simultaneously, his great suffering under discipline is valourised as the heroic means to attain bourgeois identity.

III

Byronic self-narration paves the way for but is ultimately displaced by bourgeois self-narration. As a consequence, bourgeois heroism kills off the Byronic. I do this in two ways, first by demonstrating how the representation of the Byronic in Victorian culture more generally, and Dickens's oeuvre more specifically, begins to parody the figure of the Byronic Hero, and secondly by showing how Steerforth, whilst portrayed more seriously by Dickens, is killed off to make way for the bourgeois hero.

The Byronic exercised an important influence on Victorian bourgeois literature. Thorslev observes that key features of the Byronic Hero

> reappear in England, as the dominant traits of heroes in Arnold's *Empedocles*, in much of Tennyson's work (see *The Ancient Sage*, or passages of *In Memoriam*), especially clearly in Clough's *Dipsychus*, and even in Pater's *Marius*.[36]

Similarly, Richard Lansdowne has shown how *Don Juan* had a huge influence on nineteenth-century literature, particularly as a 'transmitter and transformer of eighteenth-century fictional technique.'[37]

Byron's influence on Victorian culture, then, was pervasive. As Andrew Elfenbein observes, that influence 'affects not only the novel, poetry, and drama, but fashion, social manners, erotic experience and gender roles' in the Victorian era.[38] Elfenbein usefully observes that the idea of Byron in the Victorian period was a composite produced by his life and his work. However, Elfenbein explicitly avoids discussing 'the clichéd Byronic hero' since it 'overlooks the complexity of possible institutions, discourses, and practices that made both Byron and his influence available to Victorian writers.'[39] It is intriguing that Elfenbein does not discuss Dickens in his study, for Dickens adopts the 'clichéd Byronic hero' that Elfenbein refuses. Dickens's use of the cliché stresses the obsolescence of Byronic heroism in favour of bourgeois heroism.

Elfenbein observes that the distinctions between Byron's poetry and his public celebrity broke down as the market became saturated by novels imitating the Byronic:

> novels imitating his heroes reached an even wider audience, so that the specificity of Byron's poems was lost in the larger, more general phenomenon of imitators. The greater the market for Byron the celebrity, the less he could serve as a vehicle of cultural distinction.[40]

This offers some explanation for why the Byronic Hero becomes a composite figure in Victorian culture. Elfenbein also observes that 'the shift toward realism [...] implied a movement away not only from Byron's poetry [...] but also from Byron's imitators' and so from this composite Byronism. This is replaced by 'novels such as Charles Dickens's *Dombey and Son* (1848), William Makepeace Thackeray's *Vanity Fair* (1848), and Elizabeth Gaskell's *Mary Barton* (1848) [which] provided an alternative associated with domestic realism.'[41] As the market relations of literature establish the bourgeois novel as a dominant form, exemplified by the successful novelist David Copperfield, the Byronic either disappears or becomes the object of parody.

Indeed, most of Dickens's direct references to Byron, and there are not a huge number, invoke the Byronic cliché. Many of these references appear in Dickens's letters and are frequently throwaway remarks serving to invoke a comical figuring of the Byronic, such as in a letter of 1843 where he describes a drunken coal heaver as 'maudlin and Byronical,' says that he is himself 'in danger of turning misanthropical, Byronic and devilish,' and threatens to 'carry my misanthropical impulses into effect, and leave off my neck cloth without further notice.'[42] In Dickens's references, it is clear that the misanthropy of Byron's heroes, as represented, for example, by Childe Harold, who, when he travels, '[n]o lov'd-one now in feign'd lament could rave; | No friend the parting hand extended gave' (II.16), becomes an object of parody.

Typical of the shift from Byronic Hero to bourgeois parody is the young man, Horatio Sparkins, in the story named after him (1834) in *Sketches by Boz* (published in book form 1836). He is depicted 'with his hair brushed off his forehead, and his eyes fixed on the ceiling, reclining in a contemplative attitude on one of the seats,' whilst a group of young people exclaim, 'How like Lord Byron! [...] Or Montgomery! [...] Or the portraits of Captain Ross.'[43] Indeed, this entire story is a satire on the decline of Byronic heroism. Horatio Sparkins is first noticed at a lower-middle-class ball by the daughters of a family with bourgeois ambitions who keep 'acquaintance among the young eligible bachelors of

Camberwell, and even of Wandsworth and Brixton.'[44] Horatio Sparkins remains a mystery to them: 'to the interesting Teresa, [he] seemed like the imbodied [sic] idea of the young dukes and poetical exquisites in blue silk dressing-gowns, and ditto ditto slippers, of whom she had read and dreamt, but had never expected to behold.' However, his real identity is revealed as 'Mr Samuel Smith, the assistance at a "cheap shop"; the junior partner in a slippery firm of some three week's existence.' This is 'a dirty-looking ticketed linen-draper's shop, with goods of all kinds, and labels of all sorts and sizes in the window.'[45] This story attests to the way in which Byron has entered into general circulation as a figure associated with heroism, in this case in such a way that he is undifferentiated from explorers and military figures (also through the association of his name Horatio with Nelson), and to the way in which these models of heroism have become obsolete objects of satire in the face of high capitalism and the bourgeois order. The Byronic is conceived both by the socially climbing family and by Horatio Sparkins as a pose to be adopted for class mobility, and that pose is liable to become immediately obsolete if its connection to petite bourgeois life is revealed too clearly. Byron is a satirical cultural memory and can no longer exist under the present economic conditions.

In a similar act of bourgeois aspiration, when Nell works at Mrs Jarley's waxworks in *The Old Curiosity Shop* (1840–1841), Mrs Jarley alters the waxworks when the audiences are 'of a very superior description, including a great many ladies' boarding schools.' Mrs Jarley changes popular historical figures specifically into literary figures:

> Mr Pitt in a nightcap and bedgown, and without his boots, represented the poet Cowper with perfect exactness; and Mary Queen of Scots in a dark wig, white shirt-collar, and male attire, was such a complete image of Lord Byron, that the young ladies quite screamed when they saw it.[46]

Byron again is seen as a satirical caricature of libertinage, but this passage also offers some insight into the way in which Dickens understood Byron's morals. The schoolteacher, Miss Monflathers,

> rebuked this enthusiasm, and took occasion to reprove Mrs Jarley for not keeping her collection more select, observing that His Lordship had held certain free opinions quite incompatible with wax-work honours, and adding something about a Dean and Chapter, which Mrs Jarley did not understand.[47]

The reference to the Dean and Chapter refers to the refusal of authorities of Westminster Abbey to allow Byron to be buried there 'on the grounds of his scandalous reputation' and debates about a memorial to him there were still ongoing during the early part of Dickens's career.[48] Byron in this passage is seen to be in direct contention with bourgeois moral values as a result of his sexual libertinage.

It is perhaps telling, however, that these references to the Byronic are confined to Dickens's earlier, less carefully planned, and more explicitly comic works, and in the later novels, these caricatured images of Byron are displaced by the use of Byronic characters. I have shown Dickens to make reference to Byron in such a way as to portray him as a caricature, as a stock figure denoted by his misanthropy, moodiness, and sexual appeal. If the Byronic caricature were the only way in which the Byronic is represented in Dickens's novels, then there may be some justification to Harvey's observation that although 'Dickens found the Byronic hero a useful character type to employ in his novels, it is quite clear that he was no Byronist.'[49] Similarly, Juliet John's reading of Dickens's Byronic Heroes makes little reference to Byron's own work. Her terminology reflects this, referring to Dickens's characters as 'Byronic Baddies' in the title of her chapter, simplifying the complexity of both Dickens and Byron, as well as simultaneously infantilising both them and their readers. However, it is clear that Dickens's knowledge of Byron was attentive and thorough in spite of sometimes taking Byron and the Byronic as an object of mockery. There is a shift from Dickens's early work where the Byronic is portrayed as a caricature, to the later work, where the Byronic is deployed with more attention to Byronic texts and in order to fulfil a more complex thematic function.

Though Steerforth is taken much more seriously than these parodied Byronic characters, the novel attempts to exorcise the Byronic from the narrative by killing Steerforth, as if to say there is space for only one form of heroism. Steerforth is killed in a supremely Byronic moment, gesturing heroically and defiantly in a shipwreck at the climax of the narrative. This scene itself echoes Byronic texts. As both Harvey and Tambling point out, Steerforth's gesture of defiance, where he waves a red cap as the ship sinks, is reminiscent of *Childe Harold's Pilgrimage*, where Harold is made happier by the very futility of his life, which

> [h]ad made Despair a smilingness assume, | Which though 'twere wild, – as on the plundered wreck | When mariners would madly meet their doom | With draughts intemperate on the sinking deck, –| Did yet inspire a cheer, which he forebore to check.[50]
>
> (III.16)

This simile of sinking mariners rejoicing in their fate directly recalls Steerforth's gesture of happiness and defiance:

> The wreck, even to my unpractised eye, was breaking up. I saw that she was parting in the middle, and that the life of the solitary man upon the mast hung by a thread. Still, he clung to it. He had a singular red cap on, – not like a sailor's cap, but of a finer color; and

as the few yielding planks between him and destruction rolled and bulged, and his anticipative death-knell rung, he was seen by all of us to wave it.

(pp. 799–800)

It should be noted that there is also a long shipwreck scene in Canto II of *Don Juan*. However, in contrast to this little scene in *Childe Harold*, Don Juan explicitly prevents the sailors defiantly drinking away their deaths: '"Give us more grog," they cried, "for it will be | All one an hour hence." Juan answer'd "No!"' (II.36). Nevertheless, Harvey suggests that Steerforth's gesture is Byronic as 'a last gesture of mockery and defiance toward life,' part of a general indifference towards whether he lives or dies, 'all his abilities seem to be nothing to him. He is carelessly offhand and flippant about everything.'[51]

The rejection of Byronic heroism in *David Copperfield* is thus markedly different from the parody of the Byronic that occurred in earlier Dickens texts. At the moment of the death of the Byronic Hero, that hero gestures defiantly, asserting himself even as he is killed. The Byronic cannot be laughed out of its heroism here, at this moment, that David states, the entire narrative has been leading up to. Rather, in Steerforth's gesture of defiance, the dead Byronic comes to haunt the bourgeois heroism that it has paved the way for and which supplants it.

IV

Thus far, then, I have suggested that Dickens's work is influenced by Byron, that he portrays Byronic heroism in the character of Steerforth, that Byronic heroism paves the way for the individualised bourgeois self-narration that *David Copperfield* exemplifies in its title character, and that alongside the establishment of this individuated bourgeois heroism Byronic heroism is symbolically killed off. I want to end this chapter by suggesting that bourgeois heroism is nevertheless haunted by the Byronic in Dickens in a manner that disrupts the smooth functioning of bourgeois subjectivity. I suggest, firstly, that Steerforth, as a Byronic Hero, represents a revolutionary impulse which Dickens continues to associate with specific historical events; secondly that in the constitution of bourgeois subjectivity, Dickens, like Freud, suggests the potential for the bourgeois subject to be a revolutionary in a family context; and finally that *David Copperfield* knits these two strands together so that the specific revolutionary impulse of Steerforth is discernible in David's rebellion against the bourgeois family.

Steerforth's clearest relationship to revolution is expressed in Chapter LV, where, as I have discussed, the shipwreck bears comparison to a scene in *Childe Harold* and contrasts with a scene in *Don Juan*. In this scene, as the ship goes down, Steerforth is shown to have a singular red cap on, – not like a sailor's cap, but of a finer color; and as the few yielding planks between him and destruction rolled and bulged, and his anticipative death-knell rung, he was seen by all of us to wave it.

(p. 800)

It is clear that this cap should be taken seriously. There are a number of pointers that constrict the focus of the chapter until the cap itself is central, as though in a montage in a film that builds to a close-up. The chapter has a privileged status in the novel, insofar as the narration states that the entire narrative culminates in it:

> I now approach an event in my life, so indelible, so awful, so bound by an infinite variety of ties to all that has preceded it, in these pages, that, from the beginning of my narrative, I have seen it growing larger and larger [...] and throwing its fore-cast shadow even on the incidents of my childish days.
>
> (p. 790)

This is reinforced within the chapter. The wreck is pointed to by 'a half-dressed boatman [...] a tattoo'd arrow [...] pointing in the same direction' (p. 798). Steerforth is then a 'solitary man' at the centre of a breaking-up wreck (pp. 799–800), and finally as his 'anticipative death-knell rung, [Steerforth] was seen by us all to wave' the cap. Steerforth has been in Europe, and whilst the dating of the novel is not clear and probably does not map on to calendar time, if, as several critics have suggested, it is set in the late 1820s, within the atmosphere of revolution in the novel, and given that the novel was written with the 1848 revolutions in recent memory, it is not implausible to connect Steerforth here with the 1830 July Revolution in France.[52]

It is telling that this cap of Steerforth's is named, twice, as a *cap* rather than a hat. My contention is that this is the cap of a revolutionary, by virtue of its red colour and the fact that it is so 'singular.' It seems to be a Phrygian cap, a symbol of French Revolution. These singular red caps were worn during the 1830 revolution, and Delacroix depicts Liberty wearing one in his memorial to the July revolution, *Liberty Leading the People* (1830, first exhibited in the Salon of 1831). In an extremely interesting discussion of the iconography of the Phrygian cap in relation to psychoanalysis, Neil Hertz suggests that it is an ambivalent symbol, simultaneously a symbol of revolutionary power and the possibility of castration, by carefully tracing representations of the cap with and without a droop, and its appearance in popular images both on the head of decapitated monarchs and on the heads of those doing the decapitation.[53] This is particularly telling in the context of my argument since Steerforth is strongly linked both to revolution and to images of decapitated monarchs, to Ancient Rome and modern revolutions, and also to an ambivalent representation of the revolutionary, who creates the conditions for bourgeois subjectivity and is then killed off by it.

Steerforth's hat links him to the revolutions in France. Steerforth is also connected to the English Revolution of 1640–1660. This connection is made in a scene depicted in Chapters XIX and XX which take place at the Golden Cross, an inn which stood in what is now called Trafalgar Square. The Golden Cross is depicted twice in Dickens's work in relation to revolution, both here and in *The Pickwick Papers*. Here David dreams of 'ancient Rome, Steerforth, and friendship, until the early morning coaches, rumbling out of the archway underneath, made me dream of thunder and the gods' (p. 298). This is the same archway that has taken off 'the head of a family' in Mr Jingle's monologue in *The Pickwick Papers*, and this passage creates very curious parallels between *David Copperfield*, Dickens's semi-autobiographical novel about becoming a novelist, and the opening of *The Pickwick Papers*, Dickens's very first novel. In this remarkable scene, Mr Jingle, who Pickwick and his friends have just met, addresses them as they rumble out of the archway:

> 'Heads, heads, take care of your heads,' cried the loquacious stranger, as they came out under the low archway, which in those days formed the entrance to the coach-yard. 'Terrible place – dangerous work – other day – five children – mother – tall lady, eating sandwiches – forgot the arch – crash – knock – children look round – mother's head off – sandwich in her hand – no mouth to put it in – head of a family off – shocking, shocking. Looking at Whitehall, Sir, – fine place – little window – somebody else's head off there, eh, Sir? – he didn't keep a sharp look-out enough either – eh, sir, eh?'[54]

In this passage, then, there is a movement from the destruction of the respectable family (though curiously, this family is already slightly outside traditional bourgeois ideology since it is matriarchal), to the English Revolution, which is recalled in the reference to the execution on Whitehall of Charles I, who walked on to the scaffold from a window in the Banqueting House, but which is imagined in the domestic terms of a 'little window.' A statue of Charles I stood at the top of Whitehall by the time Dickens was writing and was visible from the Golden Cross.[55] In both cases, this is described by Mr Jingle as 'dangerous work,' but one must ask, in this paratactic utterance, for whom exactly is this dangerous work? There are several parallel meanings here. It is dangerous work to be the head of a nation or of a bourgeois family, but it also seems to be dangerous work to make connections between the bourgeois and the revolutionary and to travel in and out of the Golden Cross Inn. The parallels between this passage and that in *David Copperfield* bring David and Steerforth into the centre of a revolutionary challenge both to political systems and the traditional family. That this then is imagined in a Byronic context is stressed in what follows, for Jingle continues in a vein that Tambling suggests 'combines Byronic poetry with Byronic fighting for the revolution':

> Epic poem, – ten thousand lines – revolution of July – composed it on the spot – Mars by day, Apollo by night, – bang the field piece, twang the lyre.[56]

The doubling of these two scenes follows the parallel, associative and subterranean logic of dreams. One of the most fascinating things about Dickens's writing is the way in which extraneous material is constantly drawn into the text, making the novel rather like a labyrinth or dream-vision. Indeed, David (like several other of Dickens's characters) says, 'I could hardly believe but that I was in a dream' (p. 299), a sentiment that is repeated several times in a novel which returns insistently to dreaming (the word 'dream' and its cognates are used about 80 times in the novel). As such, Dickens's novels can be understood as dream visions, featuring the forms of transformation in dream-work that Freud identifies: condensation, displacement, secondary revision, and considerations of representation.

In this case, revolution in England and France, the destruction of the bourgeois family, and Byronism are all connected in various ways that are then centred on, or concentrated in, the figure of Steerforth. Steerforth thus gathers together Byron, political revolution, and David's personal and familial revolution. At points which are loci of his Byronism, Steerforth is a revolutionary figure, and this is part of David's own recollections. However, Steerforth is, at least in part, actually constituted as revolutionary through the consolidation of David's memories, the process through which he becomes a bourgeois hero. Hence whilst David is looking at the shipwreck, Steerforth's action 'brought an old remembrance to my mind of a once dear friend' (p. 800). At this moment, David does not recognise Steerforth but recalls him: projecting the figure of Steerforth onto the act of rebellious defiance he sees before him.

This is also a moment of madness – David fears that he is 'going distracted' (p. 800), and in the general economy of connections between different characters and points of revolution, there may be some relationship here with another character in *David Copperfield*, Mr Dick. Like in the logic of a dream, or of psychoanalysis, connections keep multiplying. Mr Dick is notable in the narrative for being mad and David, here, fears going mad, 'distracted,' which creates a connection between them. Mr Dick is obsessed with the English Civil War and has a curious relationship with the discipline of writing since the symptom of his madness is to obsessively write a 'memorial' about his life which is continually disrupted by him writing about Charles I against his will. These connections draw together psychoanalytic logic, bourgeois subjectification and political revolution, and return us to the Rat Man, whose connection to *David Copperfield* was discussed above.

Freud shows the Rat Man as a revolutionary figure in a family context and in the context of the consolidation of memory through writing. In the 'Rat Man' study, masturbation is connected with narcissism and thus the act of autobiographical writing, and these, in turn, are deeply implicated in an act of biting which rejects the authority of the father. In the case study, Freud speculates that the Rat Man has 'an ineradicable grudge against his father and had established him for all time in the role of an interferer with the patient's sexual enjoyment' (p. 205). This is based on the idea, which the Rat Man corroborates, that he has been beaten for a 'sexual misdemeanour' (p. 205). Freud suggests that this beating 'put an end to his masturbating' as a child, but the patient also informs Freud that in the patient's mother's account the punishment was due to him having '*bitten* some one [... who] might have been his nurse' (pp. 205–206). Now, reports Freud, as an adult, the Rat Man fantasies about his father returning from the dead and finding him masturbating. When the Rat Man's mother narrates the cause of the beating as his biting his nurse, she is replacing the forbidden masturbatory behaviour. Retrospectively, then, in a formal move that recalls David Copperfield retrospectively reordering his memory, biting becomes metonym for masturbating. Both represent the same thing in the family economy of power: a rejection of the authority of the father, which is then reimposed by beating, which had 'established [the father] for all time in his role of an interferer with the patient's sexual enjoyment' (p. 205). This beating shows the bourgeois production and socialisation of subjectivity occurring within the family, in contrast to Byronic militant subjectivity, which takes place in isolation from the family and in a contest between the self, its surroundings, and the broad sweep of history. Bourgeois subjectivity is formed in the relationship between the individual and the family, rather than in a heroic gladiatorial struggle with the world. However, the formation of bourgeois subjectivity, insofar as it is individual as well as familial, to some extent derives from older forms of heroism. Unlike militant subjectivity, however, that takes over everything available to it (so that the Byronic narrator becomes one with the immensity of Classical civilisation and figures far removed from him in time and space), bourgeois subjectivity's sphere is the family.

In David Copperfield's case, the rejection of the authority of the father through biting is much more explicit than in the Rat Man study since the bite is shown in the precise context of the father disciplining the child, rather than the Rat Man's mother's displaced narration. As Mr Murdstone goes to beat him: 'I caught the hand with which he held me in my mouth, between my teeth, and bit it through' (p. 68). Immediately afterwards, however, David again submits to the law of the bourgeois family. After biting his father, he describes 'how wicked I began to feel' and adds that 'it lay heavier on my breast than if I had been a most atrocious criminal' (p. 69).

With the remembrance in mind that David, after his rebellion, returns to a position under the law of the father, that he does not grow up a revolutionary but rather a bourgeois subject producing the bourgeois entertainment of the novel, I wish to argue that the rejection of the authority of the father in this family drama can be related to images of revolution elsewhere in Dickens's novel and also to Freud's suggestion that the creation of childhood memories about the family is part of a 'complicated process of remodelling, analogous in every way to the process by which a nation constructs legends about its early history' (p. 206). Freud's suggestion paves the way to what I am arguing here because it sees the process as entirely *analogous*: the creation of subjectivity is *like* the writing of official history. In *David Copperfield*, on the other hand, the analogy becomes activated, and the creation of national history (Charles I and the English Revolution) becomes intertwined with the creation of subjectivity. In the case of Mr Dick (which follows) the writing of subjectivity *is* the writing of national history. However, as the English Revolution ultimately fell to the restoration of the monarchy, David's rebellion results in the repudiation of the revolutionary in favour of bourgeois heroism. Nonetheless, the presence of the revolutionary in David's reconstruction of his past clearly shows it still asserts the cultural power to disrupt these processes.

In his essay 'Psychoanalysis and the Iconography of Revolution,' Lee Sterrenburg suggests the need to move from 'the analysis of fantasy contents per se, to the history of literary forms through which fantasy contents are mediated.'[57] Sterrenburg is responding to a now outdated form of psychoanalytic criticism in which fantasy contents of texts are used to comment biographically on the author of those texts. Sterrenburg summarises this approach by suggesting that Freud's linking of oral rebellion to long surmounted anthropophagic desires could be used to

> assume Dickens suffered a whole series of traumas in his childhood [...] these traumas were first repressed, but later given voice as a violently imagined, cannibalistic revolt against the old Dickensian nemesis of jails [...] and discredited parental authority generally.[58]

Instead, Sterrenburg suggests these insights should be analysed as part of a historical imaginary. In *David Copperfield*, the infantile traumas of the character David Copperfield, become intertwined with his narration's historical interests. Thus, the relationship between Dickens's/David's infantile trauma and the character's own historical imaginary, as well as the historical milieu in which the novel is written, become complexly interconnected. David Copperfield's original trauma is a moment of infantile oral trauma. It also results in a new awareness of identity, which is connected with the language of the phallic, '[I] saw my face in the glass, so swollen, red, and ugly, that it almost frightened me. My stripes were sore and stiff' (p. 69). The image of his face as he looks at himself in the mirror and comes into his identity as a criminal also contains a suggestion that he is looking at his erect penis for the first time. Though it is not a completely carnivalised image, the association of penis and face here suggest an inversion of the upper and lower bodily strata, and so a trace of carnivalesque resistance to authority and the law remains in the unconscious of Copperfield's discourse even as he resubmits to the law of the father.

This scene is remarkably similar to scenes recounted in the Rat Man study that connect resistance to the father's beating, the idea that the child is a criminal, and looking at the penis in a mirror. As the Rat Man rebels against his beating in 'an outburst of elemental fury,' his father comments, '"The child will be either a great man or a great criminal"' (p. 205).[59] This oral rebellion confirms the identity of the child as criminal, as rebel against the patriarchal order, both in terms of state and law and in the family. It suggests heroism stems from a rebellion against the bourgeois order, but, in David's case, his outburst of element fury, is part of the heroic self-sacrifice of submitting to it. Heroic revolt against the family is simultaneously a disruptive force and part of the process of being disciplined into conformity. Later, when the Rat Man is an adult,

> Between twelve and one o'clock at night he would interrupt his work, and open the front door of the flat as though his [now dead] father was standing outside it; then coming back into the hall, he would take out his penis and look at it in the looking-glass.
>
> (p. 204)

Freud suggests that this obsessional act is ambivalent: the opening of the door to look for his father being an expression of love for him and the masturbatory look in the mirror being an expression of defiance. Like David, the Rat Man's dilemma is a desire to rebel against the bourgeois family and be reintegrated in it. Both the Rat Man and Copperfield ultimately repudiate their revolutionary *heroism* in these experiences. Yet both remain haunted by its possibility. Though Freud may refer to him as a 'young hero,' in an earlier footnote, he observes that his father missed a third choice after 'a great man or a great criminal': 'the commonest outcome of such premature passions – a neurosis' (p. 205). The Rat Man, 'from that time forward […] was a coward – out of fear of the violence of his own rage' (p. 206). Similarly, the adult David Copperfield, narrating this event, has repudiated his childhood rebellion and remembers it with a powerful physical disgust. The idea of biting his stepfather 'sets my teeth on edge to think of it' (p. 68).

In David Copperfield's narratorial discourse he has consciously attempted to repudiate the urges in his childhood to usurp the father. As David becomes the hero of his own life by becoming a novelist, a man of letters, that involves submitting to the bourgeois law. He is not a revolutionary, and, as I have suggested, he becomes filled with a Foucauldian, disciplinary guilt that establishes him as an individuated, bourgeois subject. Nonetheless, as I have also suggested, there are still psychological reverberations of that rebellion. These also continue in the novel, outside the Oedipal family drama, in images related to, and connecting, Steerforth, the English and French Revolutions, and, finally, Byron. Embedded in the location of the hero in the bourgeois order of family, profession, and writing, then, there is not only revolutionary but also Byronic heroism. And though the narrative attempts to keep these contained in the character of Steerforth, they nevertheless bleed into David. As David consolidates himself as a bourgeois subject, he employs other counter-discourses, created through what is rejected and what is heterogeneous to David's narrative, that can never be fully subsumed into the bourgeois order.[60] These mark David because of the dream-like and dialogic structure of the novel, and because David's own heroic subjectivity, his bourgeois subjectivity, has its origins in Byronic, revolutionary heroism. As Mary Poovey points out, 'What we have in *David Copperfield*, then, is a novel in which the identity of the "hero" is never completely stabilized.'[61] As a result, despite the fact that David seems to submit to the bourgeois law in order to write novels, his discourse continues to implicate autobiographical writing with revolution, so that one cannot, as Poovey, and especially Miller, in part, do, foreclose on the question of David's simple submission to bourgeois life. To show this, I now turn to the images of the English Revolution which, as I have established already, are connected, via Steerforth, to Byron but also to the revolutionary elements of David Copperfield's character which disrupt his accession into bourgeois heroism.

I have suggested that David's desire to kill his father is itself revolutionary, but how this connects, in the dream-logic of the novel, to Steerforth's revolutionary Byronism needs some further explication. In the novel, David is consistently reminded of his immaturity, is put back into a child's position. The narration repeatedly gestures to David's youth and childishness, especially in relation to Steerforth. However, in contrast to the early beating and biting episode where David is very definitely gendered masculine by his quite literal part in the Oedipal drama, as well as by his association with phallic images, here he is placed quite definitely in the feminine position, as though the narrative wishes to stress Steerforth's patriarchal authority over David to an even greater extent than Mr Murdstone's. In Chapters XIX and XX, which are central to my argument about Steerforth's connection with revolution, David's immaturity and femininity are particularly stressed. David states that

Steerforth is 'superior' to him 'in all respects (age included),' and enjoys his 'easy patronage' (p. 299). When he is woken by the chambermaid who 'informed me that my shaving water was outside, I felt severely the having no occasion for it, and blushed in my bed' (p. 298), stressing both his immaturity but also a lack of the visible signifiers of masculinity. In this chapter, David is still known by several epithets which stress his childishness and his femininity: 'Trotwood Copperfield' (p. 295), the name he is given by Betsey Trotwood; 'little Copperfield' (p. 296); the diminutive 'Davy'; and Steerforth's new name for him, 'Daisy' (p. 297), which transforms the masculine diminutive into a woman's name and makes David something of a weak double of Rosa Dartle, also named after a flower and another unrequited lover of Steerforth. The chambermaid also wields a sort of sadistic feminine sexuality over David when she brings him his unneeded shaving water: '[T]he suspicion that she laughed too [...] preyed upon my mind all the time I was dressing; and gave me, I was conscious, a sneaking and guilty air when I passed her on the staircase' (p. 298). That 'sneaking and guilty air' again reinforces David's position as the child and is reminiscent of the guilt he feels after biting Murdstone. The atmosphere of the biting scene is conjured through the recreation of David's childhood affects. Finally, in this tightly knit section which emphasises so strongly David's immature and feminine position, he

> could not make up [his] mind to pass her at all, under the ignoble
> circumstances of the case [note the legal word here which is again
> reminiscent of David's beating, where he feels like a criminal]; but,
> hearing her there with a broom, stood peeping out of the window at
> King Charles on horseback.
>
> (p. 299)

The narrative conjures up David's childhood memories, when he rebelled against the order of the family, and then directly connects these to memories of the English Revolution.

David, in relation to Steerforth, then, is very much a child, and a cluster of images in this passage recalls the earlier childhood episode where he bites Murdstone. This is in marked contrast to his attempts to be an adult bourgeois earlier in Chapter XIX where his main object on the London coach is 'to appear as old as possible to the coachman, and to speak extremely gruff' (p. 291). He makes 'an indifferent show of being very manly' to Agnes and her father (p. 291). He also has 'half a mind to nod to my old [childhood] enemy the butcher, and throw him five shillings to drink' (p. 291), has 'given the book-keeper [of the stagecoach company] half-a-crown' (p. 292), and speaks 'condescendingly' to the coachman (p. 291). Nonetheless, it is in this attempt to show his bourgeois adulthood and respectability that he is returned to the condition of childishness and displaced by the other, proletarian characters on the roof of the coach in 'the first fall I had in my life' (p. 292). Returning David to his childhood is a small-scale proletarian revolution against this new bourgeois adult:

> [H]ere, in the very first stage, I was supplanted by a shabby man with a squint, who had no other merit than smelling like a livery-stables, and being able to walk across me, more like a fly than a human being.
> (pp. 292–294)

All of David's bourgeois heroism is gone. He describes himself as 'got up in a special great coat and shawl, expressly to do honor to that distinguished eminence,' the box seat. He 'had glorified [him]self a good deal' (p. 292). He is left feeling 'completely extinguished, and dreadfully young' (p. 294). In such scenes, the possibility of a working-class rebellion against the newly formed bourgeois subject, David, is opened up. And in succeeding passages, Steerforth, as a Byronic Hero, facilitates David's own dreams of revolution.

Against this backdrop of youth and depreciated bourgeois authority, David dreams of 'ancient Rome, Steerforth and friendship.' This is prompted by David seeing a production of *Julius Caesar*, of which he comments, '[T]o have all those noble Romans alive before me, and walking in and out for my entertainment, instead of being the stern taskmasters they had been at school, was a most novel and delightful effect' (p. 295). In his fantasy life, then, he exerts a mastery over his childhood and Roman heroes, and this, in turn, becomes associated with Steerforth in his dreams. In *Julius Caesar*, Brutus assassinates his friend, Caesar. So, in David's dream, there is an echo of him displacing Steerforth's authority and regaining his heroism. It is worth restating here that *David Copperfield* is written just a year after the 1848 revolutions in France, in which, Marx observes, the revolutionaries had been again acting 'in Roman costumes and with Roman slogans [...] imitations of Brutus [...] and Caesar himself.'[62]

The references to *Julius Caesar* alongside David's relative youth stress David's femininity and childishness, create Steerforth as an authority, and David as a potential revolutionary. Ambivalently, Steerforth's Byronic, revolutionary model threatens to recast David in its own image. Yet David is marked by a revolutionary spirit in other ways too. King Charles's execution takes on two important additional resonances beyond those which are repeated from *The Pickwick Papers*. First, the first eight instalments of *David Copperfield* were written in the year of the 200th anniversary of the execution of Charles I (1849), and this has some unconscious connection with the role of East Anglia in the English Civil War: East Anglia, as both place of David's birth and where the culminating scenes of the storm occur, took the Parliamentary side, and Cromwell himself was from Huntingdon. Dickens visited East Anglia, 'the strangest place in the world,' during the gestation of *David Copperfield*, and celebrated the anniversary of the execution that same month.[63] The remembrance of the execution in the composition of *David Copperfield* stands almost exactly contemporaneously with the year of revolutions, 1848. These facts add a revolutionary undertone to David's 'peeping out of the window at King Charles' still 'on horseback.' Secondly, the character of Mr Dick produces an extra dimension to this complex of images since he bolsters the importance of narrating the self in the novel. As he writes about Charles I, it becomes 'a Memorial about his own history that he is writing' (p. 215), which echoes the title of the novel itself. Mr Dick's attempt at writing his own history though is marred by the fact that 'for upwards of ten years,' he has 'been endeavouring to keep King Charles the First out of the Memorial; but he had been constantly getting into it' (p. 215). Here, then, the attempt to narrate the self gets constantly interrupted by an image of revolution; when David sees the memorial, he notices 'some allusion to King Charles the First's head' particularly (p. 213).

Mr Dick collapses the temporal gap between Charles I's execution and the setting of the novel: '[I]f it was so long ago, how could the people about him have made that mistake of putting some of the trouble out of *his* head, after it was taken off, into *mine*' (p. 212). Betsey Trotwood explains that this is 'his allegorical way of expressing' his madness, and this is 'his own history that he is writing' (p. 215), just as David Copperfield's own narrative is his *personal* history. Indeed, Mr Dick's allegorical writing stands as an allegory for David's own autobiographical project. Mr Dick, 'connects his illness with great disturbance and agitation, naturally, and that's the figure, or the simile, or whatever it's called, which he chooses to use' (p. 215). Thus, King Charles's head represents personal disturbance in the guise of public revolution. The wider concerns of national politics and history become absorbed by bourgeois subjectivity, as Freud suggests in his reference to the heroic formation of subjectivity being akin to a national epic. Public revolution similarly forces its way into David's narrative as he tries to describe his personal disturbances. In Chapter LV, 'Tempest,' David describes the storm as

> an event in my life, so indelible, so awful, so bound by an infinite variety of ties to all that has preceded it [...] that, from the beginning of my narrative, I have seen it growing larger and larger as I advanced.
>
> (p. 790)

David here shows that his entire narrative has been structured around a 'great disturbance and agitation,' just as Mr Dick's is. Mr Dick's writing is a model for David's.

In this respect, both David and Mr Dick are both trying to discover who the hero of their own life is, and, for both of them, King Charles figures prominently. David observes that 'I found out afterwards that Mr Dick had been for upwards of ten years endeavouring to keep King Charles the First out of the Memorial; but he had been constantly getting into it, and was there now' (p. 215). For Mr Dick, the revolution destroys his own subjectivity; it is confined within his own head and only the negative side of it, the decapitation of Charles I, informs his identity; '[T]he dead king has lost his head, and remains to haunt Mr Dick and make him "lose his head" in a different sense.'[64] In this respect, as Mr Dick tries to write his own life, his subjectivity is replaced by the memory of revolution. David's subjectivity is similarly displaced by revolution in the figures of Mr Dick and Charles I but most importantly through the figure of Steerforth – the revolutionary Byronic Hero who keeps getting into David's life – and through David's own revolutionary impulses within the Oedipal drama, which are recalled in a complex of images gathered together around the Byronic figure of Steerforth.

And whilst David, unlike Mr Dick, can make some separation of the images of the English Revolution from the rest of his subjectivity, they remain in his dreams, in his and the text's unconscious. In 'Tempest,' the revolutionary unconscious of David's subjectivity comes to confront him in the figure of the other hero of his life, Steerforth.

Chapter LV begins with David describing the storm that will kill Steerforth but also bring him back into David's life, 'like a great tower in a plain' (p. 790). This is because of the shadow it casts upon his narrative. It is metaphorically like a tower and part of his imaginary reprocessing of memory in order to write his autobiography. Yet, the sea is also like a tower: '[T]he waves on the horizon [...] were like glimpses of another shore with towers and buildings' (p. 793). David sleeps on the night of the storm and dreams that he 'fell – off a tower' (p. 797). These three identical references in such a short space suggest that the material world, David's subject-forming narration, and the dream world have become intermingled.[65] As a result, revolutionary heroism threatens to become part of David's waking subjectivity in a move from the unconscious to the conscious: David's dream here is a mutation of the one at the Golden Cross in Chapter XIX, and in it, he dreams he is 'engaged with two dear friends, but who they were I don't know, at the siege of some town in a roar of cannonading' (p. 797). Here, too, the unconscious and conscious worlds seem to mingle so that the roar of cannonading, which presumably comes from the storm outside, is equated with a dream of what seems to be the English Civil War. This dream is of friendship and so is also associated with a meeting with Steerforth, and the cannonading is reminiscent of the 'thunder and the gods.' David is brought out of it, at the same time of eight o'clock, by 'someone knocking and calling at my door' (p. 797). Yet, whereas in Chapter XIX, when David emerges from the dream, only traces of it seem to remain in the image of Charles I standing in for Julius Caesar, in Chapter LV, David wakes up *into* his dream. The storm is now laying siege; David imagines 'the fall of houses in the town,' the storm's 'raging, in lieu of the batteries' (pp. 796–797). All this puts the scene in the atmosphere of the Civil War, the last time that towns in England were placed under siege by connection with David's dream where similar images are explicitly linked with Charles I.

Whereas in David's dream in Chapter XIX, there is a movement from Julius Caesar to Charles I, in Chapter LV, the image of revolution is wrenched even further into the present. The civil war dream is replaced by the 1830 French Revolution. David is brought into the reality of the dream by a knock at the door, and the knock summons him to witness a shipwreck. As the ship goes down, David sees a 'man upon the mast hung by a thread [...]. He had a singular red cap on, – not like a sailor's cap, but of a finer color' (p. 800). Brutus, Cromwell, Byron, the 1830 revolution, and, perhaps, the revolutions of 1848 are all mustered here to climax in Steerforth's wave.

The Byronic revolutionary Steerforth must die, and David sees him not as a revolutionary but as a childhood memory, a friend who has atoned for his wrongs in the novel:

> [A fisherman] led me to the shore. And on that part of it where she and I had looked for shells, two children – on that part of it where some lighter fragments of the old boat, blow down last night, had been scattered by the wind – among the ruins of the home he had wronged – I saw him lying with his head upon his arm, as I had often seen him lie at school.
>
> (p. 801)

Despite the power of this writing, the ideology is still evident. Steerforth is neutralised, moved away from madness into the scheme of bourgeois memory. The threat of David's subjectivity being consciously further contaminated by either Byronism or revolution is averted by the novel. He is a bourgeois hero now, not a Byronic revolutionary. Despite this, though, neither David Copperfield nor the novel can erase his earlier claim, only a few pages before, that the entire narrative has led, not to this rehabilitation of Steerforth but to his defiant act – to his waving the red cap of Liberty at the height of the storm. In this consolidation of memory, Steerforth has established both Byron and revolution as the preconditions for the emergence of David's bourgeois heroism and as things that, though neutralised, indelibly mark bourgeois heroism at an unconscious level.

Notes

1 Charles Dickens, *David Copperfield*, ed. Jeremy Tambling (London: Penguin, 2004), p. 13. All further references to this work will be included parenthetically in the body of the text.

2 William R. Harvey, 'Charles Dickens and the Byronic Hero,' *Nineteenth-Century Fiction* 24 (1969), 305–316; Vincent Newey, 'Rival Cultures: Charles Dickens and the Byronic Legacy,' *The Byron Journal* 32 (2004), 85–100 (p. 85). All further references to this article will be included parenthetically in the body of this chapter.

3 Juliet John, *Dickens's Villains: Melodrama, Character, Popular Culture* (Oxford: Oxford University Press, 2001), pp. 171–198.

4 'Inventory of May 1844,' in Charles Dickens, *The Letters of Charles Dickens*, ed. Madeline House, Graham Storey, Kathleen Tillotson, et al., Pilgrim Edition, 12 vols. (Oxford: Clarendon Press, 1965–2002), IV, pp. 713, 723.

5 George Gordon and Lord Byron, *Letters and Journals*, ed. Leslie A. Marchand, 12 vols. (London: John Murray, 1973–1982), V, p. 100. This edition will be referred to throughout this chapter unless otherwise noted.

6 Byron's description of the Hockthorn would have been available when Dickens was writing *David Copperfield* in Thomas Moore's biographical edition of Byron's letters and journals, published in 1830. See George Gordon and Lord Byron, *Letters and Journals*, ed. Thomas Moore, 2 vols. (Cambridge: Cambridge University Press, 2012), II, p. 17. I am not able to find any evidence that Dickens owned a copy of this book, but as well as a keen interest in Byron, attested to in this chapter, he also had an interest in Moore, whose poetry he regularly quotes.

7 Byron, 'Alpine Journal,' pp. 104–105.

8 For Kant, being able to recognise the sublime demonstrates that the mind in its super-sensible aspect is superior to the sensible world of which we recognise we are an insignificant part of when faced with the sublime: 'Sublime is what even to be able to think proves that the mind has a power surpassing any standard of sense,' Immanuel Kant, *Critique of Judgment*, trans. Werner S. Pluhar (Indianapolis: Hackett, 1987), p. 106 (Section 25). Byron loses his subjectivity with the immensity of the sublime rather than returning to a place where subjectivity can be re-established.

9 Lukács, pp. 117–118.

10 D. A. Miller, *The Novel and the Police* (Berkeley: University of California Press, 1988), p. 196.

11 D. A. Miller, p. 199.

12 Michel Foucault, *Discipline and Punish*, trans. Alan Sheridan (Harmondsworth: Penguin, 1991), p. 193. D.A. Miller, pp. 208–209.

13 Lukács, p. 118.

14 D.A. Miller, p. 196.

15 Luc Boltanski and Ève Chiapello, *The New Spirit of Capitalism*, trans. Gregory Elliott (London: Verso, 2007), p. 8.

16 Mary Poovey, *Uneven Developments: The Ideological Work of Gender in Mid-Victorian England* (London: Virago, 1989), p. 90.

17 Jerome Christensen, *Lord Byron's Strength: Romantic Writing and Commercial Society* (Baltimore: Johns Hopkins University Press, 1993), p. xvii.

18 Poovey, pp. 104–105.

19 Weber's German word is *Beruf*, which is central to the argument of *The Protestant Ethic and the Spirit of Capitalism*, and can be translated as both 'vocation' and 'calling.' Parsons translates the world 'calling' throughout his translation since 'vocation does not carry the ethical connotation in which Weber is interested (Max Weber, The Protestant Ethic and the Spirit of Capitalism, trans. Talcott Parsons (London: Routledge, 2001), p. 141). The more recent translations by Stephen Kalberg (Oxford: Oxford University

Press, 2010) and Peter Baehr and Gordon C. Wells (London: Penguin, 2002), move between 'vocation' and 'calling' more freely.

20 Thomas Carlyle, *On Heroes, Hero-Worship, and the Heroic in History*, ed. David R. Sorensen and Brent E. Kinser (New Haven: Yale University Press, 2013), p. 136.

21 Byron, 'To John Murray, 25 March 1817,' *Letters and Journals* V, 192.

22 D.A. Miller, pp. 216–217.

23 Foucault, p. 200.

24 Foucault, pp. 203; 205–206.

25 D.A. Miller, p. 217.

26 Michel Foucault, *The History of Sexuality Volume 1: The Will to Knowledge*, trans. Robert Hurley (London: Penguin, 1998), pp. 61–62. The basis of Foucault's book is an examination of confession, but he discusses it in detail on pp. 58–64.

27 Foucault, *Discipline and Punish*, pp. 193–194.

28 Steven Marcus, 'Freud and Dora: Story, History, Case History,' in *Essential Papers on Literature and Psychoanalysis*, ed. Emanuel Berman (New York University Press, 1993), pp. 36–80 (p. 80). Interestingly enough, Byron was also born with a caul, which was sold off to a Captain James Hanson of the Royal Navy as a preventative against drowning, though he died in a shipwreck 12 years later. See Fiona MacCarthy, *Byron: Life and Legend* (London: John Murray, 2002), p. 3. Napoleon, too, was born with a caul. See Vincent Cronin, *Napoleon* (London: William Collins, 1971), p. 20.

29 Sigmund Freud, 'Notes Upon A Case of Obsessional Neurosis,' in *The Standard Edition of the Complete Psychological Works*, ed. and trans. James Strachey, 24 vols. (London: Vintage, 2001), X, pp. 151–249 (pp. 206–207). All further references to this work will be included parenthetically in the body of the text.

30 J. Hillis Miller, *Charles Dickens: The World of His Novels* (Cambridge MA: Harvard University Press, 1965), pp. 150–159 (p. 152).

31 Louis Althusser, *On Ideology*, trans. Ben Brewster (London: Verso, 2007).

32 Lukács, pp. 34–35.

33 G.W.F. Hegel, *Aesthetics: Lectures on Fine Art*, 2 vols, trans. T.M. Knox (Oxford: Clarendon Press, 1975), II, p. 1092. Jacques Rancière takes up this quotation in *The Flesh of Words: The Politics of Writing*, trans. Charlotte Mandell (Stanford: Stanford University Press, 2004), p. 71, and throughout his work in order to stress the democratising power of the fragmented heterogeneous element against the sovereign subject. I discuss Rancière's theory of the novel in more detail in Chapter 3.

34 Lukács, p. 118.

35 Miller, p. 216.

36 Peter L. Thorslev, Jr, *The Byronic Hero: Types and Prototypes* (Minneapolis: University of Minnesota Press, 1962), pp. 144–145.

37 Richard Lansdowne, 'The Novelized Poem & the Poeticized Novel: Byron's *Don Juan* & Victorian Fiction,' *Critical Review* 39 (1999), 119–141 (p. 121).

38 Andrew Elfenbein, *Byron and the Victorians* (Cambridge: Cambridge University Press, 1995), p. 9.

39 Elfenbein, p. 10.

40 Elfenbein, p. 146.

41 Elfenbein, p. 146.

42 Charles Dickens, 'To Andrew Bell, 1 February 1843,' and 'To Miss Burdett Coutts 26 February 1843,' in *Letters*, III, pp. 434 and 447. Further references to Byron in the letters, usually in the same vein, can be found in 'To

R.S. Horrell, 25 November 1840,' in *Letters*, II, p. 155; 'To the Countess of Blessington 20 November 1844,' in *Letters*, IV, p. 226; and Daniel Maclise to Charles Dickens, quoted in *Letters*, II, p. 232. The images of Byron himself, with his collars undone, were clearly in common currency. Thackeray also writes, 'Despair, Madam, is the word – Byronish – I hate mankind, and wear my shirt collars turned down,' see W. M. Thackeray, 'To Mrs Procter, 1841,' in *The Letters and Private Papers of William Makepeace Thackeray*, ed. Gordon N. Ray, 4 vols. (Oxford: Oxford University Press, 1945–1946), II, p. 22.

43 Charles Dickens, *Sketches by Boz*, ed. Dennis Walder (London: Penguin, 1995), p. 413. Another petite bourgeois parody of Byron in *Sketches by Boz* can be found in the character of Septimus Hicks in 'The Boarding-house,' see *Sketches by Boz*, p. 324.

44 *Sketches by Boz*, p. 411.

45 *Sketches by Boz*, pp. 424–425.

46 Charles Dickens, *The Old Curiosity Shop*, ed. Norman Page (London: Penguin, 2000), pp. 221–223. Elfenbein offers a very brief reading of this scene in relationship to sexuality, and particularly androgyny, in *Byron and the Victorians*, pp. 65–66.

47 *The Old Curiosity Shop*, p. 223.

48 Editor's note, *The Old Curiosity Shop*, p. 565.

49 Harvey, p. 315.

50 Harvey, p. 308; Jeremy Tambling, *Dickens' Novels as Poetry* (London: Routledge, 2015), p. 202.

51 Harvey, pp. 307–308.

52 On the late 1820s setting, see, for example, Julian Wolfreys, *Dickens's London: Perception, Subjectivity and Phenomenal Urban Multiplicity* (Edinburgh: Edinburgh University Press, 2012), p. 13.

53 Neil Hertz, *The End of the Line: Essays on Psychoanalysis and the Sublime* (New York: Columbia University Press, 1985), pp. 161–192.

54 Charles Dickens, *The Posthumous Papers of the Pickwick Club*, ed. Mark Wormald (London: Penguin, 2003), p. 26. Is there some sort of play between Mr Pickwick's name, the mad writer of *David Copperfield* Mr Dick's name, David Copperfield's name and Dickens's name, perhaps?

55 Michael Paterson, *Inside Dickens' London* (Newton Abbott: David & Charles, 2011), pp. 29–30.

56 Tambling, *Dickens' Novels as Poetry*, pp. 78–79; *Pickwick Papers*, p. 26. Tambling discusses Mr Jingle as a revolutionary figure at some length (pp. 77–92) and makes even more links between *The Pickwick Papers* and *David Copperfield*, related to areas unconnected with this chapter, such as Dickens and Copperfield learning stenography early in their careers.

57 Lee Sterrenberg, 'Psychoanalysis and the Iconography of Revolution,' *Victorian Studies* 19 (1975), 241–64 (p. 245).

58 Sterrenberg, p. 246.

59 Is the great criminal perhaps a particular new form of modern heroism? Benjamin's 'The Paris of the Second Empire in Baudelaire' quotes from Poe's 'The Man of the Crowd,' where the eponymous man 'is the type and the genius of deep crime' (p. 48). Benjamin then connects this being in the crowd with heroism: 'When Victor Hugo was celebrating the crowd as the hero in a modern epic, Baudelaire was looking for a refuge for the hero among the masses of the big city. Hugo placed himself in the crowd as a *citoyen*; Baudelaire sundered himself from it as a hero' (p. 66).

60 In *The Will to Knowledge*, Foucault describes the 'rule of the tactical polyvalence of discourses.' He states, '[W]e must not imagine a world of discourse

divided between accepted discourse and excluded discourse, or between the dominant discourse and the dominated one; but as a multiplicity of discursive elements that can come into play in various strategies.' Furthermore, this multiplicity of discursive elements is marked 'with the shifts and reutilizations of identical formulas for contrary objectives' (Michel Foucault, *The History of Sexuality Volume One: The Will to Knowledge*, trans. Robert Hurley (London: Penguin, 1998), pp. 100–102). Thus the discursive elements that David excludes from or opposes to his bourgeois subjectivity, or which, on the other hand, he deploys in mutated forms, often escape beyond the bounds of the particular deployment of power that aims to establish stable bourgeois subjectivity. This is evident not only in the fact that David does not exclude his own moments of rebellion, even though he repudiates them, but also in the fact that these elements then reappear in different forms so that the political revolution of the execution of Charles I becomes dimly connected to Steerforth's role as a father to Copperfield in his 'easy patronage' (p. 299).

61 Poovey, pp. 119–120.
62 Karl Marx, 'The Eighteenth Brumaire of Louis Bonaparte,' trans. Ben Fowkes, in *Political Writings* ed. David Fernbach, 3 vols. (Harmondsworth: Penguin/London: New Left Books), II, pp. 143–249 (p. 147).
63 Christopher Hill, *The Century of Revolution 1603–1714* (Edinburgh: Thomas Nelson, 1962), p. 30; Charles Dickens, 'To John Forster, [12 January 1849]' *Letters*, V, p. 474. Dickens's account of his trip to East Anglia is frustratingly oblique and narrated on pp. 470–474. Dickens is also oblique on the celebration of the execution, which he attributes to Walter Savage Landor's 75th birthday. See, Charles Dickens, 'To Count D'Orsay, 29 January 1849' and f.n.4, *Letters*, V, p. 481.
64 Jeremy Tambling, *Allegory* (Abingdon: Routledge, 2010), p. 102. I am reminded of the famous observation in *Doctor Zhivago* that 'everyone had gone mad in his own way' during the Russian Revolution (Boris Pasternak, *Doctor Zhivago*, trans. Max Hayward and Manya Harari (London: Vintage, 2002), p. 406). This also stresses the connection between revolution, subjectivity, and madness. David is clearly not mad, nor is everybody participating in any revolution. Nonetheless, Dickens creates intimate connections between Mr Dick and David.
65 Curiously, Mr Micawber, two instalments earlier in Chapter XLIX, has signed a letter describing himself as 'such ruined vestiges as yet Remain Of A Fallen Tower' (p. 708).

3 'I Can Pick the Right Uniform for My Century'

Napoleonic Heroism and Regimes of Representation in Stendhal's *The Red and the Black*

In this chapter, I argue that Julien Sorel, the protagonist of Stendhal's novel *The Red and the Black* (1830), creates a form of subjectivity modelled on a mutated form of Napoleonic heroism, which is here modified by the historical conditions of France around 1830. It is a mutation of heroism which reimagines the Napoleonic in the fully bourgeois conditions of 1830, rather than the transitional period of Napoleon's own rule. I connect this mutation of Napoleonic heroism to changes in representational practice in the novel. It is closely linked to the status of *The Red and the Black* as a pioneering work of modern literary realism. In responding to questions of realism, I contribute to a critical history of the novel which comments on Stendhal's distinctive use of realism, perhaps most famously articulated in Erich Auerbach's reading of the novel in *Mimesis* (1946). This consideration of realism allows me to engage with another vexed critical issue that surrounds the novel: the meaning of the ending, which depicts Julien's abrupt death on the guillotine, and so the death of his formation of Napoleonic heroism. In Chapter 34 of Book II, 11 chapters from the end, the narratorial discourse tells us something of the protagonist Julien Sorel's thoughts: 'Après tout, pensait-il, mon roman est fini' [After all, thought he, my novel is at an end].[1] This statement opens up a zone of indeterminacy about exactly what the novel is narrating. As Peter Brooks puts it, '[I]he novel – if not his, then whose? – will continue for another eleven chapters.'[2] This question of the protagonist's, the hero's, relation to the novel is central to its critical reception. In this chapter, I will separate the novel that Julien makes himself the hero of ('my novel') from the novel that continues for 11 chapters after this statement, which is entitled *The Red and the Black*.[3] This forms the basis for comparing two conceptions of heroism in the novel, both of which stand in relation to the Napoleonic, one which is killed off as obsolete on the scaffold and one which continues to haunt the realist novel.

During Napoleon's rule representations of Napoleon hover between positing him as a hero of bourgeois modernity and as heroic in a more

DOI: 10.4324/9781003160168-4

archaic way, within the representational practices of the *ancien régime*. In turn, I argue that *The Red and the Black*'s exploration and displacement of the Napoleonic into 1830 offers a way to read the remarkably split, metatextual, and eccentric style of the novel. Deploying the work of Jacques Rancière on aesthetics, I will argue that Stendhal's novel, as a pioneering text of modernity and of realism, is caught between two representative regimes and that this accounts for the novel's instability as it celebrates but is unable to sustain heroism. To conclude, I will suggest that Napoleonic heroism is riven by its own anachronism and so rendered redundant, and yet continues to haunt the novel in the mode of realism itself.

I begin by discussing the influence of Napoleon on the construction of heroism in the novel. I relate this to the important reading of the novel by Eric Auerbach, which offers a theoretical framework through which to understand the adaptation of the Napoleonic in the novel's historical context and lays out the central problem of realism in relation to this. Auerbach's rather abstract theories can illuminate concrete examples of Napoleonic heroism in the novel. This lays the ground for a discussion of how Napoleonic heroism is both killed off by the novel and continues to haunt it. Finally, I return to theoretical considerations by discussing the novel's pioneering realism and suggest that the Napoleonic continues to haunt not only the novel's content but also its form.

I

To begin with, then, I want to show how Julien creates a sense of himself as Napoleonic. This can be seen firstly in the way that Julien imagines himself as Napoleonic and secondly by the novel depicting Julien's heroism as a mutated form of Napoleonic heroism, a form of Napoleonic heroism strongly based in and influenced by the Napoleonic legacy. Julien's rise from the peasantry into the aristocratic mansions of Paris is, itself, predicated on a mutated sense of Napoleonism. These mutations of heroism are shaped by the political situation in France around the time that the novel was both composed and is set, and to the rise of capitalism more generally.

In Book I, Chapter 5, the inevitability of Julien's execution is first suggested. It is also here that Julien is established as a Napoleonic hero. This chapter specifically introduces the novel's Napoleonic and heroic themes. There is a long discussion of Julien's admiration for Napoleon:

> [F]or years now, Julien had never let an hour of his life pass without telling himself that Bonaparte, an obscure lieutenant without fortune, had made himself master of the globe with his sword. This thought consoled him for his sufferings, which he believed to be great, and increased any pleasure which came his way.
>
> (p. 26)

In this way, Napoleon becomes a sort of prosthesis to Julien's own subjectivity. All pleasures that Julien experiences are heightened by Napoleon, who is a supplement to Julien's subjectivity but who also comes to define his subjectivity. Julien identifies very closely with Napoleon: 'Why shouldn't he be adored by ["the pretty women of Paris"], just as Bonaparte, still penniless, had been adored'? (p. 26). Furthermore, for Julien, 'making his fortune meant first and foremost getting out of Verrières; he loathed his native town' (p. 26). Napoleon, too, followed a comparable trajectory and remained deeply ambivalent about the native town he left behind.

Julien, then, imagines his desire for heroism as Napoleonic and constructs his heroism around Napoleonism. As will be seen, this heroism is mutated under post-Napoleonic conditions towards a capitalist sense of Napoleonism but is still dependent on Napoleon to instigate itself. Alongside the dual construction of the novel, which sees Julien's novel and Stendhal's novel existing side by side, in Julien's attempts to imitate Napoleon, there is also a dual construction. On the one hand, the novel represents Julien's own attempts to construct his own life as a Napoleonic novel. On the other hand, the text shows Julien's Napoleonic heroism taking a very different course from Napoleon's own biography. In this respect, the novel undercuts a sense of Napoleonic heroism. Julien recognises in this chapter that to become Napoleonic means to become a priest rather than a soldier:

> When Bonaparte first made a name for himself, France was afraid of being invaded; military prowess was necessary and in fashion. Nowadays you find priests of forty earning a hundred thousand francs, in other words three times as much as the famous generals in Napoleon's army.
>
> (p. 46)

> [Quand Bonaparte fit parler de lui, la France avait peur d'être envahie; le mérite militaire était nécessaire et à la mode. Aujourd'hui, on voit des prêtres, de quarante ans, avoir cent mille francs d'appointements, c'est-à-dire, trois fois autant que les fameux généraux de division de Napoléon.]
>
> (p. 39)

Napoleonic ambition is channelled into economic accumulation.

However, since Julien's knowledge of Napoleon largely comes from a book about Napoleon in exile, the knowledge of Napoleon's fall after his meteoric rise is a precondition of Julien's own identification with Napoleon. The 'general prosperity' of the town stems from 'the fall of Bonaparte' (p. 3), and this is also what allows M. de Rênal to become mayor (p. 5). Julien's education comes from 'an old army surgeon who [...] had retired to Verrières' (p. 8). This army surgeon is a cousin of the Sorel family and not only a post-Napoleonic figure, but a Jacobin. According to the '*Ultra*' (p. 8) mayor,

> The fellow may well really have been a secret agent of the liberals. He used to say that our mountain air did his asthma good, but there's no proof of that. He had taken part in all *Buonaparté*'s campaigns in Italy, and even, so they say, voted 'no' to the Empire in the past. This liberal taught young Sorel Latin, and left him the stock of books he had brought with him.[4]
>
> (p. 14)

Thus, the opening of the narrative suggests that Julien is only able to imitate Napoleon precisely because he is in a post-Napoleonic situation. It is from a demobilised soldier whose political radicalism has forced him to the provinces that Julien gains his education, from a remnant of old Napoleonic radicalism, rather than a new or old bourgeois, or a radical of the contemporary political struggles of France. And it is through the defeat of Napoleon and the collapse of the Napoleonic regime, and the subsequent resettlement of Napoleon's supporters in the provinces, that the surgeon becomes available to Julien as an educator. It is this post-Napoleonic situation that forms the basis of his rise, which brings him out of the peasant class by providing employment for him with the anti-Bonapartist mayor and brings him his education. The revolutionary milieu, in which Julien receives his education is, moreover, been brought to the level of comedy. The disagreements between the liberal surgeon and the Ultra mayor take place over the management of the trees on an avenue in the town, which are periodically pollarded:

> The mayor's will is tyrannical [la volonté de M. le maire est despotique (p. 23)], and twice a year all the trees belonging to the commune have their branches mercilessly amputated. Local liberals claim, not without some exaggeration, that the hand of the official gardener has become far heavier since M. Maslon the curate adopted the habit of appropriating the cuttings for himself.[5]
>
> (p. 8)

There is then an alliance between tyrannical despotism and clericalism, against the Jacobin surgeon. This passage also registers the leading ideological attitude of the town since the Bourbon Restoration in the reason that the mayor gives for pollarding the trees:

> 'I like shade, and I have *my* trees pruned to give shade; I can see no other use for a tree when unlike the serviceable walnut, it *doesn't bring in any money*.' BRINGING IN MONEY: this is the key phrase which settles everything in Verrières.
>
> (p. 8)

Revolutionary politics here are anachronistic, left over from 1789 and its aftermath. And yet, the French Revolution brought about the triumph of the bourgeoisie. The mayor is an opponent of revolutionary politics but also a descendent of them, and despite being an Ultra, in some ways, his own politics are more aligned with the 1830 revolutionaries. The mayor, in his interest in making money, is clearly situated as bourgeois. Indeed, he is so bourgeois that it seems that money actually discounts more political-ideological positions. After M. de Rênal explains to his wife that Julien is not, to his knowledge, a liberal, issues of bourgeois one-upmanship come to the fore: 'It may cost me as much as a hundred crowns, but it must be reckoned a necessary expenditure to maintain our station' (p. 14). Julien's politics are less important to the mayor than the fine calculation of expenses which will prove the family's social status. In Julien's post-Napoleonic world, not only is Napoleon devalued, but the revolutionary tradition itself displaces politics for economics. So, when Julien decides to become a priest to fulfil his Napoleonic aspirations, part of the justification for this is that there are 'priests of forty earning hundred thousand francs, in other words three times as much as famous generals in Napoleon's army' (p. 26). Julien too wishes to bring in money. Nevertheless, it is not that his sense of heroism is no longer based on Napoleonism but that his Napoleonic heroism has mutated to better conform to bourgeois conditions. And that there is a mutation of the aims of Napoleonic heroism here does not change the fact that Julien's heroism is Napoleonic in origin and construction. He relies on a Napoleonic figure for his education and imagines 'bringing in money' as a Napoleonic endeavour.

Indeed, Napoleon is explicitly connected with Julien's belief in heroism in a wholly bourgeois world: 'Could I be a coward! He said to himself. *'To arms!'* [aux armes! (p. 40)] This expression, which recurred too often in the old surgeon's accounts of battles, had heroic [héroïque (p. 40)] symbolism for Julien' (p. 27). Here the reference to the Marseillaise and thus to the French Revolution is much stronger, but what is Julien's heroism? It is to '[stand up] and walk quickly in the direction of M. de Rênal's house' (p. 27), or as the French text puts it, continuing in the mood of the Marseillaise with 'marchons!': 'Il se leva et marcha rapidement vers la maison de M. de Rênal' (p. 40). The revolutionary acts of the bourgeoisie against the old feudal aristocracy, expressed in the command 'To arms!' in the Marseillaise, have become a command to begin one's job in a bourgeois household. Julien's own revolutionary act in the tradition of the Marseillaise has become the private one of him beginning his professional career. In this respect, Julien's heroism is based on a Napoleonic tradition of revolution but is simultaneously a mutation of Napoleonic heroism that, whilst haunted by this revolutionary tradition, is a Napoleonism of bourgeois life.

II

Erich Auerbach inaugurates a critical debate on the novel in terms of the relationship between history, politics, and form. Auerbach's reading is the basis on which I suggest that the focus on heroism and history in the novel are closely linked to questions of representation. I suggest that Julien's mutation of Napoleonic heroism is related to a shift in the practice of realist representation. Through a reading of Auerbach's comments on *The Red and the Black*, I argue that it is one of the earliest novels to register the historical. I then suggest that this is in part done by negotiations with anachronism, including anachronistic conceptions of heroism. The novel redirects, complicates, and unsettles these obsolete elements which are adapted to place the novel squarely in its contemporaneous present, a present of high capitalism and the consolidation of bourgeois power.

Erich Auerbach's book *Mimesis: The Representation of Reality in Western Literature* contains a chapter on Stendhal's *The Red and the Black* that has set the agenda for much of the criticism on the novel that has followed. In 'In the Hôtel de la Mole,' Auerbach argues that Stendhal is the founder of a particular form of realism that is concerned with a political and social reality. Auerbach writes that

> contemporary political and social conditions are woven into the action in a manner more detailed and more real than had been exhibited in any earlier novel, and indeed in any works of literary art except those expressly purporting to be politico-satirical tracts.[6]

Auerbach suggests that *The Red and the Black* is the first historico-political novel and places it in a history of realism based on what he sees as stylistic teleology which reaches its final expression in the Flaubertian aesthetics that combine political and historical consciousness, the serious treatment of everyday life, and a complete break with eighteenth-century aesthetics. All the novels I discuss in this book accrue details of the contemporary social condition in a way reminiscent of what Auerbach identifies in Stendhal's method: 'It is not too easy to describe Stendhal's inner attitude to social phenomena. It is his aim to seize their every nuance' (p. 463). In other words, Auerbach suggests that there is no obvious ideology that derives from the author function 'Stendhal.' Rather, there is a heterogeneous accrual of details, a gathering together of everything instead of that which accords only with his own political views. Nonetheless, this is itself on the teleological road to Flaubertian aesthetics. The difference for Auerbach seems to be in a unity of style: 'Flaubert overcame the romantic vehemence and uncertainty in the treatment of contemporary subjects' (p. 491). Whereas 'in Stendhal and Balzac we frequently and indeed almost constantly hear what the writer thinks of his characters and events,' in Flaubert, there is nothing but a rendering of events, images, and objects (p. 486) and the author disappears. Jacques Rancière observes that since Romanticism, a mode of representation has held sway in the European arts and reaches its most complete expression in Flaubert: '[E]verything is now on the same level, the great and the small, important events and insignificant episodes, human beings and things. Everything is equal, equally representable.'[7] Later in this chapter, I will return at some length to Rancière's theories of representation as a way to draw conclusions. The point here, however, is that modern realism is characterised by the endless accrual of details that exist on a plane without hierarchy. In earlier writers, according to Auerbach, it took the form of an accrual of details combined with an endless, heterogeneous, self-contradictory commentary; in Flaubert, objects speak for themselves, forming a strange sort of style which is both political and non-political simultaneously:

> Events seem to him hardly to change; but in the concretion of duration, which Flaubert is able to suggest both in the individual occurrence [...] and in his total picture of the times, there appears something like a concealed threat: the period is charged with its stupid issuelessness as with an explosive.
>
> (p. 491)

In parallel, in Flaubert, there is a unified authorial position that collects all objects, events, images, clichés, speech with the same impassive neutrality, which is itself a dispersed authorial position, that of the author who disappears since he becomes subordinate to the impassive accrual of details. This combination of impassivity and dispersal smothers any assertion of heroism. In *The Red and the Black*, on the other hand, whilst there is a similar accrual of details, this occurs around an authorial-narratorial voice that constantly intervenes in the narrative but which does not hold a solid, unified, and demarcated political position. As a result, Auerbach recognises a variety of political attitudes in Stendhal. Yet Stendhal, writes Auerbach,

> has no preconceived rationalistic system concerning the general factors which determine social life, nor any pattern-concept of how the ideal society ought to look; but in particulars his representation of events is oriented, wholly in the spirit of classic ethical psychology, upon an *analyse de coeur humain*, not upon discovery or premonitions of historical forces.
>
> (p. 463)

It is obviously true that Stendhal does not present some sort of theory of historical change, as Zola does, 40 years later, in his evolutionary schema.

Nonetheless, it seems strange that Auerbach should so strongly oppose these two options, interior psychology and a sense of history as system since it leaves no room for the possibility that literary texts register historical forces whether or not the author intends them to, or that the creation of an interiorised psychology is part of this registration of history. Furthermore, this seems to undermine Auerbach's own acknowledgement of the importance of comparative history in *The Red and the Black*. As Auerbach puts it, 'Stendhal is an aristocratic son of the *ancient regime grande bourgeoisie*, he will and can be no nineteenth-century bourgeois' (p. 464). Nevertheless, Auerbach's sense of realism as newly political and situated within certain historical conditions can then reveal how the historical situation of France in the 1820s and '30s informs the mutation of Napoleonic heroism towards the bourgeoisie.

Auerbach identifies moments of historical consciousness in Stendhal's text. He argues that Stendhal's description of the salon of the Moles is deliberately contrasted with the salons of the eighteenth century. The eighteenth-century salons

> were anything but boring. But the inadequately implemented attempt which the Bourbon regime made to restore conditions long since made obsolete by events, creates, among its adherents in the official and ruling classes, an atmosphere of pure convention [...]. In these salons [in the run-up to the 1830 revolution] the things which interest everyone – the political and religious problems of the present, and consequently most of the subjects of its literature or that of the very recent past – could not be discussed.
>
> (p. 456)

The novel itself is absolutely clear on this. The narrator of *The Red and the Black* ironically describes the atmosphere of the Moles' salon:

> Provided there was no joking at the expense of God, the clergy, the king, the powers that be, artistic and literary figures currently enjoying favour at Court, or indeed any part of the establishment; provided that no good word was spoken for Bérange, the opposition press, Voltaire, Rousseau, or anything venturing to be in any way outspoken; provided above all that there was never any mention of politics, it was permissible to discourse freely on any subject.
>
> (p. 263)

By introducing Voltaire and Rousseau, the comparison to the salons of the eighteenth century is explicit. Stendhal's comparison shows the emergence of particular ideological conditions rooted in a particular historical and social reality. What is more, literature, in a novel such as *The Red and the Black*, is doing exactly what the salons it depicts and which are exactly contemporaneous with it, are unable to do: discussing historical change. Rather,

> the discourse of the salon enacts [...] a self-perpetuating cycle of rep-etitions in which all the participants appear, in the words of the text, as 'copies les uns des autres,' as derivations of a 'patron commun' that is itself the copy of another model

the pre-Revolutionary aristocracy.[8] And what emerges in the obsoles-cence of these salons is a coming revolution that will attempt to sweep away the old forms unsuitable for the current historical reality, which will conjure up a new form of literature, which Auerbach characterises as realism, and which will both ensure and challenge the cultural, political, and economic dominance of the bourgeoisie. Salons are replaced by the literature of realism itself as the place where historical change is worked through. However, *The Red and the Black* shows how the salons them-selves are resurrected precisely to stymie political change. Whereas the events in Paris are leading up to the *bourgeois* revolution of 1830, con-versation in the salon is about 'the state of society [...] under George IV' where the *aristocracy* has 'more or less reduced George IV to the state of a Venetian doge' (p. 257). Outside the salon, the aristocracy's ascendancy is threatened; inside, they speak of the aristocracy in the ascendancy, and 'this discussion appeared to rouse the marquis from the state of torpor in which boredom had kept him submerged' (p. 257).

This contrasts with the use and mutation of Napoleonic heroism that Stendhal depicts Julien putting to work in *The Red and the Black*. In the heart of a depoliticised, obsolete, almost parodic resurrection of the salon form of the *ancien régime*, there is another resurrection in their midst: Julien Sorel's resurrection of Napoleon Bonaparte. The salons are a place where art and politics meet, or in this case fail to meet, 'after one or two elegant remarks about Rossini and the weather' (p. 263). Julien parallels the salons as the site where art and politics *do* meet. He is more akin to the salons of the past. In the char-acter Julien and in the novel *The Red and the Black*, art and politics come together as they should do in the ideal form of the salon. Julien and the novel are artistic, textual apparatus for critiquing the interac-tions between the revolutionary history of the recent French past, both Jacobin and Napoleonic, and the aristocratic and bourgeois societies whose strength is contested during the Restoration. He emerges into the dead space of the salon, which connects the revolutionary past with the blandness of the aristocratic present, as a Napoleonic bour-geois revolutionary. His role in the novel is to disrupt aristocratic com-placency. Julien uses the texts of the recent French past as a technology to construct his own intervention in the present after the model of a new kind of heroic Napoleon. The limits of Napoleonic, revolutionary heroism in relationship to the creation of bourgeois realism as a literary form are being tested here. What occurs when Julien-Napoleon enters realism in the particular, historical guise of the bourgeois-Napoleon disrupting the ossified world of the Restoration? In the next part of this chapter, I wish to show that even whilst Julien's heroism is being constructed, and Julien is constructing his own heroism, in the Napoleonic mode on the basis of precursor texts, *The Red and the Black* undermines this heroism in favour of a realism that disrupts the possibilities of heroism.

This use of Napoleon in a given historical situation can be related in other ways to the claims about mutations of form that Auerbach posits. Auerbach makes an intriguing remark about heroism in his chapter on Stendhal:

> [T]he stylistic level of [Stendhal's] great realistic novels is much closer to the old great and heroic concept of tragedy than is that of most later realists – Julien Sorel is much more a "hero" than the characters of Balzac, to say nothing of Flaubert.
>
> (p. 466)

This remark is similar to the thesis of Lukács's *Theory of the Novel* insofar as Lukács suggests that a former epic conception of the world is replaced by the novelistic one. If the novel is symptomatic of a shift from the old epic conception of literature to this something else called realism, then it would be the case that to retain the concept of the hero that belongs to epic in realism would mean that this kind of heroism is, when depicted in realism, obsolete or anachronistic, no longer suitable for either the artistic or historical conditions in which new work is written. Roger Pearson echoes this view in a different register by suggesting that Stendhal's novel is on the borderline between epic and novel since it 'appears to narrate a quest and an education, those two traditional features of the epic [and] the novel.'[9] Furthermore, Auerbach traces other anachronistic conceptions of heroism in biographical details about Stendhal. Noting Stendhal's 'conception of *esprit* and of freedom,' which is 'entirely that of the pre-Revolutionary eighteenth century,' Auerbach observes,

> Such traits make him appear a man born too late who tries in vain to realize the form of life of a past period; other elements of his character, the merciless objectivity of his realistic power, his courageous assertion of his personality against the triviality of the rising *juste milieu*, and much more show him as a forerunner of certain later intellectual modes and forms of life; but he always feels and experiences this reality of his period as a resistance.
>
> (p. 465)

There are some ambivalences here, and the complexities of Stendhal's historical position as both a child of the eighteenth century and a writer of the nineteenth century are reflected in the complexities through which Julien's heroism is represented in novelistic realism. According to Auerbach, Stendhal himself belongs to a time before the realist revolution but also at the vanguard of it. But the trait in which Auerbach most powerfully sees a forerunner of Flaubert in Stendhal's realism – the courageous assertion of personality – is this not a Napoleonic trait too? Indeed, objectivity – a second feature of Stendhal's novel that Auerbach sees as looking forward to Flaubert – could also be claimed as a Napoleonic trait. Nevertheless, as I have argued, there is an ambivalent attitude to the historical position of Napoleonic heroism in *The Red and the Black*, which parallels the way Stendhal is simultaneously a figure of the eighteenth and nineteenth centuries. He invests in the historically obsolete figure of Napoleon, but this allows him to disrupt the (also obsolete) space of the aristocratic salon, precisely in order to suggest a revolutionary potential which is attached to the 1830 revolution, bourgeois revolution more generally, and perhaps a strain of proletarian revolution since Julien's social mobility means that he is stretched across the proletarian and bourgeois classes. Stendhal invests in ideological modes that are partially obsolete, and this, in turn, also means an investment in outdated forms. However, in Stendhal's work, this investment in the obsolete, conversely, has the effect of being at the forefront of a new conception of realism which registers history. This aesthetic configuration is mirrored in Julien Sorel himself, who by investing in the obsolete figure of Napoleon brings himself closer to the historical dynamism of class relations. Thus, investment in Napoleon ushers in the bourgeois and proletarian revolutions of the nineteenth century, and a deployment of heroism introduces non-heroic realism. The very bases on which *The Red and the Black* is premised are rendered obsolete by the text that unfolds from them – yet, as we shall see, that text continues to be haunted by them.

III

I now wish to turn to the novel itself to substantiate and develop in more concrete, textual terms the theoretical conclusions I drew from Auerbach. Auerbach's conception of Stendhal-as-author comes from a textual construction. He bases it on quotations from Stendhal's autobiographical books, *La Vie de Henri Brulard* (1835–1836, published 1890) and *Souvenirs d'Égotisme* (1832, published 1892). Stendhal's depiction of complex, ambivalent Napoleonic heroism, in the character of Julien Sorel, similarly works on deployments of textual constructions. Julien adapts the textual Napoleon he admires into a Napoleonic heroism for himself in the capitalist world of 1830, meaning that Napoleon, despite his obsolescence, shapes Julien's subjectivity, but this mutated version of

Napoleonism is riddled with contradictions. Napoleonic obsolescence undermines Julien's heroism and suggests the inevitability of his execution, a theme I take up in the final sections of this chapter.

When Julien first discovers that he is to be made the tutor of the mayor's children in his hometown, Verrières, where the first half of the novel is set, he is reading a book about Napoleon, the *St Helena Chronicle* (p. 19). It is knocked out of his hands by his father, a peasant who has come to own a sawmill and who now delivers this news to Julien (pp. 20–21). This 'most precious' of books 'landed in the *public stream*' (p. 20). This gives some clue as to the fate that befalls the image of Napoleon in this novel. Napoleon is rendered useless by a peasant/petite bourgeois businessman bringing an employment opportunity from a bourgeois businessman and becomes a matter not of inherent meaning but part of the flow of public representation; that is, Napoleon becomes a technique of realism rather than a technique of heroism but also is made to be entirely unsuitable as a cultural image on which one could construct a form of heroism. Nonetheless, this is what Julien constructs his heroism on.

The book of Napoleon, which creates Napoleon as a textual construct, is destroyed by the public stream, but by entering the public stream, it also creates Napoleon as part of public flows of representation. Napoleon here enters society as part of its public circulation of discourses. I make this claim on the basis of the valuable observations that Richard Terdiman offers in his essay, 'From City to Country: An Outline of *Fluvio-Critique*,' which suggests ways of reading texts within a cultural materialist framework by particular attention to the rivers in them. Terdiman observes that watercourses both symbolically and literally connect the provinces to Paris as a site of modernity in many canonical French texts of the nineteenth century. This is most obvious in the repeated plot where the country is left behind for the city along the course of rivers, in the way that 'everything in them seems to press towards Paris in a headlong craving for acceleration – of property accumulation, of erotic intensity, of personal power,' which is the key trajectory for Julien's story.[10] For Terdiman, though, rivers flow in both directions, and the provinces are constructed 'by a series of insistent cultural meanings that emanate from the metropolis.'[11] This means that the book on Napoleon that falls into the stream 'compound[s] the layering of [the stream's] symbolic resonances.'[12] Julien's Napoleon worship is here related to a particular trajectory of modernity since the industry on the stream relates Verrières to Paris: 'As for the *public* stream which powered the saw, M. de Rênal managed to have it diverted, using the influence he commands in Paris' (p. 5). He derives this influence from 'the events of 1815 [the Bourbon Restoration],' which 'made him mayor' (p. 5). This same formulation, '*public* stream,' is used both in this context and when Julien's book on Napoleon is knocked out of his hands. Thus, the novel, in its opening, already draws together Julien's relationship with Napoleon and contemporary Parisian politics in the symbolic resonances of the stream.

In Verrières, the stream has seen an evolution from 'an artisanal (the saw mill) to a primitive industrial (the mayor's nail works) to a proto-consumer economy (the calico factory).'[13] Thus Julien's Napoleon worship symbolically frames him, in relationship to the stream, as a subject of developing capitalism and its associated politics even before he goes to Paris. There is no bucolic place outside modernity, every version of the pastoral in modernity is part of modernity. In the French context, as Marx points out, this is in part Napoleon's doing, but this simultaneously creates the conditions for the dispossession of the peasanty through the creation of urban and rural proletariats: the

> Napoleonic form of property, which was the condition for the liberation and enrichment of the French rural population at the beginning of the nineteenth century, has developed in the course of that century into the legal foundations of their enslavement and poverty.[14]

The similarities between country and city in the transition to capitalism also clarify why the move from the provinces to Paris does not seem to radically alter Julien's narrative but, rather strikingly, to repeat it in a higher social milieu.

Indeed, repetition is key in this later Parisian narrative. When Julien finally sleeps with Mme de Rênal, the narration states that 'one could say, in the novelettish style, that he had nothing left to desire' (p. 91), similarly, when he sleeps with Mathilde de la Mole, the narration states, 'It is wiser to suppress the descriptions of such excesses of folly and bliss' (p. 373). At each point, there is an absence constituted by a narratorial intervention that makes an ironic, censoring comment on what has taken place, as though the second was a repetition of the first. Each consummation of the love affair is stated with a similar rhetorical device that playfully refuses to state clearly what happens. Julien's narrative trajectory is structured by repetition: 'capitalism's revolution was spreading from centre to periphery in such a manner that the country/city bipolarity increasingly lost its clarity.'[15] In this respect, it should also be noted that Napoleon both comes from the periphery (Corsica) and imagined as an exile after his fall, continues to exert influence from the periphery.[16] Furthermore, Terdiman points out that

> the enigma and the scandal of Verrières [...] was not that rapaciousness was abroad in France, but that it had broken out in the countryside [...] it is the reproduction, in the countryside's supposed site of *difference*, of precisely the developments that a burgeoning capitalism was visibly determining in the cities.[17]

Napoleon as text falling into the public stream seems, at the very beginning of the novel, to mark Napoleon as a historical mediator between city and country, as well as bringing him together with the stream that is the driving force of capitalism in the small town, powering the nail works, sawmill, and factory, as a figure that connects the capitalist city to the countryside that it needs to survive.

Napoleon offers a form of self-representation that can be adopted by Julien in order to figure his own move from country and city as relatively homogeneous within the rise of bourgeois capitalism and as a model to make himself the hero of bourgeois life through a textual existence that heroises his connection to capitalism. This first image of the textual Napoleon in *The Red and the Black* is thus absolutely central to the novel. But whilst the legacy of his material reforms might haunt the novel in spite of his disappearance in the post-Napoleonic international order and Bourbon Restoration, much of his importance in this novel, even as a figure of material history, is specifically in relation to a book about his past military exploits falling into the public stream, connecting the circulation of images to the circulation of capital, both of which flow between the city and the country.

On the other hand, though, Napoleon is an obsolete figure, a remnant of a world and an era that ushers in but nonetheless precedes high capitalism. As such, Napoleon marks Julien's heroism as different, out of step with the world in which he lives. The *St Helena Chronicle* is a record of Napoleon's conversations on St Helena (Slater's notes, p. 533) and is 'the keystone of the Napoleonic legend.'[18] For Julien, along with 'the collected bulletins of Napoleon's great army,' it 'complete[s] his Koran' (p. 22). These works are both explicitly creations of a heroic myth of Napoleon, but the comparison to the Koran is a curious one. It implies the Otherness of Julien's Napoleon worship. This Islamic reverence for Napoleon is placed alongside Julien's Christian reading: '[H]e had learnt off by heart the whole of the New Testament in Latin. He also knew J. de Maistre's book *On the Pope*, and believed as little in the one as in the other' (p. 22). Julien's religious hypocrisy, then, juxtaposes a Napoleon worship that is constructed as sincere, Other and heretical, which must be partially hidden though is also available for public circulation, and a knowledge of Christianity that is not the basis of belief but rather held purely for its utility. He has learnt the Christian texts 'to win over old Father Chélan, on whom it was plain to him that his own future lot depended' (p. 22). However, Julien's knowledge of Latin mutates and is stressed in a different way in relation to his class mobility in the unexpected confines of the Moles' salon. Here he impresses with a knowledge of Latin literature, rather than the Vulgate and theology, which 'went down more than well' (p. 257), but the Roman Classics have been adopted for conservative reasons, acquired in order to avoid having to discuss any contemporary literature. Thus, Julien's subjectivity is split in the textual montage from which it is composed, the sincerely believed credo of Napoleon is figured as an Otherness within a hypocritically held adherence to the dominant culture of church and state; Latin literature is figured as an analogue for the ascendancy of the aristocracy, 'they talked about the state of society under Augustus and under George IV' (p. 257).

As I stress several times in this book, Marx points out the close connections between Napoleon and Ancient Rome. However, Napoleonic heroism must mutate in order to survive in the capitalist world. Elements of the separate parts of Julien's split textual identity thus bleed into one another. Napoleon is the Other to the Latin learning of church and state, but learning Latin is also Napoleonic technique, attested to by the fact that Julien learns Latin pragmatically to emulate Napoleon. In a situation where France is no longer under military threat, 'the answer is to be a priest' (p. 26) and the church offers more power and possibilities than the army. Julien is inspired because he has seen a local justice of the peace, 'a level-headed and honest man' (p. 26), passing politicised sentences (p. 25) out of fear of a priest who is 'reputed to be a spy from the Congregation' (p. 25), a religio-political secret society 'deeply involved in reactionary politics' (Slater's note, p. 533). There is a direct line, also, then, between Julien learning Latin to become a priest and his desire to be involved in political machinations. In this respect, Julien's learning Latin to emulate Napoleon, as part of his campaign against the ruling class, is not separable from the ruling class's own use of Latin. Napoleon enters the church and aristocracy that, from Julien's perspective, he stands against. But, of course, Julien learns Latin as an oppositional strategy to integrate himself subversively into the ruling structures of power, as Napoleon did. Indeed, in the salon, as Julien speaks of Latin literature, what

> actually overawed him still further was two mirrors, both eight feet high, in which from time to time he would glance at his interlocutor while speaking of Horace. His sentences were not too long for a provincial. He had beautiful eyes, and the nervousness made them shine, now hesitantly, now radiantly when he had given a good answer. He was deemed to be agreeable.
>
> (p. 256)

> [C'était, dans le fait, deux glaces de huit pieds de haut chacune, et dans lesquelles il regardait quelquefois son interlocuteur en parlant d'Horace, qui lui imposaient encore. Ses phrases n'étaient pas trop longues pour un provincial. Il avait de beaux yeux dont la timidité tremblante ou heureuse, quand il avait bien répondu, redoublait l'éclat. Il fut trouvé agréable.]
>
> (p.251)

In this passage, subject positions are partially maintained; it is clear that the 'his' and 'he' must refer to Julien. He is the only one who is provincial, who has need to be nervous, who is being judged. His interlocutor is positioned as belonging to the aristocracy in contrast to Julien: '[T]he marquis signalled to Julien's interlocutor to push him hard' (p. 256), implying some intimacy between them, and Julien sees the interlocutor as one of an abstract 'they'; the narration states that Julien is thinking 'it seems they only know this author [Horace]' (p. 256) as he is questioned. However, as Julien glances into the mirror at his interlocutor, there is a certain blurring of subject positions. At first glance, the 'he' seems to be indeterminate, especially given that the narrator has stated that Julien is looking at his interlocutor at this moment. There is something odd about these mirrors too. How is it that Julien can look into the mirror and see his interlocutor? The only arrangements possible here would be the two mirrors side by side, with Julien and his interlocutor laterally beside one another or with the mirrors facing each other so that they reflect into infinity. In either case, the arrangements suggest either a lateral equality between Julien and his interlocutor, they are not adversarially facing one another but next to each other, as though in a series, or that they are swapping places in the reflections of reflections, to infinity. This is compounded by the use of free indirect discourse here: the sentences that each begin with 'his' or 'he' could be attributed, along with the narrator, to Julien or to his interlocutor. Lacan observes in his famous essay on the mirror stage that the subject is formed when he or she looks into the mirror, but this subject formation produces 'the armour of an alienating identity.'[19] Noting the surprisingly militaristic metaphor here, Julien's subjectivity is constructed by the text here in a play of mirrors, where he comes oddly close, despite his hypocrisy, to the people he opposes. In the first instance, the Napoleonic is adopted as Julien's identity in opposition to a knowledge of Latin learning, yet this Latin learning can also, via Marx, be seen to be Napoleonic. Marx also points out that this Napoleonic-Roman costume is available for appropriation by the ruling class, and as Julien discourses with them, his identity, at a textual and psychoanalytic level, begins to be constituted by that which he has hypocritically opposed himself to – the aristocratic.[20] Julien's identity is a montage, made up of a series of Others which he alternately claims and rejects, in a movement of mirrors that goes to infinity. This is an example of Julien's Napoleonism registering, and being mutated by, historical context, to the extent that, though Napoleon clearly inspires Julien's heroism, he also renders him unstable, both in opposition to and close to the aristocratic class whose power threatens to be swept away by capitalism.

I have argued that, with the risk of Napoleon's obsolescence Julien mutates Napoleonism for the world of capitalism but that this creates instabilities and contradictions in the figure of Napoleon. These ultimately pave the way for Julien's execution. This can be seen in Julien's mutation of Napoleon from a military figure to a hero of civil society. Since Julien is a montage of texts, full of the discourses of the Other, he is not shown to be a double of Napoleon but rather a representation that is riddled with other elements. He is a representation of Napoleon that is shot through with the historical concerns of his own historical moment. As such, Julien's heroism, when compared to Napoleon's, is not directly comparable but mutated. When he is first seen with his father, his father's 'hand turned him round like a child's hand turning a tin soldier' (p. 20). Julien, then, despite imitating Napoleon, is not a soldier but a diminutive, malleable memory of a soldier. Perhaps one tentative way of thinking about him would be as a demilitarised Napoleon, given that he must display his heroism in civil society, and even after becoming a military officer, there is no sense that he is likely to go to war, but rather is 'presented as a lieutenant without ever having been a sub-lieutenant except on the books of a regiment he had never heard of' (p. 465). Given that Julien becomes an officer in 'the fifteenth regiment of Hussars, one of the most brilliant in the army' (p. 465), it seems that the real work of being a soldier is done in the unknown regiment he is only nominally in, and here his military commission is to do with status rather than military ability: 'His horses, his uniforms, his servants' livery were punctiliously maintained in a way which would have been a credit to the fastidious-ness of a great English lord' (p. 466). His heroism is not in military deeds themselves, though he models it on Napoleon, but on invading aristo-cratic society as a proletarian-petite bourgeois upstart whose description echoes the Roman context again: '[W]e should find in him shades of the rebellious plebeian [plébéien révolté (p. 436)]' (p. 459).

Alongside this mutation of the Napoleonic, there is a corresponding mutation of written form. Julien takes his Napoleon from texts that ideo-logically claim the authority of eyewitness accounts, biography, and his-tory, and yet Julien as Napoleonic hero is depicted in a very different formal context, that of the novel. There is a shift from the *St Helena Chronicle* [*Le Mémorial de Sainte-Hélène*] to the other subtitle of the novel *Chronicle of 1830* [*Chronique de 1830*] but the *Chronicle of 1830*, unlike the narratives of Napoleon that are concerned with presenting a *historical* account, never features the major historical event of 1830, its revolution.[21] Julien imagines himself as a modern upstart along the lines of Napoleon but never reaches Napoleon's interventions in society. Indeed, the novel never touches the issue of revolution directly.

These different representative modes, historical memoir and novel, have different values within the ideology of their time in so far as they make a claim to truth, but the point here is that Julien's hero worship of Napoleon is mediated by and exists around texts, and, furthermore, as I am about to discuss, he imagines his own life as a text – not a history, however, but a novel. Julien has worshipped the Napoleon of historical testimony but becomes the Napoleonic hero of a novel. In the process of becoming the hero of his own novel, Julien has imitated Napoleon but been forced to change Napoleon into a figure for the capitalist world of

1830. These mutations of Napoleonic heroism introduce contradictions into Julien's Napoleonic heroism that lay the groundwork for his own destruction as a hero.

IV

In this chapter, I use the terms 'Stendhal's novel' to demarcate *The Red and the Black* in its entirety, and 'Julien's novel' to designate the process of class mobility and subject formation that Julien is shown, within the wider narrative, to conceive of as a novel. Whilst the novel has a dual structure in this respect, the two terms are not opposites, and, furthermore, it should always be remembered that Julien's novel is part of Stendhal's novel. Whilst I call one part of the dual structure 'Stendhal's novel,' it should be remembered that Stendhal, just as much as Julien, is a textual construct, beginning with his serial use of pseudonyms. As such, Stendhal here is an 'author function,' as Michel Foucault outlines in his text 'What Is an Author?' Stendhal is not a knowable subject, no subject is, and besides, I know nothing of Stendhal, I can make no claims about him. Rather, 'Stendhal' is the name that we collectively attribute to a unifying tendency that can limit the proliferation of meaning. As Foucault puts it, the author 'is a certain functional principle by which, in our culture, one limits, excludes, and chooses [...] the author is therefore the ideological figure by which one marks the manner in which we fear the proliferation of meaning.'[22] Within our current epistemic regime, attributing an author function must be a precondition of analysis in what would otherwise be the endless play of signs. This does not presume that I must believe in some unified, knowable subject named Stendhal, especially given that the pseudonym name itself destabilises, or even mocks, the idea of a unified subject who precedes the work. But it does mean that in any reading of *The Red and the Black*, Julien's novel comes into tension with, and is ultimately killed by, Stendhal's novel. This is part of the process of rejection of the Napoleonic heroism represented by Julien in favour of the nascent realism represented by the author function Stendhal. In this section, I examine how this process occurs in the novel, prior to discussing how this relates to the mutation of form, towards realism, which Napoleon continues to haunt.

Book I Chapter 5 is key to understanding Julien as a Napoleonic hero. I suggest that at this key early moment when Julien is situated as a Napoleonic hero, the necessity of killing off the Napoleonic is simultaneously encoded in him. I discussed previously that Book I Chapter 5 contains two Napoleonic moments, a narration of Julien's history of Napoleon worship and a moment of fear where Julien rallies himself with the memory of the old surgeon from Napoleon's army and says to himself '*To arms!*' Between these two Napoleonic moments comes a decidedly odd piece of writing that has a major bearing on Julien's attempts to write a novel of his life, to make himself a hero of his own novel. In this passage, Julien is in the church of Verrières just after being engaged as a tutor to M. de Rênal the mayor's family:

> Alone in the church, he took a seat in the finest-looking pew. It bore the arms of M. de Rênal.
>   On the hassock Julien noticed a piece of paper with printing on it, spread out there as if meant to be read. He looked at it closely and saw:
>   *Details of the execution and last moments on Louis Jenrel, executed at Besançon on the...*
>   The paper was torn. On the back, the first few words of a line could be read. They ran: *The first step.*
>   Who can have put that paper there? Julien wondered. Poor wretch, he added with a sigh, his name ends like mine.
>
> (p. 27)

There is much to say about this uncanny passage, not least that its uncanniness goes two ways at once, but in both cases, there is a sense of that 'something which ought to have remained hidden but has come to light.'[23] In the first instance, there is the identification of Julien Sorel with Louis Jenrel. Louis Jenrel seems to be his double, their names 'rhyme,' an idea which is confirmed by Julien being executed later in the novel. Freud observes that the double is 'the uncanny harbinger of death' since the double threatens the individuated existence of the self. Freud explicitly connects the double with 'the constant recurrence of the same thing – the repetition of the same features or character traits or vicissitudes, of the same crimes, or even the same names.'[24] We have already seen how fundamental repetition is to Julien's narrative.

In the second instance, there is the sense that this fragment has been left for Julien to read. But just who has laid out this text for Julien 'as if meant to be read': some form of providence, the novelist, some divinatory character who is never presented, Julien's superego? There is a sense of the supernatural, of a hallucinatory premonition, which is heightened by Julien feeling a 'secret terror': 'On his way out, Julien thought he saw blood beside the stoup of holy water' (p. 27). This hallucination is revealed to have a mundane explanation, however: '[S]ome of it had been spilled, and the light coming through the red drapings over the windows made it look like blood' (p. 27). The hallucination is in the same image cluster as the execution that has connected Sorel to Jenrel. However, though the uncanny impression of blood here is quickly dispelled, it nevertheless points to Julien's own ability to experience the uncanny at this moment, where he becomes aware of the possibility of his own death. Further, 'a secret terror' is a near-perfect description of the uncanny as something that should have remained hidden but has come to light, especially since

French has no specific word for the uncanny and tends to fall back on words like *sinistre* to describe it.[25] There are other ways that this passage can be read as uncanny too. There is a sense of textual play at work here, in the depiction of Julien himself as reader interacting with text, and in the greater intensity of metafictional licence than the narrative will allow Julien to recognise. Julien seems half-aware of the metafictional play occurring at this point when he recognises that 'his name ends like mine.' However, Louis Jenrel's name does not just end like Julien Sorel's but is a half-anagram of it. The uncanny, particularly when its effects are produced by ideas of 'the double,' is itself about the production of subjectivity. As Freud suggests, 'the "double" was originally an insurance against the destruction of the ego' when the concept of the ego is in an early stage of development, and Freud also suggests it becomes part of the superego, thus 'the first step,' may be a kind of command directing Julien's own ego development. Freud suggests that uncanniness derives its affectual content from material that reminds us of these now repressed stages in the development of the ego, particularly since when these come to light, they reflect a compulsion to repeat that tends towards destruction. Thus, the superego aspects of Sorel/Jenrel bring to light the sense that they are propelling Julien towards his own death.[26]

I want to stress here the fact that the novel is engaged in a textual game that plays with two differing versions of subjectivity, one that stems from Julien presented as a subject in formation within a Freudian framework – in relation to the family romance and to castration – the other as a textual composite, which can also be read through Freud but where the novel itself is the object of psychoanalysis, rather than Julien as subject. The notion of 'the novel as subject of psychoanalysis' demands a different form of criticism from psychoanalytic criticism which treats character histories as real psychobiographies for psychoanalysis to decode and, rather, recognises texts as full of psychoanalytic structures. These two schemas would correspond to the two novels which I am suggesting run parallel to each other: Julien's novel of his own life and Stendhal's novel of Julien's life within the context of a French history that goes beyond it. In Stendhal's constitution of Julien's subjectivity, there is the premonition of his destruction, which is written into the context of French history.

Indeed, Julien's subjective sense of uncanniness is compounded by extra-textual knowledge that derives from historical context. The passage with the slip of paper in the church further complicates whose novel this is. Stendhal's sources for the plot are well known; 'The story is based on, and the novel originally inspired by, two court cases which Stendhal read about in the *Gazette des Tribunaux*,' writes Roger Pearson in his introduction to *The Red and the Black*.[27] These court cases both deal with young men who were executed for murdering their lovers, in one case that of Antoine Berthet, in similar circumstances to Julien Sorel. Again, the question is whose novel is this – Julien Sorel's, Stendhal's, or its extra-textual antecedents? It is as though Julien's own sense of uncanniness is supported by the novel that does not belong to him. This extra-textual construction of subjectivity is far beyond the textual Napoleonic subjectivity that Julien tries to construct for himself and is entirely out of his control.

Simultaneously, then, Julien's extra-textual antecedents and his own psychobiography both guarantee his eventual execution. Freud states that uncanniness is felt in the fear of castration.[28] Thus the cut of the guillotine at the end of the novel, which is the result of him usurping the name of the father to have sex with a mother figure, seems to already be known to Julien within the closed world of his subjectivity. There is a suturing of the textual and extra-textual, for Julien's uncanny affect must derive from different desires from those purportedly stated by the novel, the desire for 'the pretty women of Paris' (p. 26), but rather from desire within the family romance. In other words, if, as I have shown, he feels uncanny when he reads the scrap of paper, it must be because he is aware of his own castration complex (which makes sense given that he has just been beaten by his father, has been musing on father figures including Father Chélan and Napoleon, and knows he is going to fulfil a father role as tutor) and thus aware of his own desire for his mother. Since Julien has no mother figure present in the novel, it is then hardly surprising that on the page following this he first meets Mme de Rênal, around whom he feels a 'deep agitation,' who fears that he will beat her sons and who must at this point give up having her own sons in her bedroom as though she is making room for Julien (p. 28). This uncanny moment then sets the stage for the two love affairs that will guarantee Julien's passage to the guillotine.

The combination of the psychobiographical and the historical (based on his emulation of the historical Napoleon) in the creation of Julien points to the highly textually sedimented, highly arbitrary nature of the fictional subjectivity that is created by Stendhal and named Julien Sorel. The castration complex of an imagined, individuated subject may begin his journey to the scaffold, but this is depicted simultaneously with textual games and references to Napoleon and other historical events. Julien's subjectivity is a textual construct created by Stendhal which suggests a relationship between the Napoleonic and the ideological conditions in France in the years preceding the 1830 revolution and also a textual construct created by Julien himself based on Napoleonic texts through which he imagines himself as much more unproblematically heroic. The tension between these two constructs of heroism is attested to by the disjunction between Julien's novel and the Stendhalian text which extends beyond it.

The passage I am discussing is sandwiched between two very explicit references to Napoleon. Julien attempts to construct a heroic subjectivity in relation to Napoleon, but this occurs in relation to psychoanalytic and textual elements that destabilise this. This is implied by the marked difference between the Napoleonic form of subjectivity – particularly its militarism – and the confusion evident in Julien's own sense of Napoleonic subjectivity and the suggestion of the destruction of Napoleonic subjectivity predestined in Julien's path to the guillotine. The dual structure of the novel, where Stendhal's novel continues beyond Julien's, posits the destruction of Julien's Napoleonic novel by Stendhal's composite, bricolage novel, which, I show next, to be the basis of realism.

However, more can be extrapolated from this passage in the church, and, alongside these questions of subject formation and textual play, I wish to discuss the temporal scheme of the novel, which has bearings on both of these, particularly because it complicates what role Napoleon might play as a hero figure for Julien to imitate. There is a strange collapse of the sequential time of the novel in those words 'the first step.' The first step is the first step of Julien's Napoleonic trajectory. The first step also refers to the execution of Jenrel and designates Julien's execution as the final event of Julien's life through an inevitable repetition. Moreover, it seems to say, reading this paper is the first step towards the ultimate end of execution, though the final moment of execution paradoxically becomes the first here. This paradox is intensified by Julien's conception of his novel finishing before his execution, whilst Stendhal's novel continues beyond the execution. As I have shown, if Julien's life is articulated in relationship to events in contemporary France, then it is worth considering in more detail how this personal first step relates to its historical context.

The Red and the Black is 'a chronicle of 1830' (p. 1), as well as also bearing the subtitle, 'A Chronicle of the Nineteenth Century' (p. iii), but the 'publisher's note' on the very next page claims it was written in 1827 (p. 2). The novel was first published in November 1830, but its title page was dated 1831, 'and a reconstruction of the historical time-scale within the novel suggests that the events of the last few chapters take place also in 1831.'[29] The novel was actually written in 1829 and 1830 (Slater's note, p. 530). As many commentators have pointed out, despite the novel being set in 1830, it fails to show the events of the July Revolution, which saw the overthrow of the Bourbon Charles X and his replacement by Louis-Phillippe, 'the Bourgeois monarch.' The only reference to the July Revolution is in the fictitious 'publisher's note': 'This work was ready for publication when the great events of July supervened and left French minds rather unreceptive to creations of the imagination' (p. 2). Much of this places the novel in an untimely position, hovering on the precipice of the 1830 revolution but either not having reached it, or inexplicably eliding it. As Roger Pearson states the two subtitles are 'synonymous, for the July Revolution has changed nothing. Louis-Philippe may have succeeded Charles X, but vanity and hypocrisy still rule.'[30] I suspect Pearson is too pessimistic here because he forecloses on the proleptic potentiality of the novel's chronology to focus on the revolution's failure. Rather, I suggest, the novel hangs uneasily between the two.[31]

If Pearson is correct in situating the late events of the novel in 1831, then this scrap of paper that points to the execution of Sorel-Jenrel oddly complicates this since these final events, beyond the revolution, are actually the 'first step' towards a post-revolutionary world in a narrative whose stated aim is to chronicle the revolutionary year 1830. The publisher's note suggests that the novel was completed before the revolution of 1830 but is to be read in its context. However, there is something slightly odd about this note too. Stendhal is playing games. If the revolution of 1830 has left French minds unreceptive to works of the imagination, then why is the novel being published at this particular point, especially if it was completed much earlier? Furthermore, why does it elide the historical backdrop of the coming revolution, whose inevitability the paratexts suggest should be proleptically evident in the text, in favour of an imaginative story that only obliquely alludes to it? The novel is avoiding the revolution because somehow literature is not compatible with it, it is a work of the imagination that the revolution leaves people unsusceptible to, but it is also specifically responding to the revolution since, in the conditions of reception set out in the publisher's note, it is only by referring to the revolution rather than the imagination that the novel could stake a place for itself in the public sphere. The paratextual game leaves the novel totally ambivalent: it is unquestionably about the 1830 revolution, and it is not at all.

Given the multiplicity of different time schemes which are competing here, none with a particular claim to be the 'correct' time scheme, perhaps it is better to talk about an 'ideological' rather than a chronological time since this can be recognised in the varying temporal moments that are presented. Most of the dates presented suggest that the novel occurs prior to the 1830 revolution, even if its chronological time scheme goes beyond it, and, furthermore, it seems that the novel is unable to depict the 1830 revolution itself, ideologically, as well as in the literal facts of its composition. Nonetheless, the novel insists it is a chronicle of both 1830 and the nineteenth century, which seems to suggest that in the ideological imagination of the novel, these two things are the same, given the similarity of phrasing of the two subtitles. Thus, the question arises whether the 'first step' – that is, the execution of Jenrel-Sorel or the narrative that depicts Julien's trajectory to execution – is not also synonymous with the 1830 revolution, the first step of 1830, its initial event. In this reading, the novel hangs between revolutionary potentiality and failure; its ideological time scheme would register Julien's Napoleonic potential and his ultimate failure.

The Red and the Black then would not only be a chronicle of 1830 because it depicts Sorel as a sort of revolutionary but also as an outdated figure in French society who needs to be done away with in order for the revolution to take place. The first step is both Julien beginning his Napoleonic trajectory *and* being executed for it. Julien as Napoleonic hero is at the start of his revolutionary trajectory and unsuitable for the revolution. If his entire narrative is about representing himself as a historically modulated version of Napoleon for 1830, and 'the first step' in Napoleonic self-creation is also the first step on the path to his own execution, then the promise of his own execution is simultaneously a precondition of him becoming Napoleonic. Julien is executed because he is too like Napoleon and anachronistic, and his becoming like Napoleon can only take place in relation to the knowledge of execution. When Julien begins, Napoleon is already dead, so to imitate Napoleon is to be fated, not to the same fate as Napoleon but one more extreme. Instead of being exiled, Julien will be executed. The political uselessness of his Napoleonism is further stressed by him being executed not for political activities but for a crime of passion.

This 'first step' multiplies difficulties for itself in relation to the novel's Napoleonic plot. Julien is trying to become Napoleon, but this Napoleon figure goes through a number of vicissitudes, which begin at the moment Julien reads that scrap of paper describing his 'first step.' Julien is sitting in M. de Rênal's pew; he is about to displace M. de Rênal as the father of his family as he takes on the roles of parent to his children and lover to his wife. Nonetheless, as Peter Brooks has argued, this is part of an attempt to establish his legitimacy as a son, to find the correct father 'among possible fathers from whom to inherit.'[32] Thus, Julien's Napoleonic insurrection is part of a process of ultimately reinstating himself, not as the revolutionary Napoleon-father but as a child of the old aristocracy. Napoleon, despite being the stated ego-ideal, gradually gets displaced because Julien is attempting to become a son, not a father. And, of course, Julien's correct father is the one that gives him the commission in the hussars and an aristocratic title at the end of 'his' novel:

> [C]ould it really be possible, he wondered, that I might be the natural son of some great lord driven into exile in our mountains by the terrible Napoleon? This idea seemed less improbable to him with every passing moment... My hatred for my father would be proof of it... I shouldn't be a monster any more.
>
> Only a few days after this monologue, the fifteenth regiment of Hussars, one of the most brilliant in the army, was lined up in battle formation on the parade ground in Strasburg. M. le Chevalier de La Vernaye [Julien Sorel] was mounted on the finest horse in Alsace, which had cost him six thousand francs. He was being presented as a lieutenant without ever having been a sub-lieutenant except on the books of a regiment he had never heard of.
>
> (p. 465. Stendhal's ellipses)

Any revolutionary displacement Julien makes in the family, such as usurping the bourgeois father-substitute, M. de Rênal, is only better to reinforce conservative models of both state and class. In this passage, towards the end of the novel, Napoleon has ceased to be the father figure, the ego-ideal, but the figure who has forced Julien's fantasy legitimate father into exile. Julien's own Napoleonic revolution is nothing but an attempt to secure the most conservative father figure he can, it is a revolution against the proletarian-peasant background he comes from, the petty bourgeois world of his own father, the bourgeois world of the small town. Julien's Napoleonic trajectory is towards aristocratic conformity and ends with a repudiation of Napoleon. Napoleonic heroism is eclipsed.

An important essay by Nicholas Rand, '*The Red and the Black*, Author of Stendhal Pseudonyms and Cryptonyms of Beyle,' brings the textual-metatextual-paratextual strand and the psychoanalytic, subject-formation strand together. Rand's article is conceived as 'a complement to Peter Brooks' interpretation.'[33] In this essay, Rand uses the cryptological psychoanalytic techniques developed by Nicholas Abraham and Maria Torok in order to consider the role of the guillotine that ends Stendhal's novel. According to both Rand and Brooks, whom he quotes, the guillotine unsettles the internal coherence of the novel, it is an 'incomprehensible' ending, and both Rand and Brooks attempt to make the guillotine coherently fit into the schema of the novel.[34] To put this into the terminology I have used to describe the split in the novel, they attempt to make Julien's novel wholly congruent with Stendhal's novel to justify why the novel should continue when Julien has said his novel is finished. Brooks does this by relating the guillotine to Julien's quest for paternal legitimation. He thus interprets Julien's novel as extending beyond its stated end within Stendhal's novel. Rand, on the other hand, through his interest in Stendhal's own name, minimises the split between Julien's novel and Stendhal's novel, instead seeing them as a coherent whole, with Julien's novel a wholly subordinate element to Stendhal's novel, rather than a disrupting principle within the novel as a whole. For Rand, it is Stendhal who is executed rather than Julien.

Rand's approach, which is rich in insights about the novel aside from his main thesis, is to suggest that the pseudonym Stendhal can form the basis of an analysis that connects different parts of the novel and thus explains the role of the guillotine in the novel's structure. Thus, Rand sees associative links within the novel and even extra-textual threads that connect the different parts of the novel in unexpected ways. Quite wonderfully, he plays with the idea of Verrières and Stendhal 'as interchangeable as regards their function in the novel' since both are the names of small towns, and the narration states, at the very end of the novel, that 'to avoid tampering with personal matters, the author invented a small town.' Thus, Verrières becomes a cover for the personal in the same way that Stendhal does. They are both pseudonyms. For Rand, this means that 'the effect' of the last words of the novel 'is to topple, literally to upend, the progression of the novel by sending the guillotine back to Verrières in the first chapter.'[35] Rand uses this observation, along with a virtuoso reading of interlingual puns on guillotines in Stendhal's names, in order to argue that the reader is forewarned 'of an impending discrepancy [between Julien's trajectory and the novel's] s/he could not otherwise expect,' and that coming to recognise the integration of this discrepancy is an apprenticeship comparable to Julien's.[36] Thus Rand suggests the absolute necessity of the guillotine for the structure of the novel.

I imagine that some readers may find his method rather fanciful, though I thoroughly admire it for its sheer gleeful inventiveness and its precision. Towards the end of the essay, he goes on in a footnote to suggest that similar hidden references to the guillotine are worked into Julien's relationship with Mathilde de la Mole. Rand's rather brief suggestion here is that what continues beyond Julien's novel 'is, in part, a "historical" novel authored by Mathilde de la Mole,' an assertion he justifies through connecting her to Marguerite de Navarre, who held a procession with her lover's severed head.[37]

My problem with both Rand's and Brooks's readings is their integrationist tendencies. They work from an ideological presupposition that a novel must, ultimately, formally cohere, even though Rand's linguistic openness undermines that at the very point it insists on it. I want to suggest in what follows that the novel rather signifies its lack of integration. Could it be that the guillotine marks a split between Julien as executed anachronism and proleptic revolutionary hero and between two different modes of writing, the realism that the novel establishes and whatever representative regime (what we might call it remains to be seen) precedes it? How does this relate to Julien, then? In what follows, I wish to suggest that Julien's death, and the castration of his anachronistic, Napoleonic heroism by the guillotine, corresponds to the instantiation of a new formal mode: realism. Perhaps one could see the shift in the function of the guillotine itself. The guillotine is not used in this novel as a revolutionary instrument in the political sense, but rather as a juridical instrument of bourgeois justice. On the other hand, it retains its revolutionary history by ushering in a new phase of literary production. The revolutionary figure of Napoleon continues to haunt the novel in realism, even when Julien, the Napoleonic hero, is killed off. The temporal uncertainties of what the guillotine represents here mirror the temporal uncertainties of when the novel is set and whether it deals with revolution.

V

Julien Sorel, then, is killed off as a Napoleonic hero due to the obsolescence of the Napoleonism that defines his subjectivity. However, Napoleon continues to haunt the novel in a way that persists more enduringly. Napoleonism haunts the form of the novel as a fundamental feature of its realism.

One way to approach this dual structure of the novel at a wider formal level would be to read out from this short but, as I have shown, extremely complex episode in which Julien finds the note reading 'the first step' in church to offer further considerations of history and realism. As so much of the critical work on the novel observes, *The Red and the Black* is a major representative of the literary regime that is known as 'realism,' a highly simplistic theory of which the novel itself presents (presumably only so that it can then ceaselessly undermine it). As the narratorial discourse puts it, 'You see, sir, a novel is a mirror going along [*que se promène*] a main road. Sometimes it reflects into your eyes the azure of the sky, sometimes the quagmires of the road' (p. 371). This passage fulfils a similar function to the incident with the scrap of paper: it draws attention to the fact that the novel is not simply reflecting, as the quotation would seem to suggest it is doing, but is always drawing attention to its own constructedness, its own writtenness as a novel.[38] I want, then, to link the productions of subjectivities in *The Red and the Black* to realism as a textual strategy, and I will do that by considering how Julien comes to represent himself as Napoleon. This self-creation as Napoleon interlaces Julien's own efforts to create his own subjectivity within the space of the novel with cultural, and textual, reference points. It partakes of the textual games that characterise Stendhal's novel. It is also shaped by the temporal instabilities and problematics described earlier. Thus, whilst Napoleonic heroism is killed off by the death of Julien following his rise in what I have called Julien's novel, Napoleon continues to haunt the novel in the importance of Julien's Napoleonic heroism to Stendhal's pioneering creation of an early and paradigmatic example of literary realism.

Thus far, then, I have suggested that the novel shows two parallel productions of Julien's subjectivity, one by Julien himself in the Napoleonic model he derives from his books and another which works to ironise this by suggesting that his Napoleonic subjectivity is formed in ambivalent relation the times in which he lives, be that the aristocratic state, the emerging bourgeois state, or the time of revolutionary potentiality. I have suggested that these two versions of subjectivity are generated by a reliance on extra-textual references and metatextual play within the novel, and that these operate to illustrate the notion of heroism that Julien attempts to construct for himself and to simultaneously undermine that notion of heroism. I want to now suggest that this creation and disruption of Napoleonic heroism is specifically related to techniques for representing Napoleon. The techniques that Julien uses are obsolete in the context of the era of bourgeois capitalism. Yet they continue to haunt the novel even as these techniques are replaced by those of realism.

Just before the episode in the church, which I have discussed in so much detail in this chapter, there is a curious passage where Julien imitates Napoleon. He has come to recognise that the way to Napoleonic advancement after Napoleon is to become a priest, though this itself has been translated into the financial terms that dominate Verrières:

> Nowadays you find priests of forty earning a hundred thousand francs, in other words three times as much as the famous generals in Napoleon's army [...]. Look at that justice of the peace, such a level-headed and honest man up till now, dishonouring himself at his age for fear of displeasing a young curate of thirty! The answer is to be a priest.
>
> (p. 26)

Becoming a priest is figured as directly comparable to rising in the ranks of the Napoleonic army. Nonetheless, Julien's desire to be a priest is presented not simply as contiguous with his Napoleonic ambition but, simultaneously, in opposition to it:

> Once, in the midst of his new-found piety, when Julien had been studying theology for two years, he was betrayed by a sudden eruption of the inner fire which was consuming him. It happened at a dinner given by Father Chélan [the parish priest and his theology tutor] for a gathering of priests, at which the kindly host had presented Julien as a prodigy of learning: he went and praised Napoleon with great vehemence.
>
> (pp. 26–27)

Julien's response to this is curious: 'Afterwards, he strapped his right arm to his chest, pretending he had dislocated it while moving a fir trunk, and kept it in this uncomfortable position for two months. After this corporal punishment he forgave himself' (p. 27). Julien desires to become a priest out of Napoleonic ambition; however, that Napoleonic ambition is not actually Napoleonic, but rather concerned with the bourgeois ideology of making lots of money since his interest is based on the salary that a priest earns ('a hundred thousand francs'). Furthermore, Napoleonism is not compatible with the hypocrisy he must practice in front of the priests ('He thought it would be in the interests of his hypocrisy [hypocrisie] to make a Station in the church' (p. 25)). Julien fails to properly negotiate these difficulties and contradictions and punishes himself for them. His punishment seems to be a response to both accidentally revealing his hypocrisy and betraying his admiration for Napoleon. By admitting his admiration for Napoleon, he shows his clerical ambitions are based on a Napoleonic desire for advancement and thus hypocritical. This in turn means that, by expressing his admiration for Napoleon, he has risked damaging his prospects of Napoleonic advancement. His admiration for Napoleon causes him to lose the necessary self-control of a (highly idealised) Napoleonic hero, who views everything with a detached and steely eye. He loses his self-control. But what is this punishment? To strap up his right arm, in a gesture that looks like a parody of Napoleon's famous pose with his right hand tucked in his waistcoat, in David's painting *The Emperor Napoleon in His Study at the Tuileries* of 1812. Pearson suggests that, in this pose, Napoleon is not 'imitated but travestied.'[39] Julien re-Napoleonises himself, but this gesture, and the shifts between performing Napoleon and failing to, suggests modelling oneself on Napoleon is in crisis in the novel (Figures 3.1–3.3).

Curiously, *The Emperor Napoleon in His Study at the Tuileries* seems to suggest a partial shift away from the public space of revolution and the Napoleonic rise to power, towards the private interior of the citizen. This painting is very different from the major paintings of Napoleon by

Figure 3.1 Jacques-Louis David, *The Emperor Napoleon in His Study at the Tuileries* (1812) Courtesy National Gallery of Art, Washington.

Figure 3.2 Jacques-Louis David, *The Coronation of Napoleon* [*Sacre de l'empereur Napoléon et couronnement de l'impératrice Joséphine*] (1807). Photo © RMN-Grand Palais (musée du Louvre) / Michel Urtado

Figure 3.3 Jean-Auguste-Dominique Ingres, Detail from *Napoleon I on his Imperial Throne* [*Napoléon Ier sur le trône impérial ou Sa majesté l'empereur des Français sur son trône. Il porte le collier d'or et de diamants de la Légion d'honneur*] (1806). Photo © Paris - Musée de l'Armée, Dist. RMN-Grand Palais / Pascal Segrette

David, which depict him as the heroic soldier crossing the Alps (reproduced here in the original 'Malmaison' version (1801)) or crowning himself emperor, or in Ingres's *Napoleon I on His Imperial Throne* (1806). In *The Emperor Napoleon in His Study at the Tuileries*, Napoleon is depicted as having just finished writing the Napoleonic Code, which was enacted in 1804 and enshrines the rights of the citizen, and is the foundation for a bourgeois, private legal system. The code is visible on the desk to the right of the painting. However, Napoleon, in David's painting, despite the private space of his study or his work in creating the rights of the private citizen, is still a public figure. His relaxed, private pose is stylised; it comes from a long tradition of English portraiture in the eighteenth century when the hand-in-waistcoat pose appeared 'with relentless frequency.'[40] This style was designed to 'portray sitters pleased, in good humour, and suitably elevated in character,' and did this by adopting a 'projected,' 'idealised' vision of Classical sculpture.[41] When this pose was adopted by Napoleon it is a 'personalized revival' and 'reminting of devalued British currency,' and does not seem to have any longevity as a portrait pose after Napoleon.[42] When Julien adopts this attitude as a masochistic punishment, then, it is profoundly anachronistic. His punishment for admiring Napoleon is to make himself resemble Napoleon, whilst simultaneously experiencing (masochistic?) pain for it and having to pass it off as an accident rather than an attempt at imitation. Simultaneously, though, if his punishment is part of a lapse of self-control then Julien is re-Napoleoning himself here, refashioning himself as Napoleon, re-asserting his capacity for heroism on the basis of putting back on the Napoleonic uniform that he has let slip. It should be noted that whilst the image of Napoleon with his hand in his waistcoat is not the most heroic image of Napoleon as a military or royal figure, it shows him at his most bureaucratic, lawyerly, bourgeois, and so Julien appropriating this pose registers the mutations of heroism that he is enacting. It is, furthermore, the most familiar depiction of Napoleon. As Arline Meyer puts it, it is Napoleon's 'inimitable trademark,' though curiously *Julien is imitating it*.[43] The Napoleonic pose, then, is a received gesture handed down through an artistic tradition, which Napoleon, by being inimitable, also breaks out of. Napoleon's pose continues artistic tradition whilst breaking from it.

Napoleon is still in a uniform in this painting, though, and this has implications for Julien too. As Julien puts it, 'I can pick the right uniform for my century' (p. 336). For Julien, this declaration comes at the moment that he is holding a letter from Mlle de La Mole avowing her love for him: 'The letter which he was clutching in his hand gave him the stature and the stance of a hero' (p. 336) ['Cette lettre, qu'il tenait serrée dans sa main, lui donnait la taille et l'attitude d'un héros' (p. 325)]. However, all his Napoleon worship stands in tension with the lack of suitability of Napoleon in this fully bourgeois epoch:

As F.W.J Hemmings noted, Julien is practically the sole votary of the Napoleonic cult in *The Red and the Black*, and he learns nothing from the long, cautionary conversation at the beginning of Part II, in which a catalogue of Napoleon's ill-fated influences on French life is drawn up.[44]

This catalogue is a conversation in a stagecoach between Julien, a Bonapartist, and a liberal. Napoleon here is blamed for preventing France from becoming bourgeois more quickly, putting back the work that the 1830 revolution eventually performed:

> With his chamberlains, his pomp and his official functions at the Tuileries, he gave us a new edition of all the silly trappings of the monarchy. It had been revised, and would have done for another century or two. The nobles and priests preferred to go back to the old edition [...]. The clergy, whom Napoleon recalled with his Concordat instead of treating them as the State treats doctors, barristers or astronomers, simply seeing them as citizens, without worrying about what business they engage in to try to earn their living. Would there be impertinent gentlemen around today, if your Bonaparte hadn't created barons and counts?[45]

> (pp. 242–243)

The need that Julien has to find the correct uniform for his century then is a problem of representation since a uniform is a semiotic practice that represents position and status in society. He must represent himself in suitable terms for his time. The constellation of Napoleon represented as both monarch and private citizen, of Julien representing himself as Napoleon and as hero, and of the practices of representation that the novel itself formally engages in point to the fact that the novel marks a watershed in the poetics of representation, that markedly draws into question the status that Julien gives himself as heroic.

In terms of the history of representation, the images of Napoleon that I have reproduced in this chapter are worth considering in more detail. I have suggested already that David oscillates between depicting Napoleon as warrior and Napoleon as bourgeois, and so already tensions are evident in the image of Napoleon and his status within different historical regimes. Is he the great general, modelled on the memories of Classical civilisation (the word 'Hannibal' is visible on the rocks in the lower-left corner, making the comparison absolutely explicit), or is he a lawyerly bureaucrat? The painting by Ingres on the other hand seems to be firmly within the Classical tradition: it depicts Napoleon not as a Romantic modern general or a semi-bourgeois legislator but as a repetition of the Roman emperors. However, Ingres's painting also captures some of the ambivalence that occurs between the two David paintings at a formal level. Tellingly, Roberto Calasso connects Ingres both to Stendhal and to the new conceptions of heroism that I am articulating in this book. In Ingres's bourgeois pencil drawings, the women depicted are 'waiting to be summoned to the pages of Jane Austen and the Brontës, or of Stendhal and Balzac, all the way down to the as-yet-unborn Henry James and Proust.'[46] For Calasso, then, it is Ingres who in the visual arts stands alongside a foundational moment in the history of the modern, bourgeois novel, the invention of realism, but who also begins a genealogy that stretches to the modernism of the late nineteenth and early twentieth centuries but that remains invested in experimentally depicting bourgeois experience. Indeed, this genealogy would suggest that there is no modernist break but rather a continuation of perception between Ingres and Proust.

Roberto Calasso's *La Folie Baudelaire* devotes a significant amount of time to an intriguing reading of Ingres, which rejects his classicism and suggests he is part of the shift towards bourgeois realism and the bour-geois mutation of heroism that I am describing in this book. Speaking of Ingres's drawing of the Forestier family, produced in 1806, the same year as the painting of Napoleon, Calasso writes that 'it is an image of the new bourgeois universality' and that Ingres's drawings more generally, 'usher in the heyday of the novel' (pp. 111–112). On Ingres's paintings more generally, Calasso observes that Ingres 'continued to declare himself a *'peintre de haute histoire'* and craved official commissions for solemn cel-ebratory themes. But in the meantime he had ensured that the odalisques discreetly occupied the place reserved for the deeds of heroes' (p. 81). Thus, the hero is displaced by the courtesan, a transition which I describe in my chapter on *Vanity Fair*. However, though Calasso is dismissive of Ingres's paintings of high history, even the portrait of Napoleon partakes of the shift in the formal properties of art that Calasso describes as typi-cal of Ingres's painting. For Calasso, Ingres's work is 'the dawning of a new art, which was introduced by a painter who inveighed *against the new* every day' (p. 81, italics in the original). This new art, according to Calasso, consists of a 'fanaticism of form,' which he connects with 'the doctrine of *art for art's sake*' (p. 97, italics in the original). This is evident in two key tendencies. Firstly, 'an exclusion of air and space, that trans-position of the painting into a second nature, without atmosphere and without depth' (p. 81); that is to say, the painting turns in on itself and becomes a reflection on its own formal principles. Secondly, 'a new way to approach the inanimate' (p. 83), which is based on a gaze that, 'with equanimity [...] spreads over gloves, folds in silk, shawls, lorgnettes, fans, ribbons, cameos, fringes, bows, handkerchiefs, rings, feathers, and ruffs'; as such, 'objects, stones, fabrics, and people possess a sole nature' (p. 109). Within the closed work, then, objects take on a radical equal-ity. Art is no longer subordinated to any demands on it, other than the demands of the work itself, and it depicts everything that stands before its gaze with a serial equality, that would suggest the fungibility of all objects under capitalism. Everything has become an object of exchange, including the component parts in the work itself, which only speak of their relationship to each other. Calasso describes Ingres's objects as possessing 'the nature of the fetish' (p. 109); that is to say, things in Ingres's paintings are exchangeable on a metonymic chain and offer a phantasmagorical plenitude that disavows their metonymic nature. Any single object, or even detail, in the painting can offer itself as the central subject of the painting along the metonymic chain. The result of this is that, even in the paintings of high history, the historical subject is always potentially displaced from centrality within the image. In this respect, in the painting of Napoleon, though, according to Calasso, it is part of the second order of Ingres's work; there is a sort of turning in of the painting onto itself. Around Napoleon in that work there is a void but, also, the lavishness of the objects that not only adorn him but envelop him call into question the centrality of the emperor himself. Particularly prominent are Napoleon's golden chain of office and the folds in his robe, which occupy the central vertical axis of the painting and offer themselves, with his face, as equal foci of attention. These formal features suggest a different relationship to the historical. In this respect, it is instructive to compare David's painting of Napoleon's coronation.[47]

In this painting, with all eyes turned towards Napoleon, who is at the centre of a composition which is not an enclosed second nature but rather placed in a particular historical and geographical context, Napoleon is not displaced from the centre of the picture by what is around him. It might seem at first glance that because of the grand situation, the focus is less on Napoleon, but rather, through identification with the spectators and the generic conventions of the painting, Napoleon's position as central is absolutely confirmed. This painting is, then, very different from Ingres's painting of Napoleon where there is no hierarchy of representation that puts Napoleon in the centre of the picture but, rather, where things threaten to take the place of the emperor along a metonymic chain. Ingres is moving towards a new regime of realism where the image is not based on the importance of what is depicted but rather accrues details of the world, recalling Auerbach's description of realism in Stendhal that I outlined in Section II. That this depiction moves towards modern technologies of realism can be seen in Ingres's relationship with photography.

Calasso observes that 'Ingres did not *react* to photography, as did his peers – and generally did with repulsion [...]. Ingres *incorporated* photography into his painting long before it was invented' (p. 110). Even in the portrait of Napoleon, the stillness of the space, its second nature, and the rigid pose of Napoleon, in strong contrast to those in David, recalls early studio photography. It is almost as though Napoleon has been draped in the costumes of the emperor and had his head propped up by the supporting devices used in early photography studios because of the long exposure time. Napoleon could be in 'one of those nineteenth-century studios whose draperies and palm trees, tapestries and easels placed them somewhere between a torture chamber and a throne room,' as Walter Benjamin describes the space of bourgeois photography.[48]

What does this digression on these images of Napoleon have to do with Julien's own sense of Napoleonic heroism? As can be seen in my reading of Ingres's portrait of Napoleon, in comparison to David's, Ingres is part of a significant shift in representational practices, which can also be associated with the claim with which Auerbach inaugurates the critical tradition that places Stendhal at the vanguard of the new literary practice of realism. These representational transitions play out in relationship to Julien's creation of himself as a Napoleonic subject and wider questions of how his 'heroism' is constituted in the novel.

There is an episode in *The Red and the Black* where Julien is threatened with the loss of the social status he has gained because of a portrait of Napoleon. In Book I, Chapter 9, 'An Evening in the Country,' M. de Rênal and his servants are restuffing the mattresses, and Julien panics about having the image of Napoleon that he keeps under his mattress discovered:

> Napoleon's portrait, he said to himself, shaking his head, found hidden in the room of a man who openly professes such hatred for the usurper! found by M. de Rênal, such an extreme *Ultra* and in such a state of anger! and to crown my rashness, on the white card at the back of the portrait there are lines written in my own hand, which leave no doubt about the excess of my admiration.
>
> (p. 63)

Furthermore, Mme. de Rênal believes Julien wishes to hide this picture because it depicts an unknown lover.

Very little information is given to us about what this portrait might look like, but Porterfield and Siegfried observe that 'the flatness and strangeness' of Ingres's painting 'may have made it look too weird, too much like a popular print.'[49] Julien's picture of Napoleon, we may presume, is also a popular print. It seems unlikely that he could afford a painting. Julien's portrait of Napoleon and Ingres's portrait, then, are part of the economy of the work of art in the age of mechanical reproduction, a notion supported by Calasso's suggestion that Ingres's paintings are like photography. Julien's representation of himself as Napoleon, then, both partakes in a shift in Napoleon's image from military emperor to bourgeois professional, but it also takes part in a shift of representational practices that can be related to Ingres's new mode of representation that brings the Napoleonic closer to mechanical reproduction of the work of art. Julien's own admiration of Napoleon is structured through prints. The novel connects the formal innovations of realism with realist and popular innovations in the visual arts. To end this chapter, then, I will suggest questions of realism and heroism can be related in this new aesthetic regime, reiterate that Julien's own admiration of Napoleon is placed in the context of the end of possibilities of Napoleon heroism, which accounts for Julien's execution, and, finally, speculate about the extent to which Napoleon haunts the novel as a sign under which Stendhal's particular practice of realism is born and represents itself.

The philosopher Jacques Rancière offers a theoretical framework for understanding these shifts in representational practice. In his large body of work on the philosophy and politics of aesthetics, he describes different 'regimes of identification' that call into question received categories for thinking about the arts in the nineteenth and twentieth centuries, such as 'modernity' and 'the avant-garde.'[50] For Rancière, the category of 'modernity' cannot hold because 'it traces, in order either to exalt or deplore it, a simple line of transition or rupture between the old and the new, the representative and the non-representative or the anti-representative' (p. 24). A break can only come about within that which it breaks against, it cannot form itself from the ether, but must rather be rooted in the representational practices against which it imagines itself rebelling. Hence the direct line between Stendhal and the radical representative practices of Proust. As Rancière points out, modernism and artistic modernity claim themselves opposed to realist representational practices, and yet simultaneously their 'inaugural moment has often been called *realism*' (p. 24). With this in mind, realism, conceived as a break by Auerbach at the beginning of this chapter, must be in turn rooted in older representational practices. Analogously, then, the Napoleonic heroism in this novel, which I have demonstrated is based on representational practices, though rendered obsolete, must persist in what follows it. By describing *The Red and the Black* as a transitional novel in Rancière's terms, I will be able to reach some conclusions about heroism and the status of Napoleon in the novel.

It is worth noting at this point that in a recently translated book, Rancière has offered his own reading of *The Red and the Black*. In his essay, he suggests that Stendhal is a pioneer of the aesthetic regime of the arts, which I gloss next, but emphasises different parts of the novel with a very different inflection from my reading. Whereas I suggest that Julien's social climbing and disappearance from the narrative are both haunted by Napoleon, Rancière offers a more future-oriented reading of Stendhal, which sees Julien's happiness in prison before being executed as reminiscent of socialist utopians, which represent the 'plebeian's new happiness, the happiness of doing nothing.'[51] Using the same tools, then, Rancière sees the novel as looking forward whilst I see it looking back. This Janus-faced quality attests to its transitional status between realism and modernism.

Rather than using traditional aesthetic categories such as 'modernism,' 'modernity,' 'the avant-garde,' 'realism,' and so on, Rancière instead describes three 'regime[s] of the arts.' For Rancière, a regime of the arts is 'a specific type of connection between ways of producing works of art or developing practices, forms of visibility that disclose them, and ways of conceptualizing the former and the latter' (p. 20). In other words, the conceptualisation of a regime of art allows for an analytically rigorous definition of the relationships between the methods through which a work of art is created, the ways in which the work presents itself to its audiences, and the relationship between the two. For Rancière, defining arts through regimes of the arts prevents the confusion that traditional philosophical-critical terms present. Terms such as 'modernity' and 'the avant-garde,' for example, 'confuse two very different things: the historicity specific to a regime of the arts in general and the decision to break with the past or anticipate the future that takes place within this regime' (p. 20). The way in which works of art are created and deployed come to be seen as breaks with the contingent historical situation that informs their creation. Rancière suggests that 'realism' is also a misleading term, for reasons that have a bearing on the status of both heroism and Napoleon in Stendhal, but to explain this, a brief description of Rancière's regimes of arts is needed.

Rancière states that 'it is possible to distinguish, within the Western tradition, three major regimes of images' (p. 20). These are historically situated modes of creating and apprehending artworks, though they can also coexist. The first of these, and one that does not particularly impinge on my discussion here, is called an 'ethical regime of images,' though these images need not be plastic but include other forms of creation. In this regime, art does not have an autonomous existence but is rather subsumed under ethical questions to do with images, 'their origin (and consequently their truth content) and the question of their end or purpose, the uses they are put to and the effects they result in' (p. 20). This can be seen in the religious question of the images of the divine as well as Plato's mistrust of the arts in *The Republic*. However, Rancière calls this a regime of *images* since art itself is not fully recognisable: 'it is a matter of knowing in what way images' mode of being affects the *ethos*, the mode of being of individuals and communities. This question prevents "art" from individualizing itself as such' (p. 20).

The other two regimes Rancière names are the poetic or representative regime of the arts and the aesthetic regime of the arts. Rancière describes the representative regime of the arts as mimetic in a very specific way. In the representative regime, 'the mimetic principle is not at its core a normative principle stating that art must make copies resembling their models,' rather, 'it is [...] a pragmatic principle that isolates, within the general domain of the arts [...], certain particular forms of art that produce specific entities called imitations' (p. 21). Unlike in the ethical regime of images, art is not governed by its relationship to a concept of truth or to the uses it is put to (p. 21). Rather, there is a set of distinctive artistic regulations that exist outside the artwork and which the artwork must adhere to in order to become intelligible:

> partitions between the representable and the unrepresentable; the distinction between genres according to what is represented; principles for adapting forms of expression to genres and thus to the subject matter represented; the distribution of resemblances according to principles of verisimilitude, appropriateness, or correspondence.
>
> (p. 22)

It should be stressed that adherence to these rules literally determines whether the artwork is intelligible or not. Again, whilst this regime of arts is still operative in our cultural life, it is most clearly articulated in the Aristotelean classicism of the *ancien régime*.[52]

On the other hand, the aesthetic regime of the arts no longer depends upon outside regulations in order for the work to become intelligible; rather, 'it strictly refers to the specific mode of being of whatever falls within the domain of art, to the mode of being of the objects of art' (p. 22). In the aesthetic regime, art has become autonomous. That is to say, 'the aesthetic regime of the arts is the regime that strictly identifies art in the singular and frees it from any specific rule, from any hierarchy of the arts, subject matter, and genres,' and because of this, there is no longer any clear barrier between art and what lies outside art: '[I]t simultaneously establishes the autonomy of art and the identity of its forms with the forms that life uses to shape itself' (p. 23). For Rancière, the aesthetic regime of arts is a more accurate designation for what is vaguely designated modernity. It is historically related, then, not only to the avant-garde but also to the bourgeois revolution in the arts at the beginning of the nineteenth century and the emergence of realism. He is particularly clear that the early twentieth-century avant-garde tradition of non-representative art is not only autonomous art, but rather figurative representation and realism are also autonomous, for the criteria for the judgement of their representational practices exist only within the arts themselves. A particularly privileged site for the development of the autonomy of art is the realist novel:

> The leap outside of *mimēsis* [as defined in the representative regime of arts] is by no means the refusal of figurative representation. Furthermore, its inaugural moment has often been called *realism*, which does not in any way mean the valorization of resemblance but rather the destruction of the structures within which it functioned. Thus, novelistic realism is first of all the reversal of the hierarchies of representation (the primacy of the narrative over the descriptive or the hierarchy of subject matter) and the adoption of a fragmented or

proximate mode of focalization, which imposes raw presence to the detriment of the rational sequences of the story.

(p. 24)

This obviously differs from Auerbach, who traces different historical articulations of mimesis rather than limiting it to one aesthetically and historically particular aesthetic-political regime. Where Rancière and Auerbach do agree, though, is on the exemplary status of Flaubert. Flaubert is the exemplary articulation of a new form of realism: the 'writing style of small perceptions placed side by side,' the fragmented presentation of raw material over a rational sequence. [53] However, I wish to bring Rancière's arguments to bear particularly on the question of Napoleonic heroism.

The paintings by David and Ingres belong to representative and aesthetic regimes of art, respectively. In David's painting, the painting is presented within certain codes to make its political content fully intelligible. The royal figure is made the centre of the composition; it is a genre painting on a grand, historical scale. Similarly, David's painting of Napoleon with his hand in his waistcoat, which, as I have suggested, also subscribes to a set of gestural codes that belong to an older tradition of painting. On the other hand, Calasso essentially argues that Ingres's painting has become autonomous. Comparing the paintings of David and Ingres, then, one can see a shift from the representational to the aesthetic regime of the arts.

When Julien imitates Napoleon, when he re-fashions himself as Napoleon, when he represents himself as Napoleon, he is making himself intelligible through the codes of the representational regime of art. He believes that he can acquire meaning in the world through representing himself within a preordained tradition of representation. On the other hand, the novel itself has already broken with this tradition of representation. Auerbach may say that Stendhal is a figure of the eighteenth century in his analysis of the human heart, but this psychological insight is a series of discrete fragmented perceptions. This is clear throughout the novel but perhaps most of all in the final chapters. To take a typical example:

As he got into bed he discovered that the sheets were made of a coarse material. The scales fell from his eyes. Ah! I'm in a cell, he said to himself, because I've been condemned to death. That's only right.

(p. 504)

The psychological content emerges from small sense perceptions rather than a generalised theory of psychology.[54]

This, then, explains why Julien says that his novel is over before *The Red and the Black* is over. It is not, as Brooks and Rand argue, that the two endings need to be reconciled. Rather the novel recognises its own transitional movement. On the one hand, there is Julien who tries to represent himself as Napoleon, who tries to become a Napoleonic hero. In this novel, he follows codes of the appropriate way to represent himself, based on painterly models, on the primacy of a plot that will see him socially rise as Napoleon did. On the other hand, there is the novel of fragmented perceptions, the novel of realism. In this novel, there is no longer space for heroism because the novel has become autonomous, it has abandoned the hierarchies of subject matter that demand a hero. In the bifurcation of the novel, then, *The Red and the Black* recognises its own transition from the representational to the aesthetic regime of arts, and it continues beyond the end of Julien's novel in order to kill off this old order, which is no longer suitable for it. In this respect, it is telling that there are no longer epigraphs from seventeenth- and eighteenth-century writers in the final chapters of the novel. The chapters themselves have become autonomous from external regulations that are defined by the authors of an old regime of art.

Under the aesthetic regime of the arts, there can be no Napoleon except in the way that Ingres represents him, not as a hero but as just another photograph, as a strangely decentralised figure rather than as the figure at the zenith of a hierarchical model for heroism.

Under the aesthetic regime of the arts, the novel must execute its own hero in favour of the multiplicity of fragmented impressions of life. When Julien is executed, the narration states two things: 'Never had his head looked so poetic as at the moment it was due to fall,' and 'Everything happened simply, appropriately, and with no affectation on his part' (p. 527). When Julien is executed, he becomes poetic. Under the radical equality of subject matter in the aesthetic regime of the arts, the severed head becomes an aesthetic object which is directly compared in the same paragraph to 'the sweetest moments he had experienced in those early days in the woods of Vergy' (p. 527). And there is no affectation on Julien's part. As his execution becomes aesthetic, he ceases to imitate Napoleon.

Yet Napoleon continues to haunt the text, not as a hero, but as one paradigmatic example of a textual, reproducible, interchangeable, redeployable, re-contextualisable image. I have shown how these circulating images are the basis of the entire narrative trajectory of the novel through close readings of the passage where Napoleon's image is thrown into the public stream and the scenes where Julien Napoleonises himself, as well as the scene in the church. These scenes are key to the novel because they set the novel in motion, like the flow of the river from the country to the city. It is on the basis of circulating images of Napoleon, that do not conform to any hierarchy and can be thrown in the public stream or stored inside straw mattresses where they are mistaken for portraits of lovers, that this pioneering realist novel is built. It is not merely that these images circulate like others, but the image of Napoleon that haunts realism is the privileged circulating image on which Stendhal builds the realist novel. Perhaps this is where the proleptic potentiality of the novel's 1830 can be found.

Notes

1 Stendhal, *Le Rouge et le Noir: Chronique du XIXe siècle* (Paris: Gallimard, 1972), p. 439. Further references to the French text will be made parenthetically and refer to this edition. The two translations I have referred to render this slightly oddly given the importance of novels and other books for Julien's construction of his own subjectivity. Catherine Slater, whose translation will be the principal one I refer to offers, 'When you come to think about it, he reflected, my story's ended' (Stendhal, *The Red and the Black*, ed. and trans. Catherine Slater (Oxford: Oxford University Press, 2009), p. 626. Further references to this translation will be incorporated parenthetically into the body of the text. Roger Gard translates the phrase as '[w]ell, after all, thought he, my romance is at an end' (Stendhal, *The Red and the Black*, trans. Roger Gard (London: Penguin, 2002), p. 465). This rendering has a certain logic to it given that Julien then goes on to consider how he has 'been able to make himself loved' by Mathilde (Gard's translation, p. 465). Yet it seems to give less attention to the wider context of the chapter in which Julien discovers that so many of his youthful ambitions have been fulfilled. He has been given an aristocratic title, a commission in the Hussars, and been accepted by his aristocratic lover. This is not just the end of his romance as a lover but also the end of a novel. Of course, the French word for novel, 'roman,' hovers around the other meaning of 'romance' in English, 'a fictitious narrative, usually in prose, in which the settings or events depicted are remote from everyday life' (*OED*). *OED* notes the relationship between 'romance' and the Anglo-Norman word 'roman,' meaning a tale of chivalry in metrical verse, such as the *Roman de la Rose*. However, it is clear that whereas the French word evolved to take in the unchivalric novel which depicts everyday life, the meaning of the English 'romance' remains attached to fantastical narratives. This important echo remains in in Gard's translation, and, as he observes in his translator's preface, 'the reader ignorant of the original language is [...] shut off from the hovering possibilities and alternatives that might suggest themselves to someone who knows the language' (p. xxviii). Gard seems to have at least partially kept open the hovering possibilities.

2 Peter Brooks, *Reading for the Plot: Design and Intention in Narrative* (Cambridge, MA: Harvard University Press, 1992), p. 66.

3 Throughout this chapter, I call Julien's novel the narrative which follows the trajectory Julien imagines for himself as a Napoleonic hero, which he himself refers to as a novel, and Stendhal's novel the novel in its entirety, which narrates Julien's novel, but also undercuts it, ironically comments on it, and continues beyond it.

4 Some explanations of historical context are due here. An 'Ultra' is an ultra-royalist, a supporter of Bourbon power, and one who would thus be opposed to the 1830 revolution. Calling Bonaparte by his Corsican name is a way of expressing contempt and stressing his non-French origins. Voting against the Empire marks the surgeon out as a staunch supporter of the values of the 1789 revolution, and on page 8, it is said that he is 'both a Jacobin and a Bonapartist at once, according to the mayor.'

5 Slater's 'tyrannical' offers a nice echo of the first verse of the *Marseillaise*, though there is plenty of talk of 'les despotes sanguinaires' in the *Marseillaise* too.

6 Erich Auerbach, *Mimesis: The Representation of Reality in Western Literature*, trans. Willard R. Trask (Princeton University Press, 1974), p. 457. Further references to this work will be incorporated parenthetically into the body of the text. Whether or not this is wholly accurate is somewhat in the balance, particularly as regards one earlier novel I have discussed: Lermontov's *A Hero of Our Time*. It is striking that neither Pushkin nor Lermontov are discussed by Auerbach, and he is at pains to distance the Russian writers from the European tradition that this book describes. Auerbach argues that 'the enlightened, active bourgeoisie, with its assumption of economic and intellectual leadership, which everywhere else underlay modern culture in general and modern realism in particular, seems to have scarcely existed in Russia' in the early nineteenth century, and by the mid-nineteenth century they are only visible in the major cities, where they play a significantly different role because of the consolidation of state absolutism and the continuation of serfdom until 1861' (p. 521). In my own chapter on Russian writers, I have been at pains to stress this economic-cultural difference whilst also showing that the influence of western European writers allowed a form of politicised, realist writing which has something in common with the literature of the western European bourgeoisie.

7 Jacques Rancière, *The Future of the Image*, trans. Gregory Elliott (London: Verso, 2007), p. 120.

8 Christopher Prendergast, *The Order of Mimesis: Balzac, Stendhal, Nerval, Flaubert* (Cambridge: Cambridge University Press, 1986), p. 134.

9 Roger Pearson, *Stendhal's Violin: A Novelist and his Reader* (Oxford: Clarendon Press, 1988), p. 124.

10 Richard Terdiman, 'From City to Country: An Outline of *Fluvio-Critique*,' *NOVEL: A Forum of Fiction* 41 (2007), 53–72 (p. 53). Terdiman takes the literal reading of rivers and extends it to using them as an allegory for flows of time in which to discuss the ideology of representations of temporality in the nineteenth-century French novel.

11 Terdiman, p. 56. This is most obvious to him in his reading of Flaubert's *The Sentimental Education*, which begins with a reversal of the normal trajectory of moving towards Paris, with Frédéric Moreau leaving Paris (p. 60), but also in the way the other texts he discusses, *The Red and the Black* and Balzac's *The Peasants*, have their countryside framed by metropolitan viewers.

12 Terdiman, p. 56.

13 Terdiman, p. 63.

14 Karl Marx, 'The Eighteenth Brumaire of Louis Bonaparte,' trans. Ben Fowkes, in Political Writings, ed. David Fernbach, 3 vols. (Harmondsworth: Penguin/London: New Left Books, 1973), II, pp. 143–249 (p. 241).

15 Terdiman, p. 64.

16 This could be related to the complex vagaries of imperialism. Terdiman points out how the 'colony [...] increasingly guaranteed a mythicized stability of the nation' through "civilizing" missions that mirrored the homogenisation of the French countryside through capitalism' (p. 64). Though Terdiman points out this occurs later in French history, and though *The Red and the Black* predates the height of French colonialism, perhaps Napoleon's very specific case as a subject of a French colony could, speculatively, be brought to bear here without disregarding the fact that he came from minor aristocracy. If like the river, 'the Mediterranean and the Atlantic mediated between metropole and colony, between center and margin' (p. 64), then Napoleon, a minor aristocrat from a French colony, who never learnt to properly spell French, seems to occupy a curious place between being a privileged but nonetheless colonial subject and being the centre of the first French Empire.

17 Terdiman, p. 66. Italics in the original.
18 Gard's notes, p. 541.
19 Jacques Lacan, 'The Mirror Stage as Formative of the I Function as Revealed in Psychoanalytic Experience,' in *Écrits: The First Complete Edition in English*, trans. Bruce Fink with Héloïse Fink and Russell Grigg (New York: W.W. Norton, 2006), pp. 75–81 (p. 78).
20 Marx, 'Eighteenth Brumaire,' p. 147.
21 Could there be a sort of fetishistic disavowal here? Stendhal 'straddles the eighteenth and nineteenth centuries' as Stirling Haig observes (Stirling Haig, *The Red and the Black* (Cambridge: Cambridge University Press, 1989), p. 5). Perhaps there is a certain investment in the revolutionary tradition of the 1789 Revolution and the early Napoleon, which is seen to be fragmenting under the Empire, Restoration, and definitively bourgeois revolution of 1830. Thus *The Red and the Black* in its complex claims about the date it was written in relation to the 1830 revolution (I discuss this at more length later in this chapter) is able to acknowledge that fragmented revolution, whilst also fetishistically representing it as a more authentic or complete revolution by imagining it taking place through Julien-as-Napoleon. Of course, like the child's insistence on the mother's continuing possession of a penis in Freud's essay on fetishism, this desire comes under constant assault in the novel. I will discuss the significance of the castrating guillotine later in this chapter.
22 Michel Foucault, 'What is an Author?,' trans. Josué V. Harari, in *The Foucault Reader*, ed. Paul Rabinow (London: Penguin, 1991), pp. 101–120 (p. 119).
23 Sigmund Freud, 'The Uncanny,' in *Standard Edition of the Complete Psychological Works*, ed. and trans. James Strachey, 24 vols. (London: Vintage, 2001), XVII, pp. 218–256 (p. 241).
24 Freud, pp. 234–235.
25 Freud, p. 221.
26 Freud, pp. 235, 238.
27 Roger Pearson, 'Introduction,' in *The Red and the Black*, ed. and trans., Catherine Slater, pp. ix–xxiii (p. xi). Pearson gives an account of the sources of the novel pp. xi-xiii. Stendhal was not an inventor of plots: 'In a marginal novel to *Lucien Leuwen* he wrote that he could not carry off a witty dialogue and think of the background at the same time: "Whence the advantage of working with an already given story, like Julien Sorel"' (Haig, p. 15). Haig gives a detailed account of Stendhal's sources for *The Red and the Black*, pp. 14–26.
28 Freud, p. 231.
29 Pearson, 'Introduction,' p. ix.
30 Pearson, *Stendhal's Violin*, p. 74.
31 I echo here the 'hanging' uncertainty of revolutionary potentiality in literature described by Paul de Man in 'Wordsworth and Hölderlin,' trans. Timothy Bahti, in *The Rhetoric of Romanticism* (New York: Columbia University Press, 1984), pp. 47–65.
32 Brooks, p. 64.
33 Nicholas Rand, '*The Red and the Black*, Author of Stendhal Pseudonyms and Cryptonyms of Beyle,' *Romanic Review* 80 (1989), 391–403 (p. 391, Fn. 2).
34 Rand, p. 391.
35 Rand, pp. 396–397. The relevant passage in Slater's translation is on p. 529. Rand also observes that the same note includes a comment on morals in England and America, which connects back to the spurious Hobbes quotation that begins Chapter 1 of Book I. This is further bolstered by a remarkable series of puns that Rand offers of Verrières, including '*vers hier*, towards yesterdays,' which 'can be linked to the idea that the novel's plot is justified by

the rise and the fall of Napoleon Bonaparte' (p. 398, Fn.8). Rand also puns on *verra*, 'the third person future of the verb *voir* (to see),' *vérité* (truth), which connects with Book I's epigraph, 'The truth, the truth in all its harshness' (Stendhal, p. 3), and *verre* (glass) (Rand, p. 398), both of which connect with questions of realism that I explore elsewhere in this chapter.

36 Rand, p. 401.
37 Rand, p. 402, Fn. 12.
38 Ann Jefferson offers an insightful reading of this passage, identifying what she calls 'mimesis [...] tangled in a paradox' and the inability of any reader to authenticate the claims of realism in the novel, in her *Reading Realism in Stendhal* (Cambridge: Cambridge University Press, 1988), p. 123.
39 Pearson, *Stendhal's Violin*, p. 127.
40 Arline Meyer, 'Re-dressing Classical Statuary: The Eighteen-Century "Hand-in-Waistcoat" Portrait,' *The Art Bulletin* 77 (1995), 45–63 (p. 45).
41 Meyer, p. 47.
42 Meyer, p. 61.
43 Meyer, pp. 61–63. Meyer also states, without explanation or attribution, that Napoleon's gesture is a 'quasi-military emblem' (p. 63) despite the fact that she has stressed its versatility throughout her article.
44 Haig, p. 41.
45 The language of 'editions' in curiously similar to Marx's 'Eighteenth Brumaire,' when he describes the Napoleonic Revival of Napoleon III as a 'second edition' (p. 146). This view of Napoleon ultimately and paradoxically holding the country back from its bourgeois destiny despite his modernising reforms, which the critics of Napoleon in this passage of Stendhal do not mention, is echoed in very different terms by Marx. According to Marx, Napoleon's support for the peasants, who were an atomised social class, prevented the creation of class solidarity amongst them and resulted in them delegating all the power to the executive, which instituted a new monarchy. See the 'Eighteenth Brumaire,' pp. 239–240.
46 Roberto Calasso, *La Folie Baudelaire*, trans. Alistair McEwen (London: Penguin, 2013), p. 112. Further references to this text will be incorporated parenthetically into the body of the text
47 There is a full-length study of David's and Ingres's paintings of Napoleon in Todd Porterfield and Susan L. Siegfried, *Staging Empire: Napoleon, Ingres, and David* (University Park: Pennsylvania State University Press, 2006). In relation to my claims about Ingres here, the authors talk of a 'scattered visuality of details and emphasis on surface design,' which results in a 'disembodiment of the emperor' (pp. 11, 13). They relate this to changes in the popular understanding of the body politic after the French Revolution, which works in tandem with some of my claims about the dispersal of heroism in the bourgeois epoch.
48 Walter Benjamin, 'Franz Kafka: On the tenth anniversary of his death,' in *Illuminations*, ed. Hannah Arendt, trans. Harry Zorn (London: Pimlico, 1999), 108–135 (p. 115).
49 Porterfield and Siegfried, p. 107.
50 I am here drawing principally from his *The Politics of Aesthetics: The Distribution of the Sensible* and *The Future of the Image*. The quotation and ideas about terminology above are from Jacques Rancière, *The Politics of Aesthetics: The Distribution of the Sensible*, trans. Gabriel Rockhill (London: Continuum, 2011), p. 20. Further references to *The Politics of Aesthetics* will be incorporated parenthetically into the body of the chapter.

51 Jacques Rancière, *Aisthesis: Scenes from the Aesthetic Regime of Art*, trans. Zakir Paul (London: Verso, 2013), p. 49. Rancière's reading is on pp. 39–53.
52 For an extended reading of the operations of the representative regime of arts, see Rancière's discussion of Corneille's *Oedipe* in *The Future of the Image*, pp. 112–118.
53 Rancière, *The Future of the Image*, p. 125.
54 In *The Aesthetic Unconscious*, trans. Debra Keates and James Swenson (Cambridge: Polity, 2010), Rancière argues that the achievement of Freud is to systematise the study of the heterogeneous aesthetic fragments which form subjectivity into a non-normative psychological methodology.

4 Napoleon at Vanity Fair
Costumes of Exiled Heroism

'And so it is that the French Emperor comes in to perform a part in this domestic comedy of Vanity Fair which we are now playing, and which would never have been enacted without the intervention of this august mute personage'

Vanity Fair, Chapter XVIII

The critical response to *Vanity Fair* has long recognised the interconnection of Thackeray's complex representational practices, the issue of class, and Napoleonic heroism. The relationship between the three elements of this literary constellation, and their significance for the novel's politics, have been the subject of intense debate rather than consensus between critics. John Peck observes that *Vanity Fair* depicts the last days of aristocratic rule in Britain, and the consolidation of bourgeois political power and culture:

> By the end of *Vanity Fair*, most readers feel they have moved from Waterloo to a post-Reform Act world. This is more than a matter of chronology: a complex case about democratisation, about a shift towards middle-class values, is articulated in the second half of the novel.[1]

Peck's reading of *Vanity Fair*, in many ways, pre-empts the broader argument of this book; as the bourgeoisie reaches the end of its heroic phase and it consolidates its power, there is a shift away from heroism towards the social stability of a conservative bureaucratic and family life: 'At the opening of *Vanity Fair*, the army is the only profession open to young middle-class men who are intent on bettering themselves. But as peace takes over from war, there is a growing sense of a professional class.'[2] That Thackeray depicts this shift is not in doubt, but the critics diverge on the novel's political stance in relation to this shift. For Peck, despite a 'contempt' for the bourgeoisie, which reaches 'unrelieved disdain,' Thackeray's novel ultimately consolidates middle-class values and power: '[B]y the end of the novel Thackeray himself has begun to acquire something of a

DOI: 10.4324/9781003160168-5

middle-class outlook.'[3] This view is shared by Mary Hammond's historicist reading of the novel which firmly positions it in relationship to contemporary political and press debates about Waterloo, militarism, and the fate of Napoleon. Hammond sees the novel as working towards class integration via a critique of heroism. For her, the novel 'subtly integrated a revisioned memory of Waterloo with the vigorously imperialist but resolutely individual middle-class ambitions of the novel's present.'[4] And whilst Patricia Marks is more sceptical of Thackeray's accommodation to the new social order, she argues that *Vanity Fair* is a satire of despair, where the ability of language to speak the truth has become so unstable that social vice can no longer be named for what it is. Marks argues that Thackeray associates linguistic duplicity with the French language, and thus that in the novel, 'the British have in reality lost the war by enthroning Napoleon at home linguistically.'[5] Ultimately, in Marks's reading, linguistic duplicity becomes so pervasive that all language is essentially corrupt, untrustworthy, and false, and satire's only option is 'to fall silent.'[6] If Thackeray is reluctant to integrate with the new social order in this account, he at least capitulates to it. All three of these accounts betray a marked hostility to the character of Becky Sharp, and this hostility seems to go beyond the critique of her as a fictional textual construct. Indeed, there is a tendency in criticism of *Vanity Fair* to treat Becky as a real person, even to imply that her textual being is somehow an affront to the critic. I discuss next the text's production of Becky's existence beyond the limits of the text itself and the disruptive power of this textual move. Becky is depicted as the leading edge of the bourgeois values that Thackeray comes to integrate and also a dangerous Napoleonic invader: 'Language is as bankrupt as Becky';[7] or '[n]ot just a Napoleon invading society, Becky is the heart of that society's hypocrisy writ large in the language of commerce.'[8]

   Both of these formulations depict Becky as a capitalist figure and (unconsciously) imply a high valuation of the pre-existing society that Becky disrupts. On the other hand, critics such as Andrew Miller and David Musselwhite have argued that Becky's disruptive energy is not the bearer of capitalist values but a force which undoes both the aristocratic values of the novel's first half and the bourgeois values of its second. I outline their arguments at greater length below, and throughout this chapter, I build on their responses to the novel. It is indisputable that Becky is associated with Napoleon in *Vanity Fair* and that this is in some way related to Thackeray's attempt to grapple with the emergence of a stable bourgeois society, but what does her identification with Napoleon signify? Ultimately, not the consolidation of bourgeois society but a force for its undoing. To scramble the codes, to disrupt dominant representational practices, is not to represent moral bankruptcy, except from the perspective of the society which stabilises those codes.

   It is the contention of this chapter that in Thackeray's *Vanity Fair*, which is subtitled, 'A Novel Without a Hero,' Thackeray reactivates memories of Napoleon in order to attempt to articulate a notion of heroism, real heroism, adequate for the unheroic post-Napoleonic era.[9] Andrew Miller notes the 'many Napoleonic insurrections imaged and achieved, on the domestic front of [Thackeray's] novels.'[10] Whilst I suggest that the historical figure Napoleon has become an object of parody, he is also re-envisioned afresh in the domestic sphere in this novel. I suggest in this chapter that this form of domestic Napoleonic heroism comes closer to disrupting the forces of high capitalism than the previous models of heroism that I have discussed in this book. I begin by setting out some mutations of the cultural image of Napoleon between 1806 and 1847, focusing particularly on the change in the perception of Napoleon after his exile and suggesting that Napoleon becomes a parodic figure for Thackeray whilst still being haunted by heroic possibility. I relate the mutations of Napoleonic heroism to mutations of capitalism by reading Marx's discussion of mutations of heroism in the rise of Napoleon III in 'The Eighteenth Brumaire of Louis Bonaparte.' I suggest, following Marx, that there is an absence of heroism under capitalism and in *Vanity Fair* but that Marx sets the stage for a reactivation of heroism under capitalism which could bring revolutionary change. Perhaps this absence of heroism in Thackeray and Marx suggests the potential for a heroine. I conclude by pointing to some specific instances in *Vanity Fair* of the reactivation of Napoleon as heroic in the character of Becky Sharp, who Thackeray explicitly reveals to be a heroic mutation of Napoleonic heroism, haunted by the past but able to suggest revolutionary change for the future. I connect her destruction of signifying and representational systems to the haunting revolutionary energy of Napoleon.

I

On the 13 October 1806, very soon after he had completed writing *Phenomenology of Spirit*, G.W.F. Hegel wrote to his friend Niethammer about the arrival of Napoleon Bonaparte and the French Army in Jena. In this famous letter, Hegel describes seeing Napoleon:

> I saw the Emperor – this world-soul (*diese Weltseele*) – riding out of the city on reconnaissance. It is indeed a wonderful sensation to see such an individual, who, concentrated here at a single point, astride a horse, reaches out over the world and masters it.

Hegel goes on to describe Napoleon as an 'extraordinary man, whom it is impossible not to admire.'[11] Shlomo Avineri observes that Hegel's admiration of Napoleon was 'much more than mere infatuation [...] which was quite common among intellectuals at the time.'[12] Hegel's vision of Napoleon as a super-human figure, a being that can dominate all time, through history, and space from a single point, suggests a heroism comparable only to ancient epics, where the hero's experience is, in Lukács's phrase, that 'the world is wide and yet it is like a home.'[13] Avineri points to another fragment in Hegel, which he connects to Hegel's encounter with Napoleon since it is also from the Jena period and links 'philosophy and the actual world' by showing 'philosophical principles being realised in the political and historical realm.'[14] In this passage, which recalls modern warfare in a much wider historical frame, Hegel asserts that

> through consciousness spirit intervenes in the way the world is ruled. This is its infinite tool – then there are bayonets, cannon, bodies. But the banner [of philosophy] and the soul of its commander is spirit. Neither bayonets, nor money, neither this trick nor that, are the ruler. They are necessary like the cogs and wheels in a clock, but their soul is time and spirit that subordinates matter to its laws. An *Iliad* is not thrown together at random, neither is a great deed composed of bayonets and cannon: it is spirit that is the composer.[15]

Though it is important to differentiate Hegel's description of Napoleon as a world-soul from the notion of world-spirit (*der Weltgeist*), according to Hegel, Napoleon is the very motive force of history. In the similarity of the terms 'world-soul' and 'world-spirit,' there is the possibility of a slippage. The fragment above is markedly subjectless; there is no motive subject of history, but rather Spirit (*Geist*) that moves history from outside human subjectivity.[16] Nonetheless, Hegel's earlier description of Napoleon, put alongside this passage, suggests Napoleon as subject (rather than object), as motive force of history since for Hegel Napoleon is an embodiment of *Geist* itself, he is a world-soul, a driver of history, because he is beyond the bounds of the individual subject who is usually the object of history. Whereas Hegel suggests in the second passage that Spirit itself is the 'composer,' the motive force of history, he describes Napoleon as the figure who 'masters' the world. Napoleon is the subject in whom Spirit intervenes in the world; he is the military commander who composes the bayonets and cannons into a historical event; he is the epic poet who records his own history too. He is the closest that it seems human subjectivity can come to its own bounds before it becomes the movement of history itself. The deeds of Napoleon are imagined alongside the *Iliad*, which is explicitly paralleled with the modern warfare of bayonets and canons. Napoleon, in this moment of Hegel's imagination, embodies an epic heroism at the height of modernity. Napoleon, for Hegel, masters not only space but, through his command of history, time as well; he is a force of modernity, bringing about the modern state in the image of a hero from antiquity, a hero absolutely at home in the world because he is the world. Alexandre Koèjeve, in his *Introduction to the Reading of Hegel*, goes so far as to argue that Hegel sees the Battle of

Jena as 'the end of History properly so called.' For Koèjeve, this means that all that remains of history is an 'extension in space of the universal revolutionary force actualized in France by Robespierre-Napoleon.'[17] We may question the empirical veracity of this claim, but it is certainly useful for thinking about literature that thinks about the implications of the Napoleonic moment. It sees post-Napoleonic history as a series of Napoleonic afterlives, which attempt to repeat his revolutionary form. This afterlife, however, is subject to many vagaries.

Because Napoleon is of such world-historical importance, he invites novelistic representations, but in the examples I discuss in Thackeray, these become novelistic images of parody. Napoleon is no longer the master of space and time but becomes subject to the novelist's own mastery of space and time. Napoleon is no longer a figure filled with the world-spirit but becomes much flatter. Napoleon becomes akin to the novelistic images of language that Bakhtin discusses. For Bakhtin, the competing discourses of the novel, which originate outside it, when they are incorporated into the novel, in 'no way function [...] as the *primary means of representation*' but have 'become the object of representation, or more precisely of a representation that is parodied and stylised.'[18] In the passage from Hegel, Napoleon himself becomes the primary means of representation of Spirit, of history. By the time he reaches Thackeray's novel, he has become a parody of Spirit.

One way to illustrate this is to turn to Thackeray's own eyewitness account of Napoleon only ten years later. On 17 December 1816, when Thackeray was five years old, he was shipped, without his parents, from India to England on a ship named, curiously enough for Thackeray's later interest in him, the *Prince Regent*. During its journey, on 8 March the following year, the *Price Regent* stopped on St Helena where the child Thackeray saw Napoleon in exile.[19] Thackeray relates his memories of this visit, much later in his life, in *The Four Georges* (1855–1856, published 1860):

> Our ship touched at an island on the way home, where my black servant took me for a long walk over rocks and hills until we reached a garden, where we saw a man walking. 'That is he,' said the black man: 'that is Bonaparte! He eats three sheep every day, and all the little children he can lay hands on!' There were people in the British dominions besides that poor Calcutta serving-man, with an equal horror of the Corsican ogre.[20]

This passage is obviously parodic. In Thackeray's imperialist discourse, any awe of Napoleon becomes a joke at the expense of someone deemed a racial inferior, and any white Briton who similarly continues to revere Napoleon becomes the butt of the joke simultaneously with that 'poor Calcutta serving-man.' Nonetheless, in 1817, Napoleon still seems to bear the traces of the memory of Napoleon as Hegel saw him. The parodic Napoleon is haunted by the heroic Napoleon. True, he is no longer the spirit of history but nor has he become utterly impotent in this parody. Rather, he has become the stuff of fairy tales, an 'ogre' with a prodigious appetite who eats children and gargantuan quantities of mutton. He echoes the folk heroes of Rabelais, too, in this respect, though in a decarnivalised world. For Hegel, Napoleon seems to embody the epic past and modernity simultaneously. In 1817, Thackeray's focus has shifted. Thackeray presents Napoleon as embodying a transitional moment between the past of folk tales and legends and a modernity where such archaic heroic power is laughed at. Napoleon represents here the transitional folk tales and early novels that come before the rise of the novel proper, though we are again reminded of his modernity by his being placed in a specifically colonial context. There are traces of heroic scale in Napoleon. He becomes a sort of folk villain without the positive connotations given to him by Hegel. Nonetheless, it is worth remembering that the seemingly negative folk context, even in the early nineteenth century, can represent the possibility of utopian historical change. Bakhtin observes in *Rabelais and His World* that

> the grotesque, including the Romantic form [where the negative pole is emphasised at the expense of its regenerating possibilities], discloses the potentiality of an entirely different world, of another order, another way of life. It leads men out of the confines of the apparent (false) unity of the indisputable and stable.[21]

Through the servant's invocation of this monstrous, rapacious Napoleon, the supposedly impotent, safe confines of his exile are drawn into question. The image of the old eating the young is reminiscent of the story of Saturn, of the Golden Age, and of historical potentiality.[22] The folk villain and folk hero for Bakhtin are not opposite poles but suggest each other.

This multi-faceted view of Napoleon was not limited to a single moment. The episode had obvious importance to Thackeray for the rest of his life. He returns to Napoleon over and over again, towards the end of his life in *The Four Georges* and in his first major novel, *Vanity Fair*.

That *Vanity Fair* is written in a post-Napoleonic age, an era when the heroic potential of Napoleon is exhausted, is apparent from the fact that Napoleon, for Thackeray, has become a novelised, parodic image. This sets up two overlapping versions of the Napoleonic for Thackeray, that of the persisting heroic of history and that of parody. In *Vanity Fair*, he rewrites his own childhood experience in very different terms, giving it to Jos Sedley. It is worth quoting this passage at some length:

> Our worthy fat friend Joseph Sedley returned to India not long after his escape from Brussels. Either his furlough was up, or he dreaded

to meet any witnesses of his Waterloo flight. However it might be, he went back to his duties in Bengal, very soon after Napoleon had taken up his residence at St. Helena, where Jos saw the ex-Emperor. To hear Mr. Sedley talk on board ship you would have supposed that it was not the first time he and the Corsican had met, and that the civilian had bearded the French general at Mount St. John. He had a thousand anecdotes about the famous battles; he knew the position of every regiment, and the loss which each had incurred. He did not deny that he had been concerned in those victories – that he had been with the army, and carried dispatches for the Duke of Wellington. And he described what the duke did and said on every conceivable moment of the day of Waterloo, with such an accurate knowledge of his grace's sentiments and proceedings, that it was clear he must have been by the conqueror's side throughout the day; though, as a non-combatant, his name was not mentioned in the public documents relative to the battle. Perhaps he actually worked himself up to believe that he had been engaged with the army; certain it is that he made a prodigious sensation for some time at Calcutta, and was called Waterloo Sedley during the whole of his subsequent stay in Bengal.

(pp. 482–483)

Whereas according to Thackeray's memories, in 1817, Napoleon retained the traces of folk heroism, by 1847, he has become nothing but part of the means of parody. He has become not even parodic in his own right, but rather instrumental to the parodying of Jos Sedley. On St Helena in 1817, he was still an object of attention, as he remains for Jos himself. However, in the context of this passage, Napoleon retains a heroic stature himself only insofar as he is the adversary against which Jos can make the parodied attempt to define his own heroism. Even in Thackeray's 1817 anecdote, Napoleon retains demonic power in his voracious appetite. Here it is implied that the joke hero can make believe that he has defeated Napoleon himself. What is more, Napoleon's own heroism is increasingly subordinated to the Duke of Wellington's heroism. Wellington comes to take the position of historical hero. Jos's lies about what Wellington did at 'every conceivable moment of the day' suggests Wellington masters time that no moment of the time of Waterloo is conceivable without Wellington doing something in it, as though every single moment he exists in is a heroic moment, a moment that demands to be recorded and disseminated to prove that the witness is a witness to history. Napoleon on the other hand becomes spatially restrained. Exile flattens time into the deadness of captivity. For Napoleon, history is over – a quite different end of history from the one Hegel imagined.

It should not be forgotten though that Thackeray's 1817 reminiscence is written a significant time after *Vanity Fair* even if it recalls a period long before its composition. It is clear that in spite of the parody and insignificance that comes to surround Napoleon at moments, his memory still looms large and is able to reactivate memories of heroism. And whilst he may be threatened by parody, which kills him off as a heroic figure, Napoleon also continues to insistently haunt *Vanity Fair* as a heroic figure and model for heroism.

II

Writing a few years after the publication of *Vanity Fair*, in 'The Eighteenth Brumaire of Louis Bonaparte,' Marx recognises the inadequacy of Napoleon in the era of high capitalism.[23] As David E. Musselwhite points out, Thackeray 'lacks Marx's political insight but what is striking is the way in which they seem to share a number of metaphorical and stylistic obsessions,' particularly to do with heroism and history.[24] Musselwhite describes the links and disjunctions between Marx's and Thackeray's conceptions of heroism and history, with a particular a focus on the rhetorical strategies used to depict history itself. In what follows, I wish to draw closer comparisons between Thackeray and Marx with reference to the notion of heroism, particularly in the depiction of Napoleon.[25] In Marx's famous essay, he describes the political reaction which is instantiated at the behest of the Parisian bourgeoisie in order to stabilise the market after the destabilising effects of the democratic revolution of February 1848. This bourgeois reaction ultimately brought to power the dictatorial Napoleon III. In his description of Napoleon III, Marx makes particular reference to the inadequacy of the image of Napoleon for the bourgeois epoch. Marx describes Napoleon (along with Robespierre, Danton, and some other revolutionaries of the late eighteenth century) as 'the heroes of the old French Revolution.'[26] Echoing the sentiments of Hegel, Marx sees Napoleon having a particular power of world-historical momentum:

> [T]hen came Napoleon. Within France he created the conditions which first made possible the development of free competition, the exploitation of the land by small peasant property, and the application of the unleashed productive power of the nation's industries. Beyond the borders of France he swept away feudal institutions so far as this was necessary for the provision on the European continent of an appropriate modern environment for bourgeois society in France.
>
> (p. 147)

Napoleon, then, maintains the same heroic status for Marx as he does for Hegel. However, Marx translates this into historical materialist terms. And this is the important point. In contrast to Kojève's influential reading of Hegel, which sees Napoleon as both ultimately trans-historical and, thus, the very end of history, Marx recognises the continuation of history and Napoleon's historical limitability and mutability: 'Once the new social formation had been established, the antediluvian colossi [Napoleon, along with the Jacobins] disappeared' (p. 147).

Marx also observes that both the French Revolution of 1789 and the political formations that followed, up until the collapse of the Napoleonic Empire, imitated Roman cultural and political formations:

> But unheroic as bourgeois society is, it still required heroism, self-sacrifice, terror, civil war and battles in which whole nations were engaged, to bring it into the world. And its gladiators found in the stern classical traditions of the Roman republic the ideals, art forms and self-deceptions they needed in order to hide from themselves the limited bourgeois content of their struggles and to maintain their enthusiasm at the high level appropriate to great historical tragedy.
>
> (p. 148)

Marx claims that bourgeois society needed heroism, that heroism must be at least seen to operate to bring this society into being even when it seems to have disappeared and that this is achieved by imitating ancient Rome. However, once bourgeois society is stabilised, this heroic orientation collapses: bourgeois society, under first the Bourbon restoration and then under the July Monarchy, 'was no longer aware that the ghosts of Rome had watched over its cradle, since it was wholly absorbed in the production of wealth and the peaceful struggle of economic competition' (p. 148). In the British context, the stable bourgeois society that Thackeray depicts is created by the 1832 Reform Act, which enfranchised a section of the male urban bourgeoisie, and the 1846 Importation Act, which repealed the corn laws, marking a victory for free trade capitalism and drastically reducing the potential for popular revolution.

It is in this context that Marx's famous dictum, which begins his essay, must be read: 'Hegel remarks somewhere that all great events and characters of world history occur, so to speak, twice. He forgot to add: the first time as tragedy, the second as farce' (p. 146). For Marx, when 'the adventurer,' Louis Bonaparte (Napoleon III), hides 'his commonplace and repulsive countenance beneath the iron death-mask of Napoleon' (p. 148), when the revolutionaries of the late 1840s dressed themselves up as the former heroic revolutionaries, they were no longer heroic. In the former revolutions, states Marx,

> the resurrection of the dead served to exalt the new struggles, rather than to parody the old, to exaggerate the given task in the imagination, rather than to flee from solving it in reality, and to recover the spirit of revolution, rather than to set its ghost walking again.
>
> (p. 148)

These former revolutionaries were still establishing the whole order of bourgeois society, but once bourgeois society is established, revolutions serve only to further entrench the most barbaric aspects of bourgeois society: '[I]nstead of *society* conquering a new content for itself, it only seems that the *state* has returned to its most ancient form, the unashamedly simple rule of the military sabre and the clerical cowl' (p. 149, Marx's italics), however now to defend bourgeois rather than feudal interests. Perhaps, indeed, Hegel was not so wrong in suggesting that Napoleon leads us to the end of history, but importantly, Marx modifies what this might mean. It is not the heroic energy and actuality of Napoleon that is the end of history but his passing and the attendant ossifying of bourgeois society: 'heroes without deeds of heroism, history without events; a course of development apparently only driven forward by the calendar, and made wearisome by the constant repetition of the same tensions and relaxations' (p. 170). What Marx describes here, in a more pessimistic mode than his central revolutionary thesis, is the end of heroism under bourgeois society and therefore the end of history itself since class struggle has ended in the complacent ascendancy of the bourgeoisie. Elsewhere, of course, Marx sees the engine of history being restarted by the proletariat's class struggle with the bourgeoisie. In this context, it is only a reactivated heroism, haunted by the heroism of the past but newly revolutionary, that can restart the movement of history. Marx outlines an absence of heroism in bourgeois society but reveals a framework where future revolutionary heroism could sweep this away, haunted by the idea of a heroism of the past which it imitates in a mutated form for new historical conditions. I will return to this notion at the end of this chapter by suggesting that Becky Sharpe in *Vanity Fair* represents a renewed revolutionary heroism that is haunted by Napoleon's heroism, just as Napoleon's heroism was haunted by the heroism of ancient Rome. For now, however, I will discuss how *Vanity Fair* registers the absence of heroism in bourgeois society in order to set the stage for its renewal.

This characterisation of the surrounding historical European moment in Marx helps to contextualise Thackeray's orientation towards history and heroism in *Vanity Fair*. Thackeray subtitles *Vanity Fair* 'a novel without a hero,' and John Sutherland notes that *Novel without a Hero* was one of the provisional titles before Thackeray decided on its final title.[27] Thackeray continues to stress the absence of a hero in the text of the novel. He advises his reader to 'take warning and go elsewhere' if they admire 'the great and heroic in life and novels' (p. 8), illustrated with a particularly wonderful caricature of a bourgeois gentleman of leisure reading the novel (Figure 4.1).

Furthermore, though the novel is set during the Napoleonic Wars and their immediate aftermath, the events that both Hegel and Marx see as heroic are not depicted. Thackeray famously avoids showing the Battle of Waterloo, stating, 'We do not claim to rank among the military novelists.

Figure 4.1 William Makepeace Thackeray, *Untitled Illustration to* Vanity Fair, *Chapter I [Caricature of a Bourgeois Reader]*. Public Domain. Source: https://en.wikisource.org/wiki/Vanity_Fair_(Thackeray)

Our place is with the non-combatants' (p. 361) and later separating himself from the epic and Classical past that both Hegel and Marx associate with heroism, 'from the story of Troy down to to-day, poetry has always chosen a soldier for a hero' (p. 372).[28] *Vanity Fair*, though, is obviously prose and thus distances itself from the epic tradition. Furthermore, the narrator reflects, 'I wonder is it because men are cowards in heart that they admire bravery so much, and place military valour so far beyond every other quality for reward and worship?' (p. 372). Yet, with this question it is implied that these very qualities of heroism, amongst men at least, are impossible, precisely because they are cowards – are only available in certain forms of fictional narrative, whose own time too has passed away. Alongside this scepticism about heroism is a shift in the novel's attitude to history. As Sutherland notes, with the passing of Napoleon, the sense of history itself in *Vanity Fair* begins to pass away. Heroism drives history according to Marx, and without heroism history itself begins to wind down, the novel struggles to recognise proletarian mass history:

> [I]n the second half of the novel, after Waterloo, the historical background to *Vanity Fair* fades somewhat. As we follow the fortunes of Thackeray's characters over this most troubled of eras, one has the odd impression of social tranquillity [...]. *Vanity Fair* is blind to Peterloo, corn law riots, industrial revolution, reform agitation.[29]

Musselwhite offers a slight corrective to this view, convincingly arguing that the second half of the novel, with its supposed turn to satire, does not suppress any history whatsoever, but rather represents the historical

Figure 4.2 William Makepeace Thackeray, Untitled Illustration to Vanity Fair, *Chapter VI [Caricature of Regency Fashions].* Public Domain. Source: https://en.wikisource.org/wiki/Vanity_Fair_(Thackeray)

stoppage of history, bringing into line Marx's views of heroism and history and the depiction of history in *Vanity Fair*: '[F]or all its ostensible suppression of history, *Vanity Fair* is historical through and through – it enacts the impasse of 1848 just as Chapter 51 enacts the collapse of tragedy into farce.'[30] For Thackeray, then, the movement of history after Waterloo comes to a stop, and stable bourgeois society, from which Thackeray comes and to which he addresses the novel, need no longer pay attention to these agitations except to repress them.[31] Thackeray, in a nation of marked economic and political stability, when compared to the rest of Europe, is able to retroactively empty that past time which still had historical potentiality.[32] Not only has the movement of history stopped in the present in which Thackeray writes, but he also transfers this to the past that he writes about. This is best illustrated not by a direct reference to political history but with a transformation that Thackeray enacts within another frame of historical reference (Figure 4.2):

> It was the author's intention, faithful to history, to depict all the characters of this tale in their proper costumes, as they wore them at the commencement of the century. But when I remember the appearance of people in those days, and that an officer and a lady were actually habited like this –

I have not the heart to disfigure my heroes and heroines by costumes so hideous; and have, on the contrary, engaged a model of
rank dressed according to the present fashion.

(pp. 899–900)

This passage was an author's footnote in the first edition but removed
in later ones and would have appeared on page 75 of the text as it
stands, towards the end of Chapter VI. [33] It is very intriguing and not a
little strange with its references to heroes and heroines in what is osten-
sibly a novel without a hero, and the very conscious anachronism in
what begins (at least) as a historical novel. I think it can be explained
by recognising the ideological work that this passage is doing in comparison to the nearly contemporaneous 'The Eighteenth Brumaire of
Louis Bonaparte.' Thackeray is deheroising the past by dressing it in the
clothes of the present whilst turning the fuller heroism of the past into a
laughingstock. However, this passage also works in the opposite direction. Faced with a non-history without heroes, Thackeray attempts to
resurrect heroism. The passage simultaneously marks the subjects of the
Napoleonic War (but not, here, Napoleon himself) as heroic and brings
this heroism into the present (the mid-1840s) by borrowing 'names slogans and costumes so as to stage the new world-historical scene in this
venerable disguise' (p. 146). In order to continue to maintain the illu-
sion that a dead bourgeois stability is heroic, Thackeray, that bourgeois
novelist, must populate the costumes of the present with the heroes and
heroines of the past. The heroes and heroines of a more historically full
age appear in the costumes of the present in order to make the present
look more heroic. This strategy works ambivalently; it is a part of the
deheroising of the Napoleonic past; it also registers the Napoleonic past
haunting the present. The footnote suggests a comical discomfort about
finding that the heroism of the Napoleonic era continues to haunt the
contemporary present and attempts to find a way to accommodate the
Napoleon past in the unheroic present. Thackeray accommodates the
heroism of the past in the unheroic present by dressing his characters
up in the fashions of the 1840s so that they look like they are heroes
for now, rather than heroes in the Napoleonic past in which they are
otherwise situated.

Does this not present a contradiction though? Thackeray, as we have
seen, is a novelist who registers the absence of heroism but is here attempting to resurrect it. He avows that his is a novel without heroes, he presents
history as becoming non-historical and unheroic, and yet he simultaneously attempts to make it full, to fill the present with heroes. This possibility of heroism is what leaves the stage open for Becky Sharp, as I discuss
later in this chapter, but Becky's heroism is achieved against a backdrop
of non-heroism. The other uses of the word hero in the novel tend to
be heavily ironic, such as in this description of Jos Sedley at Waterloo:
'"Don't try and frighten *me*," the hero cried from his bed' (p. 371), or that

of 'Young Tandyman [a junior officer in Rawdon Crawley's mess], a hero of seventeen, laboriously endeavouring to get up a pair of moustachios' (p. 697). Elsewhere characters are heroic only to other characters in the novel, and thus treated with irony, such as George Osborne, about whom Amelia believes 'there never was such a face or such a hero' (p. 57, a sentiment repeated on p. 213). Thackeray's heroes are unheroic even in the Napoleonic age that Hegel and Marx claim is heroic.

This ironic heroism, which attests to the absence of heroism, particularly adheres to capitalist characters, representatives of the coming unheroic world in which Thackeray is writing. It is notable that up until the Waterloo episode, after which the novel becomes relatively ahistorical, of the male characters it is only George Osborne and Jos Sedley who are referred to as heroes. Jos Sedley is depicted as a representative of a particularly aggressive form of imperialist capitalism:

> He was in the East India Company's Civil Service, and his name appeared, at the period of which we write, in the Bengal division of the East India Register, as collector of Boggley Wollah, an honourable and lucrative post, as everybody knows.
>
> (p. 27)

As Andrew Miller notes, he is particularly associated with the commodities which envelop his person at his first introduction: 'buckskins and hessian boots, with several immense neckcloths, that rose almost to his nose, with a red striped waistcoat and an apple-green coat with steel buttons almost as large as crown pieces' (p. 24).[34] Furthermore, whilst the other capitalists are engaged in some form of social life, even if it is a deadening one, Jos is *particularly* alienated:

> He was as lonely [in London] as in his jungle at Boggley Wollah. He scarcely knew a single soul in the metropolis: and were it not for his doctor, and the society of his blue-pill, and his liver complaint, he must have died of loneliness.
>
> (pp. 27–28)

Capitalism is shown in its unheroic emptiness at a historical moment within the novel when, according to Marx, it still had a heroic potential. Thus, the dialectical relations between the novel's historical setting and the historical moment of its composition are firmly established. The impossibility of heroism in the present is rooted, in *Vanity Fair*'s discourse, very firmly in the potentially heroic near past. And yet this is firmly a *dialectical* relationship since past forms of heroism are brought into the unheroic present even as the unheroic present also changes the historical image of the past. Whilst Thackeray shows an unheroic world because he does this in dialectical tension with a past world where heroism was heroic, his unheroic capitalist characters, such as Jos, are haunted by the possibility of heroism. It is exactly this mix of heroism and non-heroism that sets the stage for the more fully Napoleonic heroism of Becky Sharp.

This dialectic can be registered in the novel's ambivalent depiction of Jos, which suggests a complex ideological stance towards him. There is something particularly poignant about Jos Sedley's parodied and failed heroism. Thackeray does not seem able to wholly condemn him as the cruel rapacious capitalist as he does particularly with John Osborne. Like Napoleon on Elba in Thackeray's recollection, who retains a sort of folk-hero stature, Jos himself carries a memory of an earlier form of heroism, and the condemnation of him is not total. Jos is reminiscent of Falstaff. He is depicted in the illustrated initial at the head of Chapter LXV (intriguingly entitled 'Full of business and pleasure,' as though suggesting head-on the clash of the Falstaffian and the capitalist) as Falstaff with Becky as Doll Tearsheet (Figure 4.3).[35]

Figure 4.3 William Makepeace Thackeray, *Illustrated Initial in* Vanity Fair, *Chapter LXV [Jos Sedley and Becky Sharp as Falstaff and Doll Tearsheet]*. Public Domain. Source: https://en.wikisource.org/wiki/Vanity_Fair_(Thackeray)

Furthermore, the false story he tells of his heroic presence at the Battle of Waterloo is reminiscent of the episode in *Henry IV Part One* when Poins and Hal surprise Falstaff and his crew at the scene of the robbery they have just committed, and then coax Falstaff into telling preposterous stories about his heroism:

FALSTAFF: What's the matter? There be four of us here have ta'en a thousand pound this day morning.

PRINCE [HAL]: Where is it, Jack? Where is it?

FALSTAFF: Where is it? Taken from us it is. A hundred upon poor four of us.

PRINCE: What, a hundred, man?

FALSTAFF: I am a rogue if I were not at half-sword with a dozen of them, two hours together. I have scaped by a miracle. I am eight times thrust through the doublet, four through the hose, my buckler cut through and through, my sword hacked like a handsaw. *Ecce signum.*[36]

This dialogue continues like this for some time in the same vein. Falstaff has, of course, like Jos, actually run away. Jos is 'a clumsy and timid horseman,' who 'did not look to advantage in the saddle,' and, as he flees, Becky acidly remarks, 'Look at him, Amelia dear, driving into the parlour window. Such a bull in a china shop *I* never saw,' as 'Mrs. O'Dowd pursu[ed him] with a fire of sarcasm' (pp. 402–405). This is all a more polite nineteenth-century version of Shakespeare's depiction of Falstaff running away from battle: 'Falstaff sweats to death | And lards the lean earth as he walks along. | Were't not for laughing, I should pity him. | How the fat rogue roared' (II.ii.105–108). Jos's connections with Falstaff are stressed by his fatness. That he is a fat man depicted in an heroic pose on an elephant, in a portrait that is sold at the auction after the family's bankruptcy, opens him to a sort of general ridicule, '"I wonder it ain't come down with him," said a professional wag, "he's anyhow a precious big one;" at which (for the elephant-rider was represented as of a very stout figure) there was a general giggle in the room' (p. 202). But whereas Falstaff 'lards the lean earth,' makes everything fertile, and, indeed, represents a universal joyousness, summarised in his pronouncement 'banish plump Jack and banish all the world' (II.iv.466–467), Jos can only raise a 'general giggle,' which is soon silenced by the expediencies of capitalism: 'Don't be trying to deprecate the value of the lot' (p. 202).

In all these examples, Jos retains the traces of a specific form of vanished heroism which is barely accessible and which is also held by Napoleon on Elba in Thackeray's earlier description – that of the carnivalesque hero. Similarly, Thackeray's heroes and heroines of the Napoleonic age, dressed in the unheroic costumes of the current fashion though, bring with them the faint echoes of past heroism.

However, not even Jos's ambivalent and fairly faint heroic potential in capitalism exists for the other key capitalists in the novel, Mr Sedley and Mr Osborne. One is from trade and registers the potential for the ossifying effects of capitalism very early in the novel, whilst the other's bankruptcy is connected to the long ending of the Napoleonic Wars. After the Battle of Leipzig, 'Old Sedley once or twice came home with a very grave face; and no wonder, when such news as this was agitating all the hearts and all the stocks of Europe' (p. 137), or, as the narrator later comments, Napoleon 'ruined the Bourbons and Mr. John Sedley' (p. 219). On the one hand, the capitalist is destroyed by the end of the Napoleonic, on the other, as in the case of Mr Osborne, they are so firmly entrenched in Thackeray's image of Vanity Fair, that there is never the possibility of heroism for them. This is the case with George Osborne, and also for Mr Osborne, his father. The narrator states that the auctions of bankrupts such as Mr Sedley are places where 'even with the most selfish disposition, the Vanity-Fairian, as he witnesses this sordid part of the obsequies of a departed friend, can't but help feel some sympathy and regret' (p. 200), and yet, 'the butler of our friend John Osborne, Esquire of Russell Square [...] came to buy some of the famous port wine to transfer to the cellars over the way' (pp. 201, 205). Osborne here is completely alienated, even from his supposed friends. Again, there is no possibility of heroism here. The world-historical events which have caused the stock market crash and bankruptcy become isolated from the results of them, which are based on capitalism's endless cycle of accumulation and crisis. This is then moved from a level of general economics to individual, alienated rapaciousness between those who are supposed to have the human connection of friendship. There is also perhaps a hint of the ways in which other former images of heroism have been emptied of their heroic potential. For example, the pirate represents a figure of resistance to capitalism and of victory over the capitalists, and Mr Osborne himself suggest that Mr Sedley's bankruptcy is connected to piracy: 'They say the *Jeune Amélie* was his, which was taken by the Yankee privateer *Molasses*' (p. 156). Sutherland notes that this is in reference to the 'armed hostility and mutual depredation of shipping between Britain and America from June 1812 until the Treaty of Ghent in 1814' (p. 912). However, the very concept of the privateer, 'an armed vessel owned and crewed by private individuals, and holding a government commission [...] authorizing the capture of merchant shipping belonging to an enemy nation,' is that of the pirate acting in state interests, and it is notable here that the name of the privateer, *Molasses*, reflects imperial trade (*OED*).[37] But insofar as Osborne's own actions at the auction of Mr Sedley are like sending out a privateer to raid Mr Sedley's cellars, this is a raid bereft of all potential heroism. Between Jos and Messrs Sedley and Osborne, we see the novel's ambivalent fluctuation between 'heroic' emerging capitalism, and unheroic high capitalism, between the novel's setting and its period of composition. Ultimately, the analysis of these characters suggests high capitalism comes to dominate as capitalism heroism vanishes.

Nevertheless, the fact that the capitalist cannot be regarded as heroic does not resolve the contradiction, constituted by an attempt to situate the purported heroism of the Napoleonic past in the present of the 1840s, of Thackeray's seemingly unironic use of heroism in the passage about costume which I quoted above. Why then this contradiction? As Terry Eagleton points out, summing up a whole history of the analysis of ideology, 'it is always a complex phenomenon, which may incorporate conflicting, even contradictory views of the world.'[38] It may well be the case that Thackeray, by deleting the passage about costume in later editions, was attempting to resolve his own contradictory ideology – it certainly has something of that effect. Removing that passage destroys any potentiality for heroism whatsoever, even in the representation of a historical moment when it could have potentially existed, and so stresses the absence of it under the stultifying values of high capitalism, or what Thackeray calls Vanity Fair. At this point in his career, Thackeray is not using the term 'capitalism' directly, as he does in his later *Pendennis* (1848–1850), but rather allegorising it through the trope of Vanity Fair. In a discussion of capitalism in his letters, though, Thackeray reveals a nostalgia for heroism, whose absence, signalled by his desire for a God-like figure to intervene in affairs, haunts him in the high capitalist world. In a letter to his mother about the 1848 revolution in Paris, he writes,

> I don't believe in communism socialism or Louis Blanc – I have been reading his Organisation du Travail lately w^h points out the evils of our present system most clearly, but proposes a remedy so absurd and detestable as it seems to me that the worst tyranny w° be more acceptable feasible and conducive to the general happiness. I can't find the end of the question between property and labour. We want something almost equal to a divine person to settle it.[39]

Thackeray, perhaps more than any other writer in this study, is reminiscent of the way that Eagleton describes the fascist modernist writers of the early twentieth century: '[I]n the absence of genuinely revolutionary art, only a radical conservatism, hostile alike Marxism to the withered values of liberal bourgeois society, could produce the most significant literature.'[40] Having described the disappearance of heroism for the bourgeoisie under capitalism, he simultaneously leaves open the possibility that old forms of heroism still haunt this world and could be reactivated with radical potential, Thackeray looks to a new subject who could more successfully embody heroism than contemporary men drained of heroic potential. For a heroism of the future, he looks towards women.

III

A novel without a hero might suggest one immediate response: does it, then, have a heroine? The narrative voice invites us to make this response to the subtitle: 'If this is a novel without a hero, at least let us lay claim to a heroine' (p. 369). And it is my contention that Thackeray applies the term 'heroine' to his two lead women in a way that is far less ironic than the way he applies the term 'hero' to men, though this claim immediately gets us into difficulties since there is probably not a single utterance in Thackeray that is not ironic, or that cannot be read ironically. Irony, beyond its obvious sarcastic uses, is perhaps the most difficult of all literary effects to isolate, and convincingly argue for, because, if irony means to say something different from what its words actually signify, then all language is irony since it can only gesture towards what it means, rather than ever becoming consonant with it. Thus, when speaking particularly about Thackeray's irony, the rejoinder 'no, that's not correct, you've missed the irony' is an ever-present threat for the critic. What I will attempt to do here, then, is offer an argument as to why I think some of Thackeray's language should not be taken as ironic, by connecting this discussion with the earlier argument I have set out in this chapter about the discourse of heroism in relationship to nineteenth-century bourgeois society and the cultural image of Napoleon Bonaparte.

Both Amelia and Becky are described as 'heroines' throughout the novel, and particularly in the first half. I will begin with Amelia because it is easier to define how the term heroine works in relation to her character. Whereas Becky is consistently described in heroic terms, and is, as I shall discuss, aligned with Napoleon and a possible heroism that offers potential political emancipation, Amelia's heroism oscillates. Thus, in contrast to Becky, in an early episode in Chapter II, when Becky throws a dictionary from the carriage window, Amelia is described as 'the heroine of this work' (p. 15). By the fourth instalment of the novel, in Chapter XII, Amelia is denied heroism, though the narration continues to faintly connect her to it: 'the life of a good young girl who is in the paternal nest as yet, can't have many of those thrilling incidents to which the heroine of romance commonly lays claim' (p. 136). Amelia has shifted now from being the heroine of the work, in the military context and historical of the Napoleonic Wars, since Chapter II is entitled 'In which Miss Sharp and Miss Sedley prepare to open the campaign,' to *not* being the heroine of a romance. Chapter XII is, nonetheless, 'Quite a sentimental chapter' (p. 131), and within a page or two of Amelia not being a heroine of romance, the novel states that 'love was Miss Amelia Sedley's last tutoress' (p. 137) and that, in contrast to 'prim and reputable virgins' (p. 137), Amelia 'loved, with all her heart [...] a man so beautiful and so clever: such a figure on horseback: such a dancer: such a hero in general,' George Osborne (p. 138). Of course, this ironises George Osborne, but Amelia is here shown to be 'a heroine of romance' in spite of the narrator's claim. This passage, and other references when Osborne breaks off his engagement with Amelia to 'how entirely her character was jeopardied' (p. 218), suggest that Amelia has already had sex with George Osborne before their marriage, again reinforcing, if also complicating, the impression of her as a heroine of romance; the risk to her 'character' is sensational. By the end of Chapter XII, however, the narrator states outright that Amelia 'wasn't a heroine' (p. 140). The narrator implies this decline in Amelia's heroism is due to a retreat to the domestic sphere: '[T]he life of a good young girl who is in the paternal nest as yet, can't have many of those thrilling incidents to which the heroine of romance commonly lays claim,' adding that 'her letters *were* full of repetition' (p. 141). There has been a movement, then, from being on campaign to absorption into the domestic sphere, and from passionate love to a love which has become commonplace, repetitious, familiar, whose aim is evidently Amelia's desire to make her life one of idealised domestic bliss, both with George Osborne, and later, without.

Musselwhite draws a similar conclusion in his reading of the novel as a whole by suggesting that whilst Thackeray depicts a crisis of history that can open up heroic potential, this crisis is contained in the 're-inscription in the family of a system of representation that has collapsed elsewhere.'[41] In short, Musselwhite argues, *Vanity Fair* reinstates the primacy of the bourgeois family over the possibilities of a fragmented history, whose refusal to be contained might suggest radical possibilities. This certainly seems to be the case with Amelia, who, in the opening number of the novel, shares vicariously in the discourse of the novel that heroises Becky as an agent of breakdown, a status I will explain in just a moment, but by the end insists on a repetition in familiar familiarity, in a similar movement to that which I have argued occurs in *David Copperfield*.

On the other hand, there is Becky, whose status as heroic in the discourse of the novel never wavers, though her social status goes through so many vicissitudes. She maintains a sort of epic quality from the beginning of the novel, where she performs the 'heroical act' of throwing the dictionary out of the carriage window (p. 13), to the very end, where she makes her 'second appearance in the character of Clytemnestra' (p. 875), reactivating the world of Greek tragedy. She remains defiant of the values and morality of the society in which she is situated. Musselwhite also suggests that Becky breaks down the whole regime of representation, an onslaught which begins with her throwing the dictionary out the window, and Musselwhite collects whole series of examples of the ways that she dissimulates and plays with language and meaning: 'what Becky "represents" – if we can use that word without confusion – is the breakdown of representation itself.'[42] Musselwhite argues that this crisis of representation is also 'major theme of the *Eighteenth Brumaire*' and its account of the inability of the bourgeoisie to recognise its own revolutionary heritage and material support in society, and in the wildly Bohemian milieu that congregates around the strictly authoritarian Napoleon III. All this is, of course, fascinating and very insightful, but there are points where I would like to push Musselwhite's argument further, and, in the final section of this chapter, I wish to do this in relation to Becky-as-hero. Musselwhite tends to idealise this breakdown of representation in Becky, who 'delights in the sheer excess of language' and thereby challenges the bourgeois family: '[M]otherless, she must become her own mother.'[43] Nonetheless, his conclusions are not satisfactory. He suggests that this crisis of representation is wholly resolved, in a conservative manner, by a recentring of the values of the home, and this, as I have shown in the case of Amelia, is partially true. However, Musselwhite's reading here has several problems. It wholly drops the radical possibilities of Becky, who is *not* reinscribed in the home and remains a free agent until the very end of the novel. It does not recognise Marx and Engels's insistence elsewhere that the crisis of 1848 and after actually loosens the ties of the home: '[T]he bourgeoisie has torn away from the family its sentimental veil, and reduced the family relation to a mere money relation.'[44] Finally, it does not recognise, as I will argue in the last section, that Becky reactivates revolutionary heroism by taking up the memory of Napoleon precisely in order to break down the bourgeois world, in contrast to Napoleon III who imitates Napoleon in order to shore up bourgeois power. Whereas the masculine heroes of this novel are treated ironically, the less ironic treatment of Becky Sharp suggests the possibility of a new revolutionary heroism which could potentially restart the stopped movement of history.

IV

I think that a close look at Becky Sharp and her relations to Napoleon can resolve some of these problems, and I will suggest that Becky is a radical free agent, perhaps the only truly disruptive revolutionary hero described in this book. It is curious that in Musselwhite's chapter, Becky is dropped despite his eulogies to her. Instead, the radical potentialities of Thackeray's art are moved on to a depiction of Napoleon that, in Thackeray's oeuvre, is both inside and outside *Vanity Fair*, in a cartoon that Musselwhite discusses at length and that Thackeray drew for an anniversary of George Osborne's fictional death.[45] Thus, Musselwhite ends his essay: 'Perhaps we should here recall the impish conclusion of the drawing of George Osborne's death – "Bony runninaway like anythink". Bony looks a little like Thackeray and the pose is rampant. Escape, then, is possible – but how does one cope with exile?'[46] Napoleon may be exiled, but he continues to haunt Thackeray even here, and I want to suggest that Napoleon returns from exile in Becky's heroism, a heroism that is also the radical novelist's work (hence 'Bony' looking like Thackeray) of undoing, or at least challenging, received forms of representation.

Napoleon's revolutionary history mutates in Thackeray's work into the ability to undo the representational schema of bourgeois society.[47]

By the time *Vanity Fair* was written, as I have argued, the idea of Napoleon as heroic had been exhausted. Nonetheless, Napoleonic heroism haunts this novel, in order to invest the capitalist with a memory of heroism that he does not possess. Becky Sharp's heroism, and her Napoleonism, are of a different order. Rather than embodying the militaristic, entrenched, and conservative elements of capitalism, she is imbued with a power of play, transformation, and mimicry that recall a different form of heroism. Becky embodies what Baudelaire calls the 'heroism of modern life.' I want to show, in this final section, how this heroism of modern life, which suggests a resistance to capitalist heroism, still has a relationship with Napoleon, the bourgeois revolutionary hero, at the point when this embodied the energy and movement of history rather than the stoppage of history.

Whilst Baudelaire does not explicitly state that Thackeray is a 'painter of modern life,' there is a persuasive constellation of references which offer the possibility of considering Thackeray in relation to Baudelaire's essay. Baudelaire refers in passing to Thackeray in 'The Painter of Modern Life':

> M. Thackeray, who, as is well known, is very interested in all things to do with art, and who draws the illustrations for his own novels, one day spoke of M.G. [Constantin Guys, the French illustrator, cartoonist and chronicler of everyday city life, to whom much of Baudelaire's essay is devoted] in a London review, much to the irritation of the latter who regarded the matter as an outrage to his own modesty.[48]

As Anne Jamison observes, '[S]ince Thackeray was much concerned with illustration and the image-word rapport, as Baudelaire mentions, and was also a Guys enthusiast, Baudelaire can claim a kind of common ground with the well-known novelist.'[49]

Turning around this relationship and seeing how it plays out in Thackeray as read through Baudelaire reveals Becky embodying elements of Baudelaire's modernity, which are explicitly connected to clothing and fashion, a key area in which the relationship to the Napoleonic is played out in Thackeray.

For Baudelaire, 'modernity is the transient, the fleeting, the contingent' (p. 403). He admonishes the traditionalist, conservative critics: 'You have no right to despise this transitory fleeting element, the metamorphoses of which are so frequent.' These metamorphoses are particularly marked in terms of costume:

> There was a form of modernity for every painter of the past; the majority of fine portraits that remain to us from former times are

clothed in the dress of their own day. They are perfectly harmonious because the dress, the hairstyle, and even the gesture, the expression and the smile (each age has its carriage, its expression and its smile) form a whole, full of vitality.

(p. 403)

Baudelaire, seemingly paradoxically, associates the transience of modernity with the unity implied by an appropriate costume for a given moment. If one fails to attend to the specificity of dress of a given historical moment, one falls into 'the emptiness of an abstract and indefinable beauty' (p. 403), rather than a beauty which, because it is specific to a historical moment, unfolds in its own transience.

But for Baudelaire, the appropriate costume for the moment – the costume dictated by fashion – is transient in another and more dizzying way, too, as fashion becomes, in his thinking, 'a fancy dress ball': 'Thus the goddesses, the nymphs and sultanas of the eighteenth century are portraits of the spirit of their day' (p. 403). And whilst Baudelaire refers to the eighteenth century here, what he describes belongs also to the nineteenth-century capitalism described by Marx and Engels, where revolutionaries don the costumes of the past in order to both enact revolutionary change and consolidate their political conservatism, and where there is a constant kaleidoscopic upheaval of society in which the present recombines elements of the past and the rapidly emerging future. The ability to constantly change costumes is here not a historical aberration, but rather in conformity with a kaleidoscopic historical moment. This is the case in Thackeray's novel too.

Baudelaire's 'fancy dress ball imposed by fashion' (p. 403) is particularly reminiscent of the charades episode in *Vanity Fair*. The charades chapter is titled 'In which a charade is acted which may or may not puzzle the reader' (p. 633), implying simultaneously the contextual specificity and accuracy of the charades that are played and their simultaneous undermining of any sense of clear representational order; they have a solution but also retain the open potential of a puzzle, the failure of the costume to give the answer. In other words, where Baudelaire identifies a modernity defined by the 'fancy dress ball[s] imposed by fashion' (p. 403), Thackeray describes a modernity always in danger of unravelling through that same fancy dress. Different costumes will be worn which may or may not offer answers for the moment of the performance.

Marx too depicts a costume ball in the *Eighteen Brumaire*, where historical figures 'borrow costumes' and 'put on [...] mask[s].'[50] For Marx, Napoleon himself was putting on costumes, but, at his historical moment, as in the Hegel passage which begins this chapter, he nonetheless seems to have a stable historical identity. What has changed by the time of Baudelaire and *Vanity Fair* is the transitoriness of these fashions and the identities they create. Napoleon had conjured up a single costume that served a certain historical purpose and, when it was no longer suitable, is thrown into exile, where he becomes a relic, a tourist attraction for Thackeray and Jos Sedley, something no longer involved in the dynamic process of history. Becky Sharp on the other hand is full of the transitory, she is full of the spirit of Baudelaire's modernity, which Thackeray echoes in his novelistic critique of the nineteenth-century bourgeois world, but which he perhaps surpasses with a more thoroughgoing sense of the challenge posed by fashion to the representational order. She is able to constantly change costumes, to alter her face, to alter what she signifies. Her ability to break down stable bonds of representation is simultaneously her ability to be absolutely modern. To sum up Becky's trajectory, she is always playing charades with no solution to the puzzle.

As Musselwhite suggests, this modernity, which breaks down representation, can lead to the proto-fascism of Napoleon III. However, it is my contention though that it is not 'Bony runninaway like anythink' which provides an image of escape but Becky Sharp herself and that Becky does this, within society, on the one hand, by assuming (both 'consciously' as a character and through the implications of the narrative) the costumes of so many exiles – of foreigners abroad, of the poor, of an independent woman, of the governess, of the Jew, of the Bohemian, and of the prostitute – and on the other assuming costumes that give her back her agency – of the social engineer, of Clytemnestra as the prostitute in another social sphere, the demimondaine, and, as a key and transitional figure in all this, of Napoleon – both spirit of history and exile. [51]

When Becky Sharp adopts the costumes of exile, she presents a model of resistance within the fictional space of the text. She is able to resist the repressive power of capitalism and the bourgeois family precisely by being able to don a multitude of costumes and identities, and thereby retaining an openness in the face of that repressive power until the text's very end. The narrator states at the outset that Becky is a 'little mimic' who makes a 'caricature' of her teacher at the finishing school 'out of her doll' (p. 17), and she continues to use this skill simultaneously to aid her social climbing and mock the people she is amongst: 'When Miss Sharp was agitated, and alluded to her maternal relatives, she spoke with ever so slight a foreign accent, which gave great charm to her clear ringing voice.' Her voice 'infatuate[s]' Captain Crawley, but also makes a mockery of his aristocratic name, using her French mimicry to claim, 'I'm a Montmorency. Do you suppose a Montmorency is not as good as a Crawley?' (p. 166). Becky's mimicry then undercuts the stable hierarchical order of society in a process reminiscent of her ability to undercut the representational order, as Musselwhite suggests, when she throws the dictionary out the carriage window. Becky even undercuts the narrator's attempt to restore representational order. The narrator ends by saying, 'Come children, let us shut up the box and the puppets, for our play is played out' (p. 878). Yet the Becky puppet remains outside the box in the illustration beneath, even as a child goes to shut the lid that bears the inscription 'FINIS,' and the facing page contains another illustration: 'Virtue Rewarded: A Booth in Vanity Fair' (p. 879). Vanity Fair continues to exist beyond the textual space of the novel, and the illustrations seem to desire that Becky's existence can somehow continue beyond it too. Again, Becky is playing a part here, that of the injured woman rather than the intriguer. The illustration depicts her running a stall at a 'Fancy Fair' for 'the benefit of […] hapless beings,' a respectable woman offering Victorian charity, whilst she is seen in Bath and Cheltenham by 'a very strong party of excellent people' as 'a most injured woman' (p. 877). However, this astonishing power of Becky to undo all structures through mimicry is particularly marked in her ability to mimic Napoleon, to adopt his costume, and make herself a kind of heroism which is haunted by Napoleonism but in keeping with the milieu in which she lives. Her fancy dress is in conformity with her own time in a manner comparable to Baudelaire's description of the eighteenth-century fancy dress being in conformity with its own time, with one key difference. Becky's conformity with the historical moment is, paradoxically, a conformity that disrupts, which breaks down the representational order that she is part of (Figures 4.4, 4.5).

In the illustrated initial at the beginning of Chapter LXIV, Becky is depicted 'in the pose of Benjamin Haydon's painting of Napoleon.'[52] This is towards the end of the novel, but Becky is also connected with Napoleon from the very outset. After her very first 'heroical act' of throwing the 'Dixionary' out the carriage window, which shows her contempt for her bourgeois education, and, as Musselwhite notes, places her against the very representational practices of power, Becky's next revolutionary act is to announce to Amelia, '[S]o thank Heaven for French. *Vive la France! Vive l'Empereur! Vive Bonaparte!*' (p. 14).[53]

S. S. Prawer also observes that several other characters mirror Napoleon and that he stands for 'not only the great enemy that Britain had to vanquish, but also for the self-made man or woman who follows his example in a more private sphere.'[54] These Napoleonic upstarts include, in addition to Becky, a non-conformist cobbler and preacher, identified by Prawer, and various servants who, Miller suggests, engage in 'napoleonic insurrections.'[55] Given the trajectory of the novel moving away from history and towards the family, Napoleon is dislodged from the historical sphere into the private one. Miller writes of 'Thackeray's deep discomfort with [the] domestic *coup d'état.*'[56] However, this seems to discount Becky's always ambiguous class position, which at her birth and during her education is barely above that of a servant, and which continues to be 'contaminated' even after her elevation to the fringes of the aristocracy. By the very end of the novel, we are told that Becky, who is now poor again, 'liked the life' of a Bohemian (p. 830). She never is, in other words, fully subsumed by the order of the bourgeoisie or aristocracy. And whilst Thackeray may have felt discomfort with the servants' Napoleonic

Figure 4.4 William Makepeace Thackeray, *Illustrated Initial in* Vanity Fair, *Chapter LXIV [Becky Sharp as Napoleon, after Benjamin Robert Haydon,* Napoléon Bonaparte *(1830)]*. Public Domain. Source: https://en.wikisource.org/wiki/Vanity_Fair_(Thackeray)

insurrections, this discomfort is never wholly transferred to Becky, who, through breaking down the representational order, is allowed to stage her own Napoleonic insurrection.

Indeed, Becky's association with Napoleon, as I have suggested, is part of a more general semiotic cluster of identities linked to Becky, each of which places her in opposition to bourgeois values and morality. Napoleon stands against English conservatism and nationalism, the prostitute stands against the bourgeois family, the devil and the Jew against the Christian religion, the exile against the home, the Bohemian against respectability, and the powerful, agency-holding woman against phallocentric domination. Many of these also suggest cosmopolitan interconnections: Napoleon's internationalist project can be compared to the prostitute's peregrinations through different classes and cultures around the city streets, where, like the prostitutes in Baudelaire, where

Figure 4.5 Benjamin Robert Haydon, *Napoléon Bonaparte* (before 1846, based on a work of 1830). © National Portrait Gallery, London.

the experience of the commodification of the body is 'turned into a means of power' since 'commodities had no advantage over them.'[57] What Becky signifies through these interconnected costumes is a general challenge to all bourgeois morality. It is telling that Thackeray probably stands alone amongst Victorian authors for neither condemning Becky for (or, at least, Becky is no more condemned than any other character within the economy of Vanity Fair) nor rescuing Becky from prostitution.

On the other hand, it is against these figures of exile and challenge that bourgeois morality is formed. Modern nationalism is in part created against Napoleon, Christianity against the Jew, the bourgeois family, particularly, out of a horror of contamination by prostitution. But this in itself points towards nothing but the contradictions of capitalism. Becky, in her affinity with Bohemia, is depicted as experiencing *pleasure* in her Bohemian life: 'Her taste for disrespectability grew more and more remarkable. She became a perfect Bohemian' (p. 822). A bourgeois account would see the family as natural against the immoral commodification of the prostitute, but, rather, the bourgeois family is just as much a creation of capitalism as modern urban prostitution and, taking into account Becky's pleasure in her life, far more deadening in its effects. Indeed, whilst 'the bourgeoisie has torn away from the family its sentimental veil and reduced the family to a mere money relation,'[58] Becky can make light of this rather than trying to hide it ideologically: 'What a charming reconciler and peacemaker money is!' (p. 121). And precisely because she is cosmopolitan, of the city, of Europe, she is never fixable as a subject; she continues to challenge the laws of representation. Thus, on the one side, there is the capitalist, fixed by deadening bourgeois values. As a circulating commodity, the novel *Vanity Fair* is part of this economy, and Musselwhite is right to say that it tends towards the creation of the bourgeois family. On the other hand, though, within the novel, but written in such a way that she seems to exist beyond its boundaries, is Becky Sharp, associated with Napoleon and the heroic, who does not like him 'runaway like anythink,' but rather circulates in a very different way from the commodity, challenging signifying practices and bourgeois values beyond 1815, beyond 1848, with continuing ramifications for critical and political practice today. But, for the purposes of this book, she is the perfect emblem of the haunting of unheroic, realist bourgeois fiction by those heroic figures that predated it, laid the ground for it but seemingly vanished from it: in her case and that of *The Red and the Black*, Napoleon; in the case of *Eugene Onegin*, *A Hero of Our Times* and *David Copperfield*, Byron. She demonstrates the extent to which the nineteenth century is novel is more invested in heroism than we like to admit – despite its best efforts to hide the fact.

Notes

1 John Peck, 'Middle Class Life in *Vanity Fair*,' *English: Journal of the English Association* 43 (1994), 1–16 (p. 11).
2 Peck, 12.
3 Peck, p. 4; 14.
4 Mary Hammond, 'Thackeray's Waterloo: History and War in *Vanity Fair*,' *Literature and History* 11 (2002), 19–38 (p. 23).
5 Patricia Marks, '"*Mon pauvre prisonnier*": Becky Sharp and the Triumph of Napoleon,' *Studies in the Novel* 28 (1996), 76–92 (p. 80).
6 Marks, 88.
7 Marks, 85.
8 Hammond, 34.
9 Napoleon turns up throughout Thackeray's career, as do questions of cosmopolitanism and internationalism, which will be discussed in this chapter. I will be limiting my reading to *Vanity Fair* for the simple reason that to discuss relevant instances in Thackeray's other work would be impossible due to the sheer volume of material. S. S. Prawer's indispensable surveys of Thackeray's French, German, Jewish, European, and Middle Eastern contexts and allusions, which I refer to in this chapter, run to approximately 1,300 pages, the

substantial bulk of which is simply accruing the references, without a huge amount of close analysis.

10 Andrew H. Miller, *Novels Behind Glass: Commodity Culture and Victorian Narrative* (Cambridge: Cambridge University Press, 1995), p. 35.

11 G. W. F. Hegel, *Hegel: The Letters*, trans. Clark Butler and Christine Seiler (Bloomington: Indiana University Press, 1985), p. 114.

12 Shlomo Avineri, *Hegel's Theory of the Modern State* (Cambridge: Cambridge University Press, 1974), p. 63. Avineri provides extensive information on the influence of Napoleon and the Napoleonic Wars on Hegel's philosophy, pp. 62–80.

13 Georg Lukács, *The Theory of the Novel*, trans. Anna Bostock (London: Merlin, 2006), p. 29.

14 Avineri, p. 64.

15 Hegel, quoted in Avineri, p. 64.

16 *Geist*, which I use interchangeably with the standard English translation 'spirit' in these opening paragraphs, is a notoriously difficult concept to define. In this context, it refers to Hegel's notion of history as directed by a force outside human subjectivity. It is, one could say, a motive force of history (amongst so many other things in Hegel's philosophy). However, it is important to realise that Hegel sees *Geist* as being a product of human thought and consciousness, rather than some mystical force beyond it, though, dialectically, this human-created force then composes human actions. This is why, for Hegel, Napoleon must be contradictory. He is both originator of *Geist* and subject to it.

17 Alexandre Koèjeve, *Introduction to the Reading of Hegel: Lectures on the 'Phenomenology of Spirit,'* assembled by Raymond Queneau, ed. by Allan Bloom, trans. by James H. Nicholas, Jr. (Ithaca: Cornell University Press, 1980), p. 160.

18 Mikhail Bakhtin, 'From the Prehistory of Novelistic Discourse' in *The Dialogic Imagination: Four Essays*, ed. Michael Holquist, trans. Caryl Emerson and Michael Holquist (Austin: University of Texas Press, 2008), pp. 41–83 (p. 44).

19 Gordon N. Ray, *Thackeray: The Uses of Adversity 1811–1846* (Oxford: Oxford University Press, 1955), pp. 65–66. Thackeray continues to portray himself as a child in *Vanity Fair*, such as in the illustration on page 104 or in the famous valediction which includes the readers as children along with Thackeray, 'Come, children, let us shut up the box and the puppets, for our play is played out' (p. 878). See William Makepeace Thackeray, *Vanity Fair*, ed. John Sutherland (Oxford: Oxford University Press, 2008). All further references to this edition will be incorporated parenthetically into the body of the text.

20 William Makepeace Thackeray, *The Four Georges* (London: Smith, Elder and Company, 1866), pp. 110–111. In Thackeray's imperialist discourse, the servant is wholly stripped of his identity. He did have a name: Lawrence Barlow (see Ray, *Thackeray: The Uses of Adversity*, pp. 65–66).

21 Bakhtin, *Rabelais and His World*, trans. Hélène Iswolsky (Bloomington: Indiana University Press, 1984), p. 48.

22 Bakhtin, *Rabelais and His World*, p. 24. Bakhtin describes the Golden Age as the time 'where there are no wars, no suffering, but material wealth' (p. 399), and links it to celebrations of the elderly god Saturn, who devoured his children before vomiting them up to form a new generation of gods, which Bakhtin connects to ideas of the simultaneity of old age and renewal (pp. 7–8).

23 Marx himself had read Thackeray. In his published writings, he makes reference to Thackeray a couple of times, knew his work well enough to make 'reference to a pun' in a letter, and he owned copies of Thackeray's writing.

See S. S. Prawer, *Karl Marx and World Literature* (Oxford: Oxford University Press, 1978), pp. 237, 252, 380, 396.

24 David E. Musselwhite, *Partings Welded Together: Politics and Desire in the Nineteenth-Century English Novel* (London: Methuen, 1987), p. 122.

25 Musselwhite, pp. 122–125.

26 Karl Marx, 'The Eighteenth Brumaire of Louis Bonaparte,' trans. Ben Fowkes in *Political Writings* ed. David Fernbach, 3 vols. (Harmondsworth: Penguin/London: New Left Review, 1973), II, pp. 143–249 (p. 147). All further references to this work will be incorporated parenthetically into the body of the text.

27 John Sutherland, 'The Composition and Publication of *Vanity Fair*,' in *Vanity Fair*, pp. xxxi–xli (pp. xxxii, xxxvii).

28 There is a similar absence of the Battle of Waterloo in Stendhal's *The Charterhouse of Parma* (1839), which also suggests the impossibility of heroism.

29 John Sutherland, 'Introduction,' in *Vanity Fair*, pp. vii–xxx (p. xix).

30 Musselwhite, p. 123.

31 I wrote the first draft of this section in August 2014, the day after attending a memorial to the dead of Peterloo in central Manchester. By the massacre's 200th anniversary (2019), a public memorial by the artist Jeremy Deller had been built – a remarkably long time to honour the democracy campaigners seeking 'Universal Liberty' in this city which prides itself on its radical heritage. The violence of Peterloo, its potentiality for real historical change, and its heroism have been conveniently ignored by the bourgeois establishment for nearly 200 years.

32 Andrew Miller elaborates compelling relationships between Thackeray's writing and that symbol of British economic and political stability, the 1851 Great Exhibition, in *Novels Behind Glass*, pp. 50–90.

33 Sutherland reproduces Saintsbury's text of 1908, which is rather erratic but includes expunged material from other incarnations of the text in the footnotes.

34 Miller, pp. 18–19. Note too that Jos's coat buttons resemble money.

35 Becky as Doll Tearsheet is another layer of the image of Becky-as-prostitute, which I discuss later in this chapter.

36 William Shakespeare, *King Henry IV Part One*, ed. David Scott Kastan (London: Arden Shakespeare, 2002), II.iv.152–162. Further references will be incorporated into the body of the main text.

37 *OED* dates this word to 1641, the very beginning of the rise of capitalism. Another early citation in *OED* comes from Pepys, who also connects privateering to imperial interests: 'We have done the Spanyard abundance of mischief by our privateers at Jamaica.'

38 Terry Eagleton, *Marxism and Literary Criticism* (London: Routledge, 2002), p. 6.

39 Gordon N. Ray, ed., *The Letters and Private Papers of William Makepeace Thackeray*, 4 vols. (Oxford University Press, 1945–1946), II, pp. 355–356. Ray notes that Thackeray was close friends with Blanc in his exile in England during the rule of Napoleon III.

40 Eagleton, p. 8. Marx himself notes something similar in spirit, though very crude in judgment, in his essay 'The English Middle Class,' published in the *New-Daily Tribune* on 1 August 1854: 'The present splendid brotherhood of fiction-writers in England, whose graphic and eloquent pages have issued to the world more political and social truths than have been uttered by all the professional politicians, publicists and moralists put together, have described

every section of the middle class from the "highly genteel" annuitant and Fundholder who looks upon all sorts of business as vulgar, to the little shop-keeper and lawyer's clerk. And how have Dickens and Thackeray, Miss Brontë and Mrs. Gaskell painted them? As full of presumption, affectation, petty tyranny and ignorance; and the civilised world have confirmed their verdict with the damning epigram that it has fixed to this class that "they are ser-vile to those above, and tyrannical to those beneath them"' (Karl Marx and Frederick Engels, quoted in Prawer, *Karl Marx and World Literature*, p. 237).

41 Musselwhite, p. 140.

42 Musselwhite, pp. 135–136.

43 Musselwhite, pp. 138, 136.

44 Karl Marx and Friedrich Engels, 'Manifesto of the Communist Party,' in *Political Writings*, I, pp. 62–98 (p. 70). This does not, of course, foreclose on the very obvious dialectical point that the destruction of the traditional ties of the family simultaneously creates the nineteenth-century bourgeois family as a repressive apparatus. I just do not think that Musselwhite gives enough attention to the dialectical pole of the destruction of the traditional family, which creates the family as a repressive institution. Though the destruction of old family relations creates the bourgeois family, it also threatens to over-whelm it entirely, leaving only parodied vestiges to haunt the novel.

45 This cartoon is reproduced on Musselwhite, p. 133, and discussed at length pp. 131ff.

46 Musselwhite, p. 142.

47 I have discussed in the previous chapter the radical work of the realist novel, which Rancière suggests undoes previous highly coded received representa-tional hierarchies in favour of an equality of subject matter.

48 Charles Baudelaire, 'The Painter of Modern Life' in *Selected Writings on Art and Artists*, trans. P.E. Charvet (Harmondsworth: Penguin, 1972), pp. 390–435 (p. 395). Further references to this text will be included within the body of the chapter. Baudelaire probably also knew Thackeray's writings on Cruikshank, who Baudelaire discusses in 'Some Foreign Caricaturists' (*Selected Writings on Art and Artists*, pp. 232–243), and he sent a review copy of *Fleurs du mal* to Thackeray's *Cornhill Magazine* (see Michèle Hanoosh, *Baudelaire and Caricature: From the Comic to an Art of Modernity* (University Park: Penn State University Press, 1992), p. 210).

49 Anne Jaimson, *Poetics En Passant: Redefining the Relationship Between Victorian and Modern Poetry* (Basingstoke: Palgrave Macmillan, 2009), p. 102.

50 Marx, 'Eighteenth Brumaire,' p. 146.

51 Prawer offers an exhaustive analysis of references to Becky's Jewishness, as well as to other references to Jews and Judaism in *Vanity Fair* in *Israel at Vanity Fair: Jews and Judaism in the Writings of W.M. Thackeray* (Leiden: Brill, 1992).

52 S. S. Prawer, W.M. *Thackeray's European Sketchbooks: A Study of Literary and Graphic Portraiture* (Oxford: Peter Lang, 2000), p. 21.

53 It is intriguing to notice that in this statement Becky is connected with the Devil. The chapter initial depicts a devil supporting a capital letter; the nar-rator states that 'to say "Love live Bonaparte!" was as much to say "Long live Lucifer!", and Becky states immediately afterwards, 'I'm no angel' (pp. 13–15). This association with the devil forms another costume for Becky that places her against the religious sensibilities of the society (and all forms of contemporary Christianity are mocked in *Vanity Fair*) and also stresses again Becky's opposition to signifying practices represented by her throwing

the dictionary from the carriage window. Given Thackeray's knowledge of Goethe (another early nineteenth-century hero whom Thackeray had met), I recall Mephistopheles in *Faust Part I*, who is consistently situated in contradiction to and against signifying stability: 'a part of the power who | Wills evil always but always works the good,' and 'the spirit of always saying no,' who, like Becky Sharp, is a spirit of modernity (see Johann Wolfgang von Goethe, *Faust: The First Part of the Tragedy*, trans. David Constantine (London: Penguin, 2005), p. 46, ll.1336–1337,1339). For Thackeray's encounter with Goethe see S. S. Prawer, *Breeches and Metaphysics: Thackeray's German Discourse* (Oxford: Legenda, 1997), p. 18ff. Details of Thackeray's German reading are included throughout Prawer's study. Thackeray first read Goethe's *Faust*, in Weimar, in 1830 (Prawer, p. 25).

54 Prawer, *Thackeray's European Sketchbooks*, p. 21.
55 Miller, pp. 35, 16–18.
56 Miller, p. 17.
57 Walter Benjamin, 'The Paris of the Second Empire in Baudelaire,' in *Charles Baudelaire: A Lyric Poet in the Era of High Capitalism*, trans. Harry Zohn (London: New Left Books, 1973), pp. 9–106 (pp. 56–57).
58 Marx and Engels, *Communist Manifesto*, p. 70.

Conclusion

The bifurcated structure of this book, with two chapters dealing with Byron's influence and two chapters dealing with Napoleon's influence, raises certain comparative questions, which I wish to address in this conclusion. The book argues for a repeated structure of influence that transcends the differences between the two figures. In each chapter, I argue, the Byronic or Napoleonic Hero is figured as revolutionary; this revolutionary origin is shown to be necessary for the development of bourgeois subjectivity; the Byronic or Napoleonic is then killed off in favour of bourgeois subjectivity, which is itself imagined as heroic, but that original, revolutionary iteration continues to haunt the new bourgeois hero, to a greater or lesser degree, with disruptive effects. I have shown in each chapter the varying extent of that disruption under different socio-economic, national, and formal conditions as they are depicted in each text. There is, then, a tension between, on the one hand, a metanarrative that suggests that the institution of bourgeois heroism in relationship to Byronic or Napoleonic heroism follows the same logic in each case across national boundaries, variations in socio-economic situations, and formal conditions and, on the other hand, marked specificities which differentiate the texts and threaten to undermine that metanarrative.

In this conclusion, then, I wish to make explicit some of the comparisons and contrasts evident in the Byronic and Napoleonic sections and across the literary and national contexts represented by the four chapters. Why is it that the metanarrative of the Byronic and Napoleonic Hero being replaced by the bourgeois and then haunting the bourgeois seems to recur in each of these texts? What is the difference between the Byronic and Napoleonic strands of this book, and within these, what is the difference between the specific texts discussed? To answer these questions, I turn to the shared condition of these texts as products of revolutionary flashpoints of the nineteenth century and the difference between Byronic and Napoleonic heroism in terms of a production of subjectivity and a production of history.

DOI: 10.4324/9781003160168-6

Each text in this book is written alongside one of the several revolutionary flashpoints of the nineteenth century or responds to revolutionary moments of the past. Chapter 1 shows the influence of the Decembrist Revolt of 1825 on Pushkin and Lermontov. The Decembrist Revolt sought to institutionalise a constitutional monarchy and assert individualistic rights for members of the aristocracy in Russia. Pushkin was directly involved in the revolt, and, as I show in my chapter, *Eugene Onegin* responds directly to it. Lermontov's *A Hero of Our Time*, by self-consciously responding to *Eugene Onegin* establishes its own relation to the Decembrists.

However, even as the directly political references recede in *A Hero of Our Time*, the legacy of the Decembrists still subsists in the focus on duelling. I discuss, in that chapter, how duelling was adopted by the Decembrists as an assertion of bodily autonomy in the face of an autocratic society that denied autonomy to the aristocracy who were obliged to do service for the state. As such, duelling is figured as bourgeois, even when practiced by aristocrats. When the Decembrists duelled, it expressed their bodily autonomy, their status as individuals. They imagined this practice as bourgeois, and for them, duelling was connected to the rights of the individual laid out in the French Revolution of 1789.

Chapter 2 shows how Dickens imagines Steerforth in *David Copperfield* returning from the 1830 revolution in France. It also discusses the influence of the English Revolution of the mid-seventeenth century on Dickens and highlights the novel's composition during the 200th anniversary of the execution of Charles I in 1649, as well as in the immediate aftermath of the 1848 revolutions which swept Europe. In Chapter 3, I explore the influence of the 1830 revolution in France, to which *The Red and the Black*, published in 1830 with the subtitle *Chronicle of 1830*, simultaneously refers to and disavows. I also stress the continuing influence of the 1789 French Revolution and its aftermath on the narrative. In Chapter 4, I show that *Vanity Fair* is written directly under the influence of the 1848 revolutions, and I also argue that, more than any other text in this book, Becky Sharp is shown to be a revolutionary character in her own right.

Each text, then, is a response to one of the revolutionary moments that took place over a 23-year period in Europe between the Decembrist Revolt and the 1848 revolutions but also to a longer tradition of revolutionary thought, belonging to the English Revolution and the French Revolution of 1789. And in one of the guiding texts of this book, Marx's 'The Eighteenth Brumaire of Louis Bonaparte,' Marx suggests that responses such as these are typical of revolutionary phenomena. He observes that 'Luther put on the mask of the Apostle Paul, the Revolution of 1789–1814 draped itself alternately in the guise of the Roman Republic and the Roman Empire' and that

Cromwell and the English people had borrowed from the Old Testament the speech, emotions, and illusions for their bourgeois revolution. When the real goal had been achieved and the bourgeois transformation of English society had been accomplished, Locke supplanted Habakkuk.[1]

In other words, Marx offers a metanarrative that spans a much wider historical time and geographical space but is still rooted in the transition into bourgeois society: each revolution models its own revolutionary heroism on past revolutions. This book follows this broadly Marxist metanarrative. The more or less bourgeois heroes of the works I study institute a revolutionary moment that borrows from a Byronic or Napoleonic model of heroism, associated with revolution, to create a bourgeois form of heroism. Marx also points to the second aspect of my own metanarrative when he states that 'Locke supplanted Habakkuk' since this implies that in the aftermath of the revolutionary change the revolutionary hero of the past is killed off in favour of a bourgeois hero of the present. However, Marx is not always consistent about this process of killing off, which assumes a much more central importance in this book.

Marx, in the opening of 'The Eighteenth Brumaire' also imagines this as a formal shift: 'the first time as tragedy, the second time as farce.'[2] What may seem like a quip or a maxim here takes on much more importance in this book too, though the metanarrative elements here, though still clear, are not so stable and the terms of the formal shifts I am identifying are different. I have shown how each of these texts invents new formal possibilities that occur symbiotically with their responses to revolution, though the shift here is not from 'tragedy' to 'farce' but from poetry to prose. In *Eugene Onegin* and *A Hero of Our Time*, I argued that the Decembrist Revolt was echoed in these texts by a formal shift from lyric poetry and the verse epic to the novel. *Eugene Onegin* posits itself as generically in-between, a 'novel-in-verse,' neither verse epic nor fully realised novel in a culture that had yet to fully develop the dominance of novel form that had already been established in Western Europe. Already though, as I showed through my analysis of Lensky's poems and the literary allusions in the work, the generic devaluation of the poem in favour of the novel is already at work and is fully realised in *A Hero of Our Time* which takes many of the elements of *Eugene Onegin* and completes its mutation into a novel in conversation with other European novels and alongside a celebration of bourgeois subjectivity and individuation. These two works are unique in this book insofar as a very clear correlation can be made between the specific content of the revolution they engage with and the formal changes that the works enact. The Decembrist Revolt was an attempt to establish a more strongly individuated subjectivity that was imagined in bourgeois terms, and these works develop the novel explicitly in order to develop and to depict a new sense of individuated subjectivity in the Western European form that had been engaged in this same project since the eighteenth century. Elsewhere in this book such a strong connection between the aims of a revolution and the formal mutations of the work do not exist. Rather, revolution is conjured to stress a sense of historical change and the revaluation of values. And, indeed, direct references to revolution are more diffuse. Dickens alludes to the English Revolution, Roman Republicanism, and the 1830 revolution in France; Stendhal shies away from depicting the 1830 revolution that he refers to; Thackeray whilst writing against the backdrop of the 1848 revolution depicts only a fictional revolution within the spaces that Becky Sharp inhabits.

Nevertheless, each of the texts discussed here adopts and develops that fundamentally bourgeois form of fictive prose – realism – to articulate their responses to revolutionary possibility.

What we see here is formal change at different points along the same trajectory. Whereas the Russian writers are moving towards the formal strategies of Western novel writing, Dickens is charting a much less clear future that the Russian novels cannot yet envisage. What he depicts is not the creation of bourgeois subjectivity but rather its consolidation, where the last elements of the epic are not shed to create a new form of writing but are used metaphorically to create a much more fully elaborated form of subjectivity. Freud, as I discuss, writes that the consolidation of individual subjectivity is 'analogous in every way to the process by which a nation constructs legends about its early history.'[3] Dickens seems to be reaching these Freudian insights some half-century before Freud, and, as such, his revolutionary moment in form, the rendering of proto-Freudian experience, is the deployment of the historically mature novel in an early elaboration of a complex Freudian bourgeois subject long before this is theorised in psychology.

The Red and the Black is different again. Here there is, as in *Eugene Onegin* and *A Hero of Our Time*, a self-reflexive depiction of mutation in the form of the novel itself. This time not the creation of the form of the novel, but rather an elaboration of the principles of European novelistic realism. As such, this mutation also has something akin to *David Copperfield* insofar as it represents a formal change in the history of the novel that gathers more importance after its initial elaboration, in its critical responses. Hence the importance of the theory and history of forms provided by Auerbach and Rancière in my analysis of this work. This time, the revolution in form is not the deployment of a wholly new form, the novel, but rather the honing of a formal approach to its material – realism – that is coupled to, and gives novelistic form to, a new philosophical attitude to that material: the radical equality of all subject matter that Rancière relates to the aesthetic regime of the arts.

Vanity Fair is something of an anomaly here since I have not argued for any sort of major formal change, nor can I see one. *Vanity Fair* is very much in the tradition of the satirical English novel and the picaresque with elements of the nineteenth-century realist novel. It does not offer the same experiments with novelistic form or forms of subjectivity that the other works in this book offer. The only major formal peculiarity in Thackeray is the *extent* to which images are used alongside text since the mere use of illustration is not itself peculiar. This use of illustration as a formal innovation is not particularly remarked upon by the text. The text does not seem self-conscious of it in the way that the other novels I discuss self-reflexively reflect on their formal innovations in the realm of generic form and forms of subjectivity. However, these images do introduce the kaleidoscopic shifting of Becky Sharp's character through a number of costumes: Clytemnestra, Napoleon, prostitute, Jew, Doll Tearsheet, penitent, proletarian, bourgeois, aristocrat, mimic, Bohemian. This is what differentiates *Vanity Fair* from the other works but also links it to them in as much as we here see this novel borrowing from the past, its masks in order to engage with revolutionary change and possibility. But elsewhere, the power of bourgeois revolution is sublimated into form in order to consolidate its bourgeois nature. In *Eugene Onegin* and *A Hero of Our Time*, the failure of the Decembrist Revolt in actuality sees its aims played out in literature. In *David Copperfield*, the revolution in the subject creates a better, more compliant bourgeois. In *The Red and the Black*, realism never depicts the revolution that it seems to emerge from, settling instead into a kind of radical formal democracy. In each case, the hero becomes bourgeois through and through.

The result of this, in most of the texts discussed, is an inability on the part of these heroes to participate in the making of history. The heroes eventually retreat from revolution rather than engaging in it. However, *Vanity Fair*, in this respect, seems to be different. It introduces a hero, Becky Sharp, who rather than have her revolutionary impulses sublimated into formal change retains a revolutionary impulse which is given to her by much more minor formal innovation. Thackeray, precisely through his borrowing of the 'revolutionary' masks of the past, allows her to resist capitulating to bourgeois stasis and allows him to actively imagine her as a figure constantly engaged in insurrections – nomadic, undertaking lines of flight, chameleonic, in a rebellion that exceeds the bourgeois parameters of the book.

Curiously, though, this is achieved with the resources already available to the novel form rather than through explicit innovation. As such, the direct relationship between formal and revolutionary change, which is suggested by the presence of Byronic and Napoleonic heroism, does not have the same sort of strong, metanarrative coherence that the institutions of Byronic and Napoleonic heroism have in the other texts. Nevertheless, all of these novels borrow, appropriate, and then negotiate around these models in their engagements with revolution and subsequent creations and/or subversions of bourgeois subjectivity and social order, and it is this fact that this book is at pains to foreground, explore, and better understand.

That said, can any broad differences between the two strands, the Byronic and the Napoleonic, be detected, and what might they signify? I would like to suggest a broad distinction between the Byronic and Napoleonic halves of this book. What unifies the two texts discussed in the Byronic strand is a particular focus on the development of new models of subjectivity: nascent bourgeois subjectivity in Pushkin and Lermontov and proto-Freudian subjectivity in Dickens. The texts in the Napoleonic strand, on the other hand, privilege historical processes: the development of a democratic novelistic realism in Stendhal and revolution itself in Thackeray, represented by Becky Sharp who does not ultimately withdraw from revolutionary possibility. Here subjectivity is much less important. Julien's subjectivity becomes a combinable element in the rich tapestry of realist equality and Becky Sharp's kaleidoscopic picara privileges the dissolution of subjectivity as a means to a social end. The development of new formal features in the Byronic texts are less enacted in their own right, as in Stendhal, but rather used as a necessary precondition for developing a new model of bourgeois subjectivity.

This can be attributed to the ways in which the Byronic and Napoleonic bequeath themselves to these texts. Byron is received by these writers in terms of text. His poetry is directly engaged with. As I have suggested, Byron's and the Byronic Hero's importance to these writers is as a representation of a transition in subjectivity – in Lukácian terms from an epic to a bourgeois subjectivity. This has implications for form but it is a mutation in subjectivity primarily, from a mingling with the world to an individuated closedness. In contrast, Napoleon comes to these writers through images, the images that Julien Sorel carries and imitates, the costume of Napoleon that Becky Sharp is drawn in, based on a painting. Here, questions of social representation predominate over subjectivity: how is the heroic subject positioned in society, and how does this relate to political history? As such, the Napoleonic strand of this book stresses the history of novelistic forms and their direct intervention in political processes much more strongly. In a dialectical reversal, whereas Pushkin and Lermontov refer most directly to revolution, but ultimately shy away from it in favour of a textual bourgeois subjectivity, Becky Sharp, whose novel refers only obliquely to revolution, exceeds the text in order to suggest revolutionary change.

Perhaps, as a concluding thought, this difference between the Byronic and Napoleonic can be returned to Carlyle's taxonomy of heroism that I discussed in the introduction. There, I suggested that Carlyle imagines the hero as king heroically making himself in the king's image, and through force of will bringing about historical change. Carlyle's taxonomy does not directly represent the heroism of Julien Sorel and Becky Sharp, but it does accord with the concern in Stendhal with exploring that creation of power through images to bring about historical change, which then manifests itself in Becky Sharp's mimicry, which offers the possibility of real revolution.

In the Byronic strand, this political, revolutionary change is subordinated to a change in subjectivity which the writers subtract from the political.[4] The Byronic, then, we might put in conversation with the hero as man of letters described by Carlyle. For Carlyle, it is the writer who offers the possibility of deep spiritual insight and political change. But this potential has not yet been realised. For Carlyle, any claim for the influence of literature on public affairs is 'sentimental' and the men of letters 'wander like unrecognised Ishamelites among us.'[5] Carlyle has every faith that substantial political influence will occur, '[T]he *best*' that literature can offer our political life 'is coming; advancing on us [...] this is a prophecy one can risk.'[6] I have my doubts that it has come about, but, writing at the beginning of the 2020s, when politicians condone persecution based on subjectivity and new permutations of fascism continue to threaten our societies, perhaps the utopian hope of a literature of new subjectivities allied with one of political radicalism is what is needed.

Notes

1 Karl Marx, 'The Eighteenth Brumaire of Louis Bonaparte,' trans. Ben Fowkes in *Political Writings*, ed. David Fernbach, 3 vols (Harmondsworth: Penguin/London: New Left Review, 1973), II, pp. 143–249 (p. 148).
2 Marx, p. 146.
3 Sigmund Freud, 'Notes Upon A Case of Obsessional Neurosis,' in *The Standard Edition of the Complete Psychological Works*, ed. and trans. James Strachey, 24 vols. (London: Vintage, 2001), X, pp. 151–249 (pp. 206–207).
4 In different contexts, of course, mutations of subjectivity can be the most political acts.
5 Thomas Carlyle, *On Heroes, Hero-Worship, and the Heroic in History*, ed. David R. Sorensen and Brent E. Kinser (New Haven: Yale University Press, 2013), p. 140.
6 Carlyle, pp. 141–142.

Bibliography

Adorno, Theodor W., *'Free Time,'* in *The Culture Industry: Selected Essays on Mass Culture*, ed. J.M. Bernstein (London: Routledge, 1991), pp. 162–170.

Allen, Elizabeth Cheresh, *A Fallen Idol Is Still a God: Lermontov and the Quandaries of Cultural Transition* (Stanford: Stanford University Press, 2007).

Althusser, Louis, *On Ideology*, trans. Ben Brewster (London: Verso, 2007).

Arnold, Matthew, *Poetical Works*, ed. C. B. Tinker and H. F. Lowry (Oxford: Oxford University Press, 1969).

Auerbach, Erich, *Mimesis: The Representation of Reality in Western Literature*, trans. Willard R. Trask (Princeton: Princeton University Press, 1974).

Avineri, Shlomo, *Hegel's Theory of the Modern State* (Cambridge: Cambridge University Press, 1974).

Bainbridge, Simon, *Napoleon and English Romanticism* (Cambridge: Cambridge University Press, 1995).

Bakhtin, Mikhail, *The Dialogic Imagination: Four Essays*, ed. Michael Holquist, trans. Caryl Emerson and Michael Holquist (Austin: University of Texas Press, 2008).

———, *Problems of Dostoevsky's Poetics*, ed. and trans. Caryl Emerson (Minneapolis: University of Minnesota Press, 1984a).

———, *Rabelais and His World*, trans. Hélène Iswolsky (Bloomington: Indiana University Press, 1984b).

Barrett, Thomas M., 'Lines of Uncertainty: The Frontiers of the North Caucasus,' in *Imperial Russia: New Histories for the Empire*, eds. Jane Burbank and David L. Ransel (Bloomington: Indiana University Press, 1998).

Bataille, Georges, *The Absence of Myth: Writings of Surrealism*, ed. and trans. Michael Richardson (London: Verso, 2006).

Baudelaire, Charles, *Les Fleurs du Mal*, trans. Richard Howard (London: Picador, 1987).

———, *Selected Writings on Art and Artists*, trans. P.E. Charvet (Harmondsworth: Penguin, 1972).

Beaton, Roderick, and Christine Kenyon Jones (eds.), *Byron: The Poetry of Politics and the Politics of Poetry* (Abingdon: Routledge, 2017).

Benjamin, Walter, *Charles Baudelaire: A Lyric Poet in the Era of High Capitalism*, trans. Harry Zohn (London: New Left Books, 1973).

———, *Illuminations*, ed. Hannah Arendt, trans. Harry Zorn (London: Pimlico, 1999).

Berman, Marshall, *All That Is Solid Melts Into Air: The Experience of Modernity* (London: Verso, 1983).

Boltanski, Luc and Ève Chiapello, *The New Spirit of Capitalism*, trans. Gregory Elliott (London: Verso, 2007).

Brecht, Bertolt, *The Life of Galileo*, trans. Desmond I. Vesey (London: Methuen, 1971).

Bristow, Joseph, *Empire Boys: Adventures in a Man's World* (Abingdon: Routledge, 2016).

Brooks, Peter, *Reading for the Plot: Design and Intention in Narrative* (Cambridge, MA: Harvard University Press, 1992).

Byron, George Gordon, Lord, *Letters and Journals*, ed. Leslie A. Marchand, 12 vols. (London: John Murray, 1973–1982).

———, *Letters and Journals*, ed. Thomas Moore, 2 vols. (Cambridge: Cambridge University Press, 2012).

———, *Major Works*, ed. Jerome J. McGann (Oxford: Oxford University Press, 2008).

———, *Works*, ed. Ernest Hartley Coleridge, 7 vols. (London: John Murray, 1903).

Calasso, Roberto, *La Folie Baudelaire*, trans. Alistair McEwen (London: Penguin, 2013).

Callaghan, Madeline, *The Poet-Hero in the Work of Byron and Shelley* (London: Anthem Press, 2019).

Cardwell, Richard (ed.), *The Reception of Byron in Europe*, 2 vols. (London: Bloomsbury, 2004).

Carlyle, Thomas, *On Heroes, Hero-Worship, and the Heroic in History*, ed. David R. Sorensen and Brent E. Kinser (New Haven: Yale University Press, 2013).

Chandler, James, *England in 1819: The Politics of Literary Culture and the Case of Romantic Historicism* (Chicago: University of Chicago Press, 1998).

Christensen, Jerome, *Lord Byron's Strength: Romantic Writing and Commercial Society* (Baltimore: Johns Hopkins University Press, 1993).

Cochran, Peter, 'From Pichot to Stendhal to Musset: Byron's Progress Through Early Nineteenth-Century French Literature,' in *The Reception of Byron in Europe*, ed. Richard Cardwell, 2 vols. (London: Thoemmes Continuum, 2004), I, pp. 32–70.

Cronin, Vincent, *Napoleon* (London: William Collins, 1971).

de Man, Paul, *The Rhetoric of Romanticism* (New York: Columbia University Press, 1984).

Diakonova, Nina and Vadim Vatsuro, '"No Great Mind and Generous Heart Could Avoid Byronism": Russia and Byron,' in *The Reception of Byron in Europe*, ed. Richard Cardwell, 2 vols., (London: Thoemmes Continuum, 2004), II, pp. 333–352.

Dickens, Charles, *David Copperfield*, ed. Jeremy Tambling (London: Penguin, 2004).

———, *The Letters of Charles Dickens*, ed. Madeline House, Graham Storey, Kathleen Tillotson, et al., Pilgrim Edition, 12 vols. (Oxford: Clarendon Press, 1965–2002).

———, *The Old Curiosity Shop*, ed. Norman Page (London: Penguin, 2000).

———, *The Posthumous Papers of the Pickwick Club*, ed. Mark Wormald (London: Penguin, 2003).

————, *Sketches by Boz*, ed. Dennis Walder (London: Penguin, 1995).

Eagleton, Terry, *Marxism and Literary Criticism* (London: Routledge, 2002).

Elfenbein, Andrew, *Byron and the Victorians* (Cambridge: Cambridge University Press, 1995).

Foucault, Michel, *Discipline and Punish*, trans. Alan Sheridan (Harmondsworth: Penguin, 1991a).

————, *The Foucault Reader*, ed. Paul Rabinow (London: Penguin, 1991b).

————, *The History of Sexuality Volume 1: The Will to Knowledge*, trans. Robert Hurley (London: Penguin, 1998).

Freud, Sigmund, *The Standard Edition of the Complete Psychological Works*, ed. and trans. James Strachey, 24 vols. (London: Vintage, 2001).

Gilmour, Robin, *The Idea of the Gentleman in the Victorian Novel* (London: George Allen & Unwin, 1981).

Goethe, Johann Wolfgang von, *Faust: The First Part of the Tragedy*, trans. David Constantine (London: Penguin, 2005).

Groce, Alexander, 'Aleksandr Pushkin's *The Captain's Daughter*: A Poetics of Violence,' *Ulbandus Review* 13 (2010), 64–78.

Haig, Stirling, *The Red and the Black* (Cambridge: Cambridge University Press, 1989).

Hammond, Mary, 'Thackeray's Waterloo: History and War in *Vanity Fair*,' *Literature and History* 11 (2002), 19–38.

Hanoosh, Michèle, *Baudelaire and Caricature: From the Comic to an Art of Modernity* (University Park: Penn State University Press, 1992).

Harvey, William R., 'Charles Dickens and the Byronic Hero,' *Nineteenth-Century Fiction* 24 (1969), 305–316.

Hegel, G.W.F., *Aesthetics: Lectures on Fine Art*, 2 vols, trans. T.M. Knox (Oxford: Clarendon Press, 1975).

————, *Hegel: The Letters*, trans. Clark Butler and Christine Seiler (Bloomington: Indiana University Press, 1985).

Hertz, Neil, *The End of the Line: Essays on Psychoanalysis and the Sublime* (New York: Columbia University Press, 1985).

Hill, Christopher, *The Century of Revolution 1603–1714* (Edinburgh: Thomas Nelson, 1962).

Hirschkop, Roy, *Mikhail Bakhtin: An Aesthetic for Democracy* (Oxford: Oxford University Press, 1999).

Jaimson, Anne, *Poetics En Passant: Redefining the Relationship Between Victorian and Modern Poetry* (Basingstoke: Palgrave Macmillan, 2009).

Jameson, Frederic, *The Political Unconscious* (Abingdon: Routledge, 2002).

Jefferson, Ann, *Reading Realism in Stendhal* (Cambridge: Cambridge University Press, 1988).

John, Juliet, *Dickens's Villains: Melodrama, Character, Popular Culture* (Oxford: Oxford University Press, 2001).

Kant, Immanuel, *Critique of Judgment*, trans. Werner S. Pluhar (Indianapolis: Hackett, 1987).

Kelly, Laurence, *Diplomacy and Murder in Tehran: Alexander Griboyedov and Imperial Russia's Mission to the Shah of Persia* (London: I.B. Tauris, 2006).

————, *Lermontov: Tragedy in the Caucasus* (London: Constable, 1977).

Kelsall, Malcolm, *Byron's Politics* (Brighton: Harvester Press, 1987).

———, 'Byron's Politics,' in *The Cambridge Companion to Byron*, ed. Drummond Bone (Cambridge: Cambridge University Press, 2004), pp. 44–55.

Koèjeve, Alexandre, *Introduction to the Reading of Hegel: Lectures on the 'Phenomenology of Spirit'*, assembled by Raymond Queneau, ed. by Allan Bloom, trans. by James H. Nicholas, Jr. (Ithaca: Cornell University Press, 1980).

Lacan, Jacques, *Écrits: The First Complete Edition in English*, trans. Bruce Fink with Héloïse Fink and Russell Grigg (New York: W.W. Norton, 2006).

Lansdown, Richard, 'The Novelized Poem & the Poeticized Novel: Byron's *Don Juan* & Victorian Fiction,' *Critical Review* 39 (1999), 119–141.

Layton, Susan, *Russian Literature and Empire: Conquest of the Caucasus from Pushkin to Tolstoy* (Cambridge: Cambridge University Press, 1994).

Leatherbarrow, W.J. (ed.), *The Cambridge Companion to Dostoevskii* (Cambridge: Cambridge University Press, 2002).

Lermontov, Mikhail, *A Hero of Our Time*, trans. Vladimir Nabokov and Dmitri Nabokov (Oxford: Oxford University Press, 1984).

Lukács, Georg, *The Theory of the Novel*, trans. Anna Bostock (London: Merlin, 2006).

Lutz, Deborah, *The Dangerous Lover: Gothic Villains, Byronism, and the Nineteenth-Century Seduction Narrative* (Columbus: Ohio State University Press, 2006).

MacCarthy, Fiona, *Byron: Life and Legend* (London: John Murray, 2002).

Marcus, Steven, 'Freud and Dora: Story, History, Case History,' in *Essential Papers on Literature and Psychoanalysis*, ed. Emanuel Berman (New York: New York University Press, 1993), pp. 36–80.

Marks, Patricia, '"*Mon pauvre prisonnier*": Becky Sharp and the Triumph of Napoleon,' *Studies in the Novel* 28 (1996), 76–92.

Marx, Karl, *Grundrisse: Foundations of the Critique of Political Economy*, trans. Martin Nicolaus (London: Penguin, 1993).

———, *Political Writings*, ed. David Fernbach, 3 vols. (Harmondsworth: Penguin/ London: New Left Review, 1973).

McDayter, Ghislaine. *Byromania and the Birth of Celebrity Culture* (Albany: State University of New York Press, 2009).

McGann, Jerome, *Byron and Romanticism*, ed. James Soderholm (Cambridge: Cambridge University Press, 2002).

———, *"Don Juan" in Context* (London: John Murray, 1976).

Meyer, Arline, 'Re-dressing Classical Statuary: The Eighteen-Century "Hand-in-Waistcoat" Portrait,' *The Art Bulletin* 77 (1995), 45–63.

Miller, Andrew H., *Novels Behind Glass: Commodity Culture and Victorian Narrative* (Cambridge: Cambridge University Press, 1995).

Miller, D. A., *The Novel and the Police* (Berkeley: University of California Press, 1988).

Miller, J. Hillis, *Charles Dickens: The World of His Novels* (Cambridge MA: Harvard University Press, 1965).

Moers, Ellen, *The Dandy: Brummell to Beerbohm* (London: Secker & Warburg, 1960).

Moretti, Franco, *The Bourgeois: Between History and Literature* (London: Verso, 2014).

Mozer, Hadley J., '"I Want a Hero": Advertising for an Epic Hero in "Don Juan,"' *Studies in Romanticism* 44 (2005), 239–260.

Musselwhite, David E., *Partings Welded Together: Politics and Desire in the Nineteenth-Century English Novel* (London: Methuen, 1987).

Nabokov, Vladimir, 'On Translating "Eugene Onegin,"' *New Yorker*, 8 January 1955, p. 34.

Newey, Vincent, 'Rival Cultures: Charles Dickens and the Byronic Legacy,' *The Byron Journal* 32 (2004), 85–100.

Nietzsche, Friedrich, *Beyond Good and Evil: Prelude to a Philosophy of the Future*, trans. Marion Faber (Oxford: Oxford University Press, 2008a).

———, *Twilight of the Idols, or, How to Philosophize with a Hammer*, trans. Duncan Large (Oxford: Oxford University Press, 2008b).

Osborne, Peter, 'The Postconceptual Condition, or, the Cultural Logic of High Capitalism Today,' *Radical Philosophy* 184 (2014), 19–27.

Pasternak, Boris, *Doctor Zhivago*, trans. Max Hayward and Manya Harari (London: Vintage, 2002).

Paterson, Michael, *Inside Dickens' London* (Newton Abbott: David & Charles, 2011).

Pearson, Roger, *Stendhal's Violin: A Novelist and his Reader* (Oxford: Clarendon Press, 1988).

Peck, John, 'Middle Class Life in *Vanity Fair*,' *English: Journal of the English Association* 43 (1994), 1–16.

Poovey, Mary, *Uneven Developments: The Ideological Work of Gender in Mid-Victorian England* (London: Virago, 1989).

Porterfield, Todd and Susan L. Siegfried, *Staging Empire: Napoleon, Ingres, and David* (University Park: Pennsylvania State University Press, 2006).

Prawer, S. S., *Breeches and Metaphysics: Thackeray's German Discourse* (Oxford: Legenda, 1997).

———, *Israel at Vanity Fair: Jews and Judaism in the Writings of W.M. Thackeray* (Leiden: Brill, 1992).

———, *Karl Marx and World Literature* (Oxford: Oxford University Press, 1978).

———, *W.M. Thackeray's European Sketchbooks: A Study of Literary and Graphic Portraiture* (Oxford: Peter Lang, 2000).

Praz, Mario, *The Hero in Eclipse in Victorian Fiction*, trans. Angus Davidson (Oxford: Oxford University Press, 1969).

Prendergast, Christopher, *The Order of Mimesis: Balzac, Stendhal, Nerval, Flaubert* (Cambridge: Cambridge University Press, 1986).

Price, John, *Everyday Heroism: Victorian Constructions of the Heroic Civilian* (London: Bloomsbury, 2014).

Pushkin, Alexander, *Eugene Onegin*, trans. Roger Clarke (Richmond: Alma, 2015).

———, *Eugene Onegin: A Novel in Verse*, trans. James E. Falen (Oxford: Oxford University Press, 1998).

———, *Eugene Onegin: A Novel in Verse*, rev. edn., trans. Charles Johnston (London: Penguin, 2003).

———, *Eugene Onegin: A Novel in Verse*, trans. Stanley Mitchell (London: Penguin, 2008).

———, *Eugene Onegin*, trans. Vladimir Nabokov, 2 vols (Princeton: Princeton University Press, 1990).

————, *A Journey to Arzrum, in Mikhail Lermontov, A Hero of Our Time*, trans. Boris Pasternak Slater (Oxford: Oxford University Press, 2013), pp. 141-184.

Radzinsky, Edvard, *Alexander II: The Last Great Tsar*, trans. Antonia W. Bouis (New York: Free Press, 2005).

Ram, Harsha, *The Imperial Sublime: A Russian Poetics of Empire* (Madison: University of Wisconsin Press, 2003).

Rancière, Jacques, *The Aesthetic Unconscious*, trans. Debra Keates and James Swenson (Cambridge: Polity, 2010).

————, *Aisthesis: Scenes from the Aesthetic Regime of Art*, trans. Zakir Paul (London: Verso, 2013).

————, *The Flesh of Words: The Politics of Writing*, trans. Charlotte Mandell (Stanford: Stanford University Press, 2004).

————, *The Future of the Image*, trans. Gregory Elliott (London: Verso, 2007).

————, *The Politics of Aesthetics: The Distribution of the Sensible*, trans. Gabriel Rockhill (London: Continuum, 2011).

Rand, Nicholas, '*The Red and the Black*, Author of Stendhal Pseudonyms and Cryptonyms of Beyle,' *Romanic Review* 80 (1989), 391–403.

Rawes, Alan, 'Marino Faliero: Escaping the Aristocratic,' in *Liberty and Poetic Licence: New Essays on Byron*, eds. Bernard Beatty, Tony Howe and Charles Robinson (Liverpool: Liverpool University Press, 2008), pp. 88–102.

Ray, Gordon N., *Thackeray: The Uses of Adversity 1811–1846* (Oxford: Oxford University Press, 1955).

Reyfman, Irina, *Ritualized Violence Russian Style: The Duel in Russian Culture and Literature* (Stanford, CA: Stanford University Press, 1999).

Scotto, Peter, 'Prisoners of the Caucasus: Ideologies of Imperialism in Lermontov's "Bela,"' *PMLA* 107 (1992), 246–260.

Shakespeare, William, *King Henry IV Part One*, ed. David Scott Kastan (London: Arden Shakespeare, 2002).

Shelley, Percy Bysshe, 'A Defence of Poetry,' in *Poetry and Prose*, 2nd edn., ed. Donald H. Reiman and Neil Fraistat (New York: W.W. Norton, 2002), pp. 509–535.

Stabler, Jane, *Byron, Poetics and History* (Cambridge: Cambridge University Press, 2002).

Stendhal, *The Red and the Black*, trans. Roger Gard (London: Penguin, 2002).

————, *The Red and the Black*, ed. and trans. Catherine Slater (Oxford: Oxford University Press, 2009).

————, *Le Rouge et le Noir: Chronique du XIXe siècle* (Paris: Gallimard, 1972).

Sterrenberg, Lee, 'Psychoanalysis and the Iconography of Revolution,' *Victorian Studies* 19 (1975), 241–264.

Tambling, Jeremy, *Allegory* (Abingdon: Routledge, 2010).

————, *Dickens' Novels as Poetry* (London: Routledge, 2015).

Terdiman, Richard, 'From City to Country: An Outline of *Fluvio-Critique*,' *NOVEL: A Forum of Fiction* 41 (2007), 53–72.

Thackeray, William Makepeace, *The Four Georges* (London: Smith, Elder and Company, 1866).

————, *The Letters and Private Papers of William Makepeace Thackeray*, ed. Gordon N. Ray, 4 vols. (Oxford: Oxford University Press, 1945–1946).

————, *Vanity Fair*, ed. John Sutherland (Oxford: Oxford University Press, 2008).

Thorslev, Jr, Peter L., *The Byronic Hero: Types and Prototypes* (Minneapolis: University of Minnesota Press, 1962).

Todd III, William Mills, *Fiction and Society in the Age of Pushkin: Ideology, Institutions, and Narrative* (Cambridge, MA: Harvard University Press, 1986).

Trigos, Ludmilla A., *The Decembrist Myth in Russian Culture* (Basingstoke: Palgrave Macmillan, 2009).

Webb, Timothy, *The Violet in the Crucible: Shelley and Translation* (Oxford: Clarendon Press, 1976).

Weber, Max, *The Protestant Ethic and the Spirit of Capitalism*, trans. Talcott Parsons (London: Routledge, 2001).

———, *The Protestant Ethic and the "Spirit" of Capitalism and Other Writings*, ed. and trans., Peter Baehr and Gordon C. Wells (London: Penguin, 2002).

———, *The Protestant Ethic and the Spirit of Capitalism: The Revised 1920 Edition*, trans., Stephen Kalberg (Oxford: Oxford University Press, 2010).

Wesling, Molly W., *Napoleon in Russian Cultural Mythology* (New York: Peter Lang, 2001).

Wilkes, Joanne, '"Infernal Magnetism": Byron and Nineteenth-Century French Readers,' in *The Reception of Byron in Europe*, ed. Richard Cardwell, 2 vols. (London: Thoemmes Continuum, 2004), I, pp. 11–31.

Williams, Raymond, *Culture and Society 1780–1950* (Harmondsworth: Penguin, 1966).

Wilson, Frances (ed.), *Byromania: Portraits of the Artist in Nineteenth- and Twentieth-Century Culture* (Basingstoke: Palgrave, 1999).

Wolfreys, Julian, *Dickens's London: Perception, Subjectivity and Phenomenal Urban Multiplicity* (Edinburgh: Edinburgh University Press, 2012).

Wolfson, Susan J., *Romantic Interactions: Social Being and the Turns of Literary Action* (Baltimore: Johns Hopkins University Press, 2010).

Wootton, Sarah, *Byronic Heroes in Nineteenth-Century Women's Writing and Screen Adaptation* (Basingstoke: Palgrave Macmillan, 2016).

Index

Note: Page numbers in italics denote figures, and n denotes a note

Milton Keynes UK
Ingram Content Group UK Ltd.
UKHW020209011223
433593UK00010B/78

9 780367 749057